KANT AND THE SPIRIT OF CRITIQUE

THE COLLECTED WRITINGS OF JOHN SALLIS

Volume III/3

KANT AND THE SPIRIT OF CRITIQUE

John Sallis

Edited by Richard Rojcewicz

Indiana University Press

This book is a publication of

Indiana University Press
Office of Scholarly Publishing
Herman B Wells Library 350
1320 East 10th Street
Bloomington, Indiana 47405 USA

iupress.indiana.edu

© 2020 by John Sallis

Part One based on a lecture course presented in the Fall of 1978 at Duquesne University, with supplementary material from lecture courses of Fall 1975 and Spring 1976 at Duquesne University.

Part Two based on a lecture course presented in the Fall of 1976 at Duquesne University.

Part Three based on a lecture course presented in the Spring of 2011 at Boston College, with supplementary material from a lecture course of Spring 2019 at Boston College.

Part Four based on lectures presented in July 2011 at the Collegium Phaenomenologicum, Città di Castello, Italy.

All rights reserved
No part of this book may be reproduced or utilized in any form or by any means, electronic or mechanical, including photocopying and recording, or by any information storage and retrieval system, without permission in writing from the publisher. The paper used in this publication meets the minimum requirements of the American National Standard for Information Sciences—Permanence of Paper for Printed Library Materials, ANSI Z39.48–1992.

Manufactured in the United States of America

Cataloging information is available from the Library of Congress.

ISBN 978-0-253-04979-7 (hdbk.)
ISBN 978-0-253-04980-3 (pbk.)
ISBN 978-0-253-04981-0 (web PDF)

1 2 3 4 5   25 24 23 22 21 20

Contents

	Key to the Citations of Kant's Works	vii

Part One. Kant, *Critique of Pure Reason*

I.	Hermeneutical Preface to Reading Kant	3
II.	Introduction to the Course	6
III.	The Transcendental Aesthetic	20
	Space	26
	A. Metaphysical Exposition of Space	26
	B. Transcendental Exposition of the Concept of Space	32
	C. Conclusions as Regards Space	34
	Time	36
	A. The Expositions of Time	36
	B. The "General Observations" of §8	37
IV.	The Transcendental Analytic	41
	A. Introduction: The Idea of Transcendental Logic	41
	B. Book I: Analytic of Concepts. Chapter I: Pure Concepts	44
	C. Book I: Analytic of Concepts. Chapter II: The Transcendental Deduction	55
	D. Book II: Analytic of Principles. Chapter I: Schematism	73
	E. Book II: Analytic of Principles. Chapter II: Principles	75
	F. Conclusion of the Analytic and Glance Ahead to the Dialectic	93
V.	Conclusion to the Course	100

Part Two. Kant's Practical Philosophy

I.	The Problem of Practical Philosophy	105
II.	The Preface of the *Critique of Practical Reason*	109
III.	*Foundations of the Metaphysics of Morals*	116

IV. *Critique of Practical Reason* — 144
    A. The Introduction of the *Critique of Practical Reason* — 144
    B. Chapter I of the Analytic of the *Critique of Practical Reason*: Principles of Pure Practical Reason — 145
    C. Chapter II of the Analytic of the *Critique of Practical Reason*: The Concept of an Object of Pure Practical Reason — 152
    D. Chapter III of the Analytic of the *Critique of Pure Reason*: The Incentives of Pure Practical Reason — 157
    E. The Dialectic of Pure Practical Reason — 161

V. Conclusion to the Course — 173

Part Three. Kant, *Critique of Judgment*

I. Introduction — 179

II. Judgment — 186

III. Aesthetic Judgment — 200

IV. Analytic of the Beautiful — 205

V. Analytic of the Sublime — 221

VI. Interest in the Beautiful — 233

VII. Art — 239

VIII. Conclusion to the Course — 250

Part Four. The Truth of Beauty

I. Introduction — 253

II. Truth — 255

III. Aesthetic Judgment — 258

IV. The Turn in the Analysis of Aesthetic Judgment — 265

V. Couplings — 267

VI. Conclusion to the Course — 272

    Editor's Afterword — 273
    Index — 275

Key to the Citations of Kant's Works

THE MAIN WORKS of Kant cited in these lectures will be referenced according to the following abbreviations. The quoted translations are at times alterations of the published versions.

Kritik der reinen Vernunft, 1781.
Translated as *Critique of Pure Reason*
by Norman Kemp Smith.
London: Macmillan, 1958.
Page references are to the
first (A) and second (B)
edition in the Akademie Ausgabe,
indicated in the margins of Smith's translation.

Prolegomena zur einer jeden künftigen Metaphysik, die als Wissenschaft wird auftreten können, 1783.
Translated as *Prolegomena to Any Future Metaphysics*
by Paul Carus with revisions by Lewis White Beck.
NY: Macmillan, 1950.
Page references are to the translation,
abbreviated as *Pro*.

Grundlegung zur Metaphysik der Sitten, 1785.
Translated as *Foundations of the Metaphysics of Morals*
by Lewis White Beck.
Indianapolis: Liberal Arts Press, 1959.
Page references are to the translation,
abbreviated as *FM*.

Kritik der praktischen Vernunft, 1788.
Translated as *Critique of Practical Reason*
by Lewis White Beck.
Indianapolis: Liberal Arts Press, 1956.
Page references are to the translation,
abbreviated as *CPr*.

Kritik der Urteilskraft, 1790.
Translated as *Critique of Judgment*
by Werner S. Pluhar.
Indianapolis: Hackett, 1987.
Page references are to the translation,
abbreviated as *CJ*.

KANT AND THE SPIRIT OF CRITIQUE

Part One.
Kant, *Critique of Pure Reason*

Lecture course presented at Duquesne University
Fall 1978

With supplementary material from lecture courses at Duquesne University
Fall 1975 and Spring 1976

I. Hermeneutical Preface to Reading Kant

THE *CRITIQUE OF Pure Reason* is one of the pivotal texts in the history of metaphysics. Our task is to begin reading that text.

To read such a text, however, is anything but a straightforward affair. In light of the work of Heidegger, Gadamer, and Derrida, we have begun to realize the immense problems posed by an appropriate reading, that is, begun to appreciate the incredibly difficult requirements to which a reading must subject itself if it is to be genuinely critical and reflective.

This course is not the place for a general consideration of hermeneutics or even for a systematic consideration of the specific hermeneutical issues pertaining to Kant's texts. Nevertheless, let me at least open up those issues with a "hermeneutical preface."

First of all, we need to see that hermeneutics in its contemporary sense bears on our reading of Kant only in view of a certain disengagement of the text from the author's explicit intentions. The point is that as long as the text is merely the realization of those intentions, the author is the privileged interpreter. In a sense, the author is the only possible interpreter, since any other one would simply set out to duplicate the author's intentions, reconstructing them from the text. Anything brought to the text by an interpreter other than the author could only distort that text, falsify it. This position amounts to a kind of "hermeneutical positivism."

On the other hand, suppose a text is *not merely* the realization of its author's intentions. Or, rather than put it negatively, suppose there can be layers of sense in the text that exceed the author's intention. Then the author would not have the kind of privilege just spoken of. Instead, it would be possible for another interpreter to expose layers of sense that remained unthought and unintended by the author. In other words, a productive interpretation would then be possible.

In such a case, one might say that the interpreter can understand the author better than the author understood himself. Now, what is remarkable is that Kant himself openly acknowledges this possibility. In the midst of a discussion of

Plato's use of the word "idea," Kant writes: "I need only remark that it is by no means unusual, upon comparing the thoughts an author has expressed in regard to his subject, whether in ordinary conversation or in writing, to find that we understand him better than he has understood himself. As he has not sufficiently determined his concept, he has sometimes spoken, or even thought, in opposition to his own intention" (A314/B370).

So at a quite explicit level, Kant's text grants the very condition which becomes an issue for hermeneutics. In other words, his text opens up a "hermeneutical space"—opens it up and situates itself within such a space.

In addition, there are Kantian texts outlining certain formal hermeneutical principles. I will mention two such principles:

The first is a canon of classical hermeneutics and pertains to the relation between whole and part. Kant expressed it initially in a letter to Christian Garve (August 7, 1783). Here it does not appear explicitly as a hermeneutical principle with the governing relation that of interpreter to text but as a compositional or methodological principle with the governing relation that of writer to text. According to Kant: "Another peculiarity of this sort of science is that one must have a conception of the whole in order to rectify each of the parts, so that one has to leave the matter for a time in a certain condition of rawness, in order to achieve this eventual rectification" (Kant, *Philosophical Correspondence 1759–99*, tr. A. Zweig, Chicago: University of Chicago Press, 1967, p. 101).

What is prescribed here is that the movement through parts to whole must be supplemented by a regression from whole to parts: the whole must be understood through the parts and vice versa. This demand is a hermeneutical principle, and in the *Critique of Practical Reason*, Kant accuses some of his critics of failing to observe it. Kant writes that the nature of human knowledge requires that one "begin with an exact and . . . complete delineation of parts." Yet, "a more philosophical and architectonic procedure . . . is to grasp correctly the idea of the whole, and then to see all those parts, in their reciprocal interrelations, in the light of their derivation from the concept of the whole" (*CPr*, p. 10).

So in reading a Kantian text, we will want to be attentive to the interplay of whole and part. In order to install such an interplay in our interpretation, I will begin with a provisional glance at the whole and will do so specifically with a series of formulations of the Kantian problem in general. Then, through detailed textual work or, in other words, through the parts, we will try to move back toward that whole, toward regaining it through the parts, toward a "synoptic view."

The second principle relates the issue of whole and part to the question of definition. Kant writes: "Such a precaution against making judgments by venturing definitions before a complete analysis of concepts has been made (usually only far along in a system) is to be recommended throughout philosophy, but it is often neglected. It will be noticed throughout the critiques of both the theoretical and the practical reason that there are many opportunities to remedy inadequacies and to correct errors in the old dogmatic procedure of philosophy which were detected only when concepts, used according to reason, are given a reference to the totality of concepts" (*CPr*, pp. 9–10, footnote).

So this principle is a warning against venturing definitions, conclusive determinations of parts, prior to the return from the whole to those parts. In other words, it prescribes a certain initial indeterminacy, one necessary at the outset and only gradually removed in the course of the text. In still other words, it prescribes a certain stratification of the text corresponding to different degrees of determinacy.

This principle is especially important for understanding the typically Kantian way of appropriating traditional concepts: they are taken over with a certain degree of indeterminacy, allowing them to be progressively redetermined at several stages of the text.

So we will want to be attentive to this kind of structure in our reading of Kantian texts. That will require a certain reticence, a certain holding back from the demand for completely determinate concepts.

II. Introduction to the Course

By way of introduction to the *Critique of Pure Reason*, that is, to the problem with which the text is engaged, I want to:

(1) indicate what the general problem is,
(2) show how, in the development of Kant's thought, it came to be a problem, and
(3) present a series of formulations elaborating the problem as a whole and moving from a more general level, that of the Prefaces and Introduction of the *Critique of Pure Reason*, to more fundamental levels.

(1) The general problem.

The general problem of the *Critique of Pure Reason* is metaphysics. We need to ask how it comes about that metaphysics is a problem for Kant. In what way does it present itself to him as something questionable, problematic? What does he see that is questionable in metaphysics?

Kant exhibits this questionableness by focusing on two features of traditional metaphysics. First, metaphysics is the highest science, in the sense that it deals with the ultimate questions, the most important questions for man, namely, questions concerning God, freedom, and immortality. Kant formulates it this way in the "Doctrine of Method": "What can I know? What ought I do? What may I hope?" (A805/B833). Metaphysics, since it deals with these ultimate questions, is indispensable. It represents an "inward need" of man, a "natural disposition." It is not an ornament. Kant maintains that there has always been metaphysics and always will be.

Second, for all its importance, metaphysics has remained a battlefield of endless controversies. It has not been able to enter upon the path of genuine science.

In summary, as Kant writes at the beginning of the Preface in A: "Human reason has this peculiar fate that in one species of its knowledge it is burdened by questions which, as prescribed by the very nature of reason itself, it is not able to ignore but which, as transcending all its powers, it is also not able to answer" (A vii).

This predicament is not, for Kant, a mere accident, a result of error by some people, their failure to work out some problems adequately. It is not a problem that could have impeded mathematics or physics. Rather, its source is a conflict of reason with itself.

The conclusion Kant draws from the plight of metaphysics is the need for a tribunal charged with settling the dispute, assuring lawful claims and distinguishing them from groundless pretensions. This tribunal would resolve the conflict and set metaphysics on the path of genuine science.

The demand for such a tribunal is "a call to reason to undertake anew the most difficult of all its tasks, namely, that of self-knowledge" (A xi). Thus the tribunal takes the form of a self-critique of reason; that is what the *Critique of Pure Reason* is all about in the first instance. According to Kant: "I mean a critique . . . of the faculty of reason in general, in respect of any knowledge after which it may strive *independently of all experience*. It will therefore decide as to the possibility or impossibility of metaphysics in general and will determine its sources, its extent, and its limits—all in accord with principles" (A xii).

Thus Kant's problem is metaphysics, and an interrogation of metaphysics takes the form of an interrogation of *reason*—specifically, an interrogation of reason with respect to its capacity to gain knowledge independently of experience or, in other words, an interrogation of *pure* reason. Such a critique is a necessary propaedeutic to metaphysics.

(2) Development of the problem (Inaugural Dissertation).

How did metaphysics come to be a problem for Kant? That is, how did the capacity of reason to gain knowledge independently of experience become questionable?

We can glimpse the answer by looking at the last of Kant's "pre-critical" works: the Inaugural Dissertation of 1770, presented on the occasion of his inauguration as professor at the University of Königsberg. What is most important is that in the Dissertation, metaphysics is *not* questionable the way it is in the *Critique*; thus the transition from the former to the latter is precisely the calling of metaphysics into question.

The general framework of the Dissertation is expressed in the title: "On the form and principles of the sensible and intelligible worlds." Accordingly, the general framework is provided by the distinction between the intelligible world (things as they are in themselves) and the sensible world (things as they appear to our senses, things as given in experience). Along with this distinction, a connection is posited between the two worlds distinguished: the intelligible world is understood as the substrate or ground of the sensible one.

This is a venerable old distinction and way of understanding it, detached by the tradition from Book 5 of Plato's *Republic*. In general, it is akin to the Leibnizian distinction between the realm of nature (extended things, phenomena) and the realm of grace (monads, substances). The distinction is duplicated on the side of the subject in the contrast between sensibility and intelligence:

> Sensibility is the receptivity of a subject by which it is possible from the subject's own representative state to be affected in a definite way by the presence

of some object. Intelligence (rationality) is the faculty of a subject by which it has the power to represent things which cannot by their own character come before the senses. The object of sensibility is the sensible; that which contains nothing but what is to be known through the intelligence is the intelligible. In the schools of the ancients the first was called a phenomenon and the second a noumenon. (Inaugural Dissertation, §3. *Selected Pre-critical Writings*, trans. G. B. Kerferd and D. E. Walford, Manchester University Press, 1968)

Sensible things appear to sensibility. This does not entail, however, that intelligence has no relation to sensible things. It can indeed relate to them, but only in its "logical use." Intelligence can do no more than compare and reflect conceptually on what is given to sensibility.

On the other hand, intelligence also has a "real use." That is crucial; through the real use of intelligence, we are able to know the intelligible, that is, know things as they are in themselves. According to Kant: "Insofar as intellectual things strictly as such are concerned, where the use of the intellect is real, such concepts, whether of objects or relations, are given by the very nature of the intellect. They have not been abstracted from any use of the senses, nor do they contain any form of sensible knowledge as such" (§6).

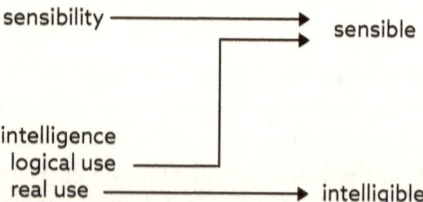

The concept of metaphysics is determined in reference to this real use of the intelligence: "The philosophy which contains the first principles of the use of the pure intellect is metaphysics" (§8). Thus metaphysics has to do with knowledge of the intelligible, that is, with our knowing things in themselves independently of experience.

The transition from the Dissertation to the *Critique of Pure Reason* is precisely Kant's calling into question the ground and thus the possibility of such knowledge. He questions the objective validity of those pure concepts he had previously taken as providing such knowledge. That is, he raises this problem: how can a concept apply to an object we do not create, an object independent of us, without the concept being derived from a sensible presentation of that object?

Kant's raising of this problem is documented in his famous letter to Marcus Herz (February 21, 1772). Let me cite an extended passage from that letter:

I noticed I still lacked something essential, something that in my long metaphysical studies I, as well as others, had failed to heed and that, in fact, constitutes the key to the whole secret of hitherto still obscure metaphysics. I asked myself: what is the ground of the relation to an object of that in us which we call the "representation" of it? If a representation is only a way the subject is affected by the object, then it is easy to see how the representation is in conformity with this object, namely, as an effect in accord with its cause, and it is easy to see how this modification of our mind can represent something, that is, have an object. Thus the passive or sensuous representations have an understandable relation to objects, and the principles derived from the nature of our soul have an understandable validity for all things insofar as those things are supposed to be objects of the senses. In the same way, if that in us which we call "representation" were *active* with regard to the object, that is, if the object itself were created by the representation (the way divine cognitions are held to be the archetypes of all things), the conformity of these representations to their objects could be understood. Thus the possibility of both an *intellectus archetypi* (on whose intuition the things themselves would be grounded) and an *intellectus ectypi* (which would derive the data for its logical procedure from the sensuous intuition of things) is at least intelligible. Our understanding, however, through its representations, is not the cause of the object (except in the case of moral ends), nor is the object the cause of the intellectual representations in the mind (*in sensu reali*). Therefore, the pure concepts of the understanding cannot be abstracted from sense perceptions, nor can they express the reception of representations through the senses; but although they must have their origin in the nature of the soul, they are neither caused by the object nor do they bring the object itself into being. In my dissertation I was content to explain the nature of intellectual representations in a merely negative way, namely, by stating they were not modifications of the soul brought about by the object. But I silently passed over the further question of how a representation that refers to an object—without being in any way affected by it—can be possible. I had said: the sensuous representations present things as they appear and the intellectual representations present them as they are. Yet by what means are these things given to us, if not by the way they affect us? And if such intellectual representations depend merely on our inner activity, whence comes the agreement they are supposed to have with objects—objects that are nevertheless not possibly produced thereby? (*Philosophical Correspondence 1759-99*, pp. 71-72)

So the aporia is as follows. If the object causes representations in the mind, then there is a ground for a relation and conformity between them, namely, in this causality. The same holds if the representation causes the object, in a way which, as we will see later, Kant associates with creative, divine knowing. But in the case of concepts given in the real use of the intelligence, "pure concepts of the understanding," neither alternative holds. These concepts, since they are independent of sensibility, are not caused by objects; nor do they cause objects. So the question the Dissertation "silently passed over" is this: how can pure concepts possibly provide knowledge of objects? That question is what leads from the Dissertation to the *Critique of Pure Reason*.

Let us briefly relate this development to Leibniz. In the transition to the first *Critique*, Kant does bring into question, and eventually under radical criticism, the Leibnizian view regarding knowledge of the intelligible. Nevertheless, Leibniz' thought in general remained the contextual background of the *Critique*. That is to say, Kant proceeds from Leibnizian concepts and formulations, the concepts of phenomenon and noumenon, for example. Kant begins with Leibnizian concepts, although he will go on to transform them radically.

This general Leibnizian background is best seen in a polemical work by Kant from the year 1770 entitled "On a discovery according to which any new critique of pure reason has been made superfluous by an earlier one" (in H. E. Allison, *The Kant-Eberhard Controversy*, Baltimore: Johns Hopkins University Press, 1973, pp. 107–160). Kant wrote this polemic in response to a scathing criticism the first *Critique* received at the hands of a Wolffian philosopher named Eberhard. The charge was that everything of importance in Kant's *Critique of Pure Reason* could be found in Leibniz and everything else in the book was the work of a sophist.

In his response, Kant shows how Eberhard's whole attack depends on a misapprehension of the distinction between sensibility and intelligence (understanding), whereby Eberhard compounds rather than clears up this problem as it was treated by Leibniz. Then, in the last part of the work, Kant turns the tables on Eberhard. Kant sets himself up as the defender of Leibniz and shows how various Leibnizian themes, such as the principle of sufficient reason, the monadology, and the doctrine of a pre-established harmony, are actually anticipations of Kant's own critical philosophy. At the very end of his response, Kant says: "The *Critique of Pure Reason* can thus be seen as the genuine apology for Leibniz."

(3) Preparatory view of the whole.

I want to present a series of four formulations meant to elaborate the critical problem as a whole while moving to more and more fundamental levels.

A. First formulation: the critical problem as a problem of the unity of reason.

This formulation predominates in the Preface to A and in parts of the Preface to B. Kant says: "pure reason as such is a perfect unity" (A xiii). But, as the history of metaphysics shows, reason is actually in conflict with itself. Kant's word is *Mißverstand*: "misunderstanding" in the dual sense of error (being deceived) and also dissension (being in conflict). Thus there is a disruption of reason's perfect unity with itself. This disruption will become visible especially in the antinomies—for instance, in the first one: the world does have/does not have a beginning in time. So the critical problem is to resolve the self-conflict and restore reason to that condition of unity proper to it.

Three issues need to be mentioned in this regard.

First, what is involved in this conflict, this misunderstanding? That is to say, what sets reason against itself? At B xxiv, Kant points to the general answer. He refers to those principles by which speculative reason comes into conflict with itself, and then he says: "These principles properly belong not to reason but to sensibility, and when thus employed they threaten to make the bounds of sensibility coextensive with the real and hence to supplant reason in its pure (practical) employment" (B xxiv–xxv). So reason's coming into this conflict is in some way connected with sensibility, with reason's relation to sensibility.

Second, the limiting of speculative reason, a limiting necessary for a resolution of the conflict, is carried out in order to free reason to that practical employment which is proper to it. Thus Kant's famous statement in the Preface to B: "I have therefore found it necessary to deny knowledge in order to make room for faith" (B xxx). Accordingly, speculative reason is to be reestablished in its proper unity in order that the unity of pure reason as such, speculative and practical, might be instituted.

Third, the essential unity of reason is also of methodological significance and is so in two senses. The initial sense has to do with completeness. Because of the unity of reason, the critique of reason can be complete: "In this inquiry I have made completeness my chief aim, and I venture to assert that there is not a single metaphysical problem which has not been solved or for the solution of which the key at least has not been supplied" (A xiii).

Kant proceeds immediately to speak of reason as "so perfect a unity." The point is that reason is a unity in the sense of being self-enclosed, involving nothing "from without," nothing accidental, contingent, that might render the account of it intrinsically incomplete: "I am to deal with nothing save reason itself and its pure thinking; and to obtain complete knowledge of these, there is no need to go far afield, since I come upon them in my own self" (A xiv).

This indicates the other sense in which the unity of reason has methodological significance. This sense corresponds to a conception of unity in terms of presence, that is, a conception of reason's unity as oneness with itself, presence to itself. The point is that the critique of reason is a matter of self-knowledge. The critique is reason's investigation of itself. In other words, the genitive in "critique of reason" is both subjective and objective. And such self-investigation is possible precisely on the basis of a certain presence to self, a presence of reason to itself. Kant broaches the issue as follows: "For metaphysics is nothing but the inventory of all our possessions through pure reason, systematically arranged. In this field nothing can escape us. What reason produces entirely out of itself cannot be concealed but is brought to light by reason itself as soon as the common principle has been discovered" (A xx).

Note the tension here, bordering on contradiction. Reason is essentially one and yet can be set against itself (can be twofold, antinomous) in a way that seems not to be merely accidental. Also, reason is self-enclosed and yet can be related to its other, namely, sensibility, in a way that leads it into conflict with itself. Third, reason is self-present and cannot be concealed from itself and yet can fall into *Mißverstand* and even "dialectical illusion."

I suggest the appropriate response is not to try to eliminate this tension but rather to be watchful for how it functions, often covertly, in Kant's text.

B. Second formulation: the critical problem as a problem of synthetic apriori judgments.

According to Kant, "Reason is the faculty which supplies the principles of apriori knowledge. Pure reason is, therefore, that which contains the principles whereby we know anything absolutely apriori" (A ii). So the *Critique of Pure Reason* has to take up the question of the possibility and limits of apriori knowledge. In this connection, we need to consider the distinctions by which Kant delimits such purely "rational" knowledge. There are two distinctions:

The first differentiates apriori from aposteriori (empirical) knowledge. This distinction is made in terms of the source of the knowledge. Apriori knowledge is absolutely independent of all experience; its source is not in any way experience. Aposteriori knowledge is empirical, derived from experience. The criteria of apriori knowledge are necessity and strict (not inductive) universality. Either one, necessity or universality, is sufficient to indicate apriori knowledge.

The second distinction is between analytic and synthetic judgments. Kant expresses this distinction in three ways:

(i) "A is B" is analytic provided "the predicate B belongs to the subject A as something covertly contained in this concept A" (A7). For example: "man is rational." One can analyze the concept of the subject (rational animal) and find the predicate contained therein, find an identity between the predicate and a component part of the subject.

(ii) According to the *Prolegomena*, an analytic judgment is one which "depends wholly on the law of contradiction" (*Pro*, p. 14). This is equivalent to the first definition.

(iii) The third definition is almost the same but adds the element of thought, although it is not clear why: "Analytic judgments are therefore those in which the connection of the predicate with the subject is thought through identity" (A7).

Kant proceeds to combine these two distinctions:

	analytic	synthetic
a priori	analytic *a priori*	synthetic *a priori*
a posteriori	~~analytic *a posteriori*~~	synthetic *a posteriori*

Kant notes that all judgments of experience (aposteriori) are synthetic. There are no analytic aposteriori judgments. Thus three permutations remain, and Kant poses the question of synthesis in each case. What is the ground (x) allowing the subject and predicate to be connected?

i) Analytic (apriori): x = the principle of identity.
ii) Synthetic aposteriori: x = experience.
iii) Synthetic apriori: x = ? We do have synthetic apriori knowledge (for example, mathematics), but how is it possible? That is the critical problem in its second formulation: how are synthetic apriori judgments possible?

Kant develops this formulation by indicating in a general way how apriori synthetic knowledge could be possible. This development occurs in the context of his proposed "Copernican revolution" (Preface to B, xvi–xvii). In effect, Kant proposes a revolution in philosophy analogous to the one Copernicus brought about in astronomy. The proposal involves two steps.

(i) Kant discusses sciences other than metaphysics and asks: how does such a science originate, that is to say, how does it get established as a science, as happened with mathematics among the Greeks? Kant answers: it originates through revolution, through a sudden insight first establishing it as a science. Specifically, this insight is one into the proper method.

Kant considers the question of origin especially in reference to modern physical science. There the proper method is experimentation. But what is the experimental method? It is not simply a matter of proceeding empirically. Thus Kant is not contrasting modern with pre-modern science in the usual way of saying that modern science is more empirical, has a higher regard for facts. Rather, what is decisive is that modern science has a *different way* of regarding facts. The contrast, as Kant sees it, is that modern science does not simply observe, does not simply heed the facts, but rather *constrains* nature "to give answers to questions of reason's own determining" (B xiii). That means reason itself poses the questions, sets forth certain principles. Experimentation then consists not in mere observation, but in devising experiments in systematic accord with these principles. Thus Kant says that "we can know apriori of things only what we ourselves place into them" (B xviii).

(ii) Kant proposes to bring into play an analogous insight in metaphysics, a "Copernican revolution." Kant writes:

> The examples of mathematics and natural science, which by a single and sudden revolution have become what they now are, seem to me sufficiently remarkable to suggest our considering what may have been the essential features in the changed point of view by which they have so greatly benefited. Their success should incline us, at least by way of experiment, to imitate their procedure so far as may be permitted by the analogy which they, as species of rational knowledge, bear to metaphysics. Hitherto it has been assumed that all our knowledge must conform to objects. But every attempt to extend our

knowledge of objects by establishing something in regard to them apriori, by means of concepts, has on this assumption ended in failure. We must therefore make trial whether we may not have more success in the tasks of metaphysics if we suppose that objects must conform to our knowledge. This would agree better with what is desired, namely, that it should be possible to have knowledge of objects apriori, determining something in regard to them prior to their being given. We should then be proceeding precisely on the lines of Copernicus' primary insight. Failing of satisfactory progress in explaining the movements of the heavenly bodies on the supposition that they all revolved around the spectator, he tried for better success by making the spectator revolve while the stars remained at rest. A similar experiment can be tried in metaphysics, as regards the intuition of objects. If intuition must conform to the constitution of the objects, I do not see how we could know anything of them apriori, but if the object (as object of the senses) must conform to the constitution of our faculty of intuition, I have no difficulty in conceiving such a possibility. (B xvi–xvii)

Some comments are in order. The first has to do with the sense of the analogy. It would seem that Kant is doing the opposite of Copernicus, for the latter instituted a shift *away from* the human subject: the earth is no longer the center. But that is not the point. The point of the analogy is that Copernicus explained the apparent movement of the planets by taking into account the movement of the observer. In other words, the apparent movement is treated as the resultant of two movements: the actual movement of the planet and the movement of the observer. In the same way, for Kant the object (appearance) is treated as the "resultant" of the thing itself and that which is contributed by the subject.

The second comment concerns the outcome of Kant's proposed revolution, which is that the possibility of apriori knowledge of objects becomes intelligible. Specifically, such knowledge is knowledge of the conformity the object must make in order to be an object (of experience), that is, knowledge of what must be characteristic of the object in order for it be an object. In other words, if a thing must conform (meet conditions, have a certain character) in order to be an object of experience, then I can know in advance that any object of experience is so conformed. I can know this independently of my experience of that object.

Thus what would need to be discovered is the required conformity. This could be discovered through an investigation of the faculty of knowledge, that is, through reason's investigation of itself. Accordingly, just as science requires insight into method and hence into the appropriate way of interrogating objects, so in philosophy there must be insight into the conditions reason prescribes for the experience of objects. And just as modern science constrains nature to answer reason's questions, so reason requires that nature conform to reason's requirements.

The third comment is that this revolution places severe limitations on our knowledge. On the one hand, we have no access to things independently of our knowing. On the other hand, as known, a thing must already have become conformed to the mind. Thus we can know the thing only as so conformed, not as it is independently of this conforming, not as it is in itself. In other words, we can know only appearances, not things in themselves.

Fourth, how does this revolution affect metaphysics? To what extent does it resolve the problem of metaphysics?

In order to grasp the import of Kant's answer, consider the traditional division of metaphysics, as first formulated by Baumgarten (cf. the "Architectonic" of the *Critique of Pure Reason*):

1. *Metaphysica generalis* (ontology, for Kant "metaphysics in its first part"), the consideration of being qua being.
2. *Metaphysica specialis* ("metaphysics in its second part"). It breaks down into:
   Rational theology—consideration of God
   Rational psychology—consideration of the human soul
   Rational cosmology—consideration of the world as a whole.

Kant says that his revolution promises to put "metaphysics in its first part" on the path of science. It makes possible a science of the necessary determinations of objects of experience as such, thus the science of being qua being ("qua being" means: as an object, an appearance).

On the other hand, by limiting knowledge to the domain of objects of experience, Kant's "Copernican revolution" radically undermines metaphysics in its second part. More precisely, it undermines the claim of speculative reason to knowledge of the supersensible. It undermines this, however, in such a way as to prepare a transition from speculative to practical reason.

Accordingly, in the "Architectonic," Kant replaces the traditional division. He divides metaphysics as follows:

1. Metaphysics of nature—consideration of the speculative employment of pure reason
2. Metaphysics of morals—consideration of the practical employment of pure reason.

Finally, what is the relation of the first *Critique* to metaphysics as reconstituted in this way, that is, to the "system of pure reason," "transcendental philosophy"?

The *Critique of Pure Reason* is a propaedeutic, a preparation for this metaphysics in its proper tasks. Kant's most general articulation of the preparatory work is couched in an architectural metaphor: materials and plan.

The first need is to estimate the materials available for the metaphysical edifice, that is, to determine the source, possibility, and principles of purely rational knowledge. Second, the plan of the edifice, that is, the formal conditions of a complete system of pure reason, would need to be projected. The plan would include a Transcendental Doctrine of Elements and a Transcendental Doctrine of Method.

C. Third formulation: the critical problem as a problem of objectivity.

The "Copernican revolution" introduces a duality into human knowledge, a duality of spontaneity and receptivity. The spontaneity corresponds to what is contributed by the mind; the receptivity corresponds to what is contributed by the object. On this basis, the revolution renders intelligible the possibility of an apriori synthetic knowledge but also separates appearances from things in themselves.

At this point, we reach the limit of the analogy; beyond this, the presentation of the critical problem in terms of a Copernican revolution becomes misleading. The difficulty is that this revolution makes it seem as though the discrepancy between an appearance and a thing in itself is simply a result of the spontaneity of knowing, a result of what the mind contributes. It then seems that if knowing were purely receptive, this discrepancy would not exist, since the mind would contribute nothing. Hence a perfect knowing would be purely receptive.

But that is not so at all. Perfect knowing, divine knowing, is a purely *spontaneous* knowing, in no way dependent on an object. Kant refers to such perfect knowing in several places in the *Critique of Pure Reason* (we will discuss them in detail later). For instance, at B145 he speaks of "an understanding which is itself intuitive," and he adds, "as, for example, a divine understanding which would not represent to itself given objects but through whose representation the objects would themselves be given or produced." Thus, perfect, divine knowing is purely spontaneous. It is not dependent on an object but rather produces its object in knowing it.

It is against such knowing that Kant contrasts human (finite) knowing: "our mode of intuition is dependent on the existence of the object and is therefore possible only if the subject's faculty of representation is affected by that object" (B72). This says that human knowing requires affection and hence receptivity. Human knowing cannot be purely receptive, however. That is the genuine point made in Kant's discussion of his Copernican revolution. If apriori synthetic knowledge is to be possible (and it must be possible, since it is actual), knowing must not be a mere conforming of the mind to the object, must not be mere receptivity. Rather, the object must also conform to the mind. Or, more adequately expressed, the object must be brought to conformity by means of a spontaneity intrinsic to knowing.

At the beginning of the Introduction in B, Kant indicates the character of this spontaneity within human knowing: "There can be no doubt that all our knowledge begins with experience. For how could our faculty of knowledge be awakened into action did not objects affecting our sense partly of themselves produce representations, partly arouse the activity of our understanding to compare these representations, and by combining or separating them work up the raw material of the sensible impressions into that knowledge of objects which is entitled experience?" (B1).

So in human knowing there is an activity of comparing, combining, and separating by which from "the raw material of the sensible impressions" an object is built up, composed. In other words, that which is given by our receptivity (fragmentary sensible impressions) is taken up into spontaneity and built into an object by this spontaneous activity. That means the fragmentary "given" is connected together into the form of an object, gathered up into the form of connection proper to objects.

Now a crucial step occurs. In order for a subject to be able to connect the "givens" together into this proper form, the subject must know in advance how they are to be connected, that is, must know the rules for connecting them. Accordingly, the form of connection proper to objects must in some way be already "in view," already known.

The form of connection proper to objects may be called simply "objectivity." Thus objects of experience, as having to be built up through the spontaneity of the subject, presuppose an apriori knowledge of objectivity. This knowledge of objectivity is the apriori synthetic knowledge at issue in the *Critique of Pure Reason*. It is a synthetic knowledge not only independent of experience but also *prior* to experience. Expressed better, this knowledge constitutes the condition of the possibility of experience. So the third formulation of the critical problem as a problem of objectivity comes down to a problem of exhibiting the elements of this knowledge of objectivity.

D. Fourth formulation: the critical problem as a problem of gathering.

The main shortcoming of the second and third formulations is that they are limited to the first half of the *Critique of Pure Reason*. We will now generalize from the third formulation and will do so in such a way as to deepen the entire issue.

According to the third formulation, central to the critical problem is the knowledge of that objectivity which is prior to experience. Such knowledge is central because of the directive function it performs. Specifically, it is directive for our spontaneity, for that distinctive activity, intrinsic to human experience, which *gathers* the "givens" into the form of connection proper to objects.

Expressed more generally, this gathering is one of an indeterminate (fragmentary) manifold into a unity, into a proper connectedness. If the manifold consists in the sensibly given, and if the unity amounts to objectivity, then we have here the kind of gathering with which the Transcendental Analytic is concerned.

But such gathering may take other forms. For example, the gathering may be one of the manifold of appearances into the unity of the idea of the world as a whole. Or it may be a gathering of the manifold of all created things into the unity of the idea of a creator. The critical problem then involves exhibiting these other forms of gathering in their essential dynamic structure and determining their possibility and limits. That is the concern of the Transcendental Dialectic.

Note that through all forms of gathering, there runs a duality between a positing or "knowing" of the unity into which something is to be gathered and the fragmentary manifold that is to be gathered up. The problem in each case will be to determine how and within what limits the manifold can be gathered into unity. In other words, to what extent does the manifold as gathered coincide with the unity posited?

The problem can thus be expressed as that of a connection between certain unities and the corresponding multiplicities. We can thereby begin to translate the Kantian problem into Greek and can do so in several ways.

Most directly, the problem has to do with unity, that is, one, ἕν, and with multiplicity, that is, many, πολλοί.

Or, if we focus on the character of the manifold as indeterminate, then this manifold corresponds to what, according to Aristotle, Plato called the "indeterminate dyad," ἀόριστος δυάς.

Or, suppose we focus not so much on unity and multiplicity, but on the *gathering* of the manifold into unity, and further, on the character of this gathering as bringing forth the object of experience, that is, as bringing it into presence. Then this gathering is a gathering into presence. Thereby we get a glimpse of that archaic sense of λόγος/λέγειν recovered by Heidegger in his interpretations of Heraclitus. Recall that λόγος was translated into Latin as *ratio*, from which comes *Vernunft*, "reason." Thus I am indicating a reversal of that translation and pointing to a level at which the archaic sense of reason is still alive in the Kantian conception.

The third and fourth formulations take us far beyond the level of the Prefaces and Introduction of the *Critique of Pure Reason*. Those formulations are meant to give some gauge of the depth of the critical problem and prevent our assuming we have reached the most basic level as soon as we have understood Kant's initial formulations. What we have to undertake now is to regain through the text the level of the problem we have at this point only anticipated in these introductory sketches.

* * *

Before proceeding, let me pause and remind you that the difficulty of Kant's texts, especially the *Critique of Pure Reason*, is legendary. Yet we need to distinguish two—at least two—kinds of difficulty in a text. There is the difficulty resulting from a mere lack of clarity in the language and in the conceptuality. And there is the difficulty resulting from a lack of clarity intrinsic to the matter itself. We might then say a text is genuinely clear only if it lets what is inherently unclear remain so and does not introduce a sham clarity, which would only serve to conceal the questionableness of the matter.

Let me then conclude my introduction to the *Critique of Pure Reason* with a seemingly outrageous statement by Heidegger and suggest it is to be understood in reference to such a conception of clarity. According to Heidegger:

> In spite of all differences and the extent of the historical interval, Kant has something in common with the great Greek beginning, which at the same time distinguishes him from all German thinkers before and after. That is the incorruptible clarity of his thinking and speaking, which by no means excludes the questionable and the unbalanced and does not feign light where there is darkness. (Martin Heidegger, *What is a Thing?*, tr. W. B. Barton and V. Deutsch, Chicago: Regnery, 1967, p. 56)

III. The Transcendental Aesthetic

BEFORE WE ENTER into the actual analyses, let us consider the preparatory matters Kant takes up at the very end of the Introduction of the *Critique of Pure Reason* and at the beginning of the Transcendental Aesthetic. We will take up:

(1) Kant's presentation of the fundamental distinction between sensibility and understanding (last paragraph of the Introduction).
(2) Kant's sketch of the general context of the Transcendental Aesthetic (opening paragraphs of the Transcendental Aesthetic).

(1) Sensibility and understanding.

The distinction is presented in the final paragraph of the Introduction. Kant is discussing the divisions and subdivisions of the *Critique of Pure Reason*, and, having postponed detailed discussion of the grounds of the subdivisions, he continues: "By way of introduction or anticipation, we need only say that there are two stems of human knowledge, namely, sensibility and understanding, which perhaps spring from a common, but to us unknown, root. Through the former, objects are given to us; through the latter, they are thought" (A15/B29).

This statement and the distinction it introduces are of the utmost importance. I will bring out three points. First, as the context indicates, the distinction provides the ground for a primary subdivision in the *Critique of Pure Reason*, namely, that of the Transcendental Doctrine of Elements into the Transcendental Aesthetic (sensibility) and Transcendental Logic (understanding or, more generally, reason). We can then sketch the overall structure of the entire *Critique of Pure Reason*:

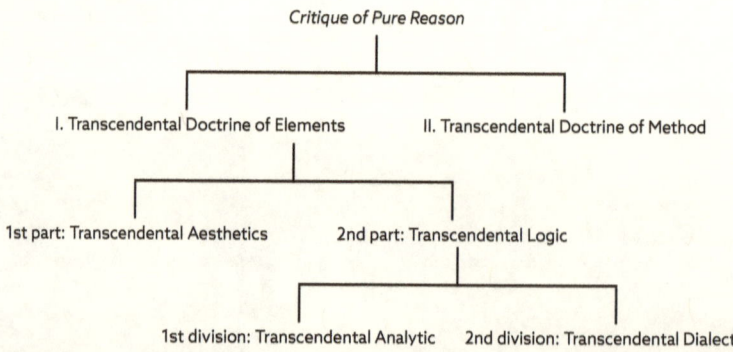

Along with the division into Aesthetic and Logic, there is also operative another fundamental division crossing it, a division into positive and negative. The Transcendental Aesthetic and Analytic form the positive part of the *Critique of Pure Reason*, and the Transcendental Dialectic forms the negative part. This latter division into positive and negative corresponds roughly to Kant's position on *metaphysica generalis* versus *metaphysica specialis*.

We can already glimpse from these general indications that the "architectonic" is not just some external form Kant thoughtlessly imposes on the *Critique of Pure Reason* but is instead grounded in the matters at issue in the book. Whether grounded adequately or not is another question, and that question assumes we have some idea of what adequacy would mean here.

Second, the distinction between sensibility and understanding is formulated in explicit opposition to the position of Leibniz and Wolff (cf. A43–44). In other words, Kant insists that sensibility is *not* just confused understanding. Specifically, Kant argues that the difference between confused and clear is merely logical (formal), whereas the difference between sense and understanding is one of content. In this connection, Kant points out (cf. Dissertation, §7) that sensible things can be very clear, as in geometry, and intellectual things extremely confused, as in metaphysics.

Third, Kant says in the passage just quoted that through sensibility "objects are given to us" and that through understanding "they are thought." So this distinction corresponds in general to that between receptivity and spontaneity. Thus it would seem that through sensibility something is received and through understanding (the active power of thought) something is added, something stemming from the subject, something apriori. But in the very next sentence, Kant proceeds to complicate matters: "Now insofar as sensibility may be found to contain apriori representations constituting the condition under which objects are given to us, it will belong to transcendental philosophy" (A15/B29–30).

This says that even within sensibility (receptivity), there are certain apriori representations. That is, not all apriori representation falls on the side of spontaneity and thought, as the initial formulation suggested. In other words, if we continue to link the apriori with spontaneity, then even within receptivity there is a dimension of spontaneity. Thereby we touch on the deeper problem running throughout the Transcendental Aesthetic: how can there be something apriori, a dimension of spontaneity, within the sphere of the given, within receptivity?

(2) General context of the Transcendental Aesthetic (§1).

On the surface, §1 looks like a mere string of definitions, a lexicon. But in fact it is a remarkably clear and concise sketch of the entire problematic within which the Transcendental Aesthetic is situated. Thus it is a sketch of the general context of the Transcendental Aesthetic.

Indeed, this is only the initial context, the *beginning* of the *Critique of Pure Reason*, and, recalling what we said earlier about the stratification of a text, we can anticipate that eventually this beginning may prove to be merely one level. Nevertheless, we can gain access to other levels only from here.

Kant begins: "In whatever manner and by whatever means a mode of knowledge may relate to objects, intuition is that through which it is in immediate relation to them . . ." (A19/B35). This says that in all knowledge of objects, all synthetic knowledge, intuition has a certain primacy; intuition is that by which knowledge stands in *immediate* relation to its object. Whatever else might be involved in the full structure of the relation of knowledge to its object, intuition is what gives knowledge its element of immediacy. Intuition is what contributes the immediate content of objective knowledge.

Thus any other elements that may belong to knowledge must be considered in reference to the primacy of intuition. Kant then concludes the first sentence by referring to intuition as that "to which all thought as a means is directed." So intuition and thought are, at least at this initial level, not simply coordinate. Thought is only a means; thought is *in service* to intuition.

Kant continues: "But intuition takes place only insofar as the object is given to us" (A19/B33). In other words, intuition, that by which knowledge is in immediate relation to its object, requires that the object be *given*. The question is: in what way can the object be given? What forms can such giving assume? There are two primary ways: the giving may proceed from the side of the subject or from the side of the object. That is, the subject may give itself the object, or the object may give itself to the subject.

Consider the two alternatives:

For the subject to give itself the object would mean for the subject to bring the object forth, create it in the very act of knowing it. The intuition corresponding to such a way of giving is called by Kant "original intuition" or "intellectual intuition" (cf. B72). Such intuition is available only to God, not to any dependent, limited, finite, being. Furthermore, Kant says about God: "all his knowledge must be intuition, and not thought, for the latter always involves limitations" (B71).

The point is that divine intuition is complete, involves no imperfection, and so has no need of thought, of that means which must come to supplement limited, imperfect modes of intuition. Therefore, God does not think.

As regards giving, the other alternative is that the object may give itself to the subject. In this case, the subject would be dependent on something it does not create, dependent on something announcing itself, affecting the subject. The intuition corresponding to this way of giving is called "derivative intuition" (B72). Kant identifies this second way of giving as the only one possible for human beings.

In turn, this second way is possible for us "only insofar as the mind is affected in a certain manner" (A19/B33). That is, in order for the object to affect the subject, the subject must have the capacity to be affected. The subject must have the capacity for receiving the object in its giving itself; the subject must have a receptivity. Thus Kant continues by introducing this receptivity, under the name "sensibility": "The capacity (receptivity) for receiving representations through the mode in which we are affected by objects is entitled sensibility" (A19/B33).

At this point, Kant summarizes: "Objects are *given* to us by means of sensibility, and it alone yields us intuitions. . . ." Then Kant adds: "Intuitions are thought through the understanding" (A19/B33).

So, unlike divine knowing (original intuition), human knowing involves not only intuition but also thought. More precisely, human intuition, *because* it is derivative (limited, dependent, finite), requires the additional element of thought, which, Kant already said, is in service to intuition, a means. Thought, as so connected to intuition, as supplementary to intuition, as required by the finitude of our intuition, is what Kant intends by the term "understanding."

So it is on account of the finitude of human intuition that there are two stems of human knowledge. Once again, these two stems are not simply coordinate. Instead, understanding is subordinate to intuition, in service to it. Kant expresses the bond of understanding to sensibility as follows: "From the understanding arise concepts. But all thought must, directly or indirectly, by way of certain characters, relate ultimately to intuitions and thus, for us, to sensibility, because in no other way can an object be given to us" (A19/B33).

This says that for us, for us humans, for human knowing, thought can relate to objects, can be a genuine representing of things, only mediately, only through sensibility, only when thought takes the form of *understanding*. One implication is that thought can represent things only as they appear, not as they are in themselves.

Here again we see that decisive transition Kant has made between the Dissertation and the *Critique of Pure Reason*. Kant no longer makes any allowance for that pure thought, that "real use" of the intellect, by which things would be known as they are. Of course Kant has not demonstrated this negative conclusion, this limitation of thought. In a sense, he is presupposing it here, but he will demonstrate it in the Transcendental Dialectic, where he will expose all forms of pure thought as belonging to the "sophistry of pure reason." In this sense, one could say of the entire Transcendental Dialectic what has often be said of its middle section on the antinomies: it is the cradle of the critical philosophy.

Kant's subordination of thought to intuition needs to be seen within the history of metaphysics. In effect, this subordination destroys a basic ontological schema that has determined Western thought since the Greeks. The traditional schema correlates two distinctions, thought and sensibility, being and appearance:

{ thought — being (what truly is, things as they truly are)
{ sensibility — mixture of being and non-being, appearance

What Kant does is to deny that thought has access to true being. Instead, Kant makes thought, as a means, subordinate to sensibility. Hence he constrains thought to the domain of appearances.

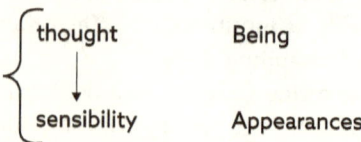

One could connect this development to what comes after Kant. From the perspective of Nietzsche, this development appears as a decisive stage in the collapse of the distinction between the "true world" (the supersensible) and the "world of appearance." It is a stage in what Nietzsche calls "the history of an error," a history he recapitulates under the title "How the true world finally became a fable." The outcome of this history, the complete collapse of the supersensible, is what Nietzsche calls "the death of God," "the advent of nihilism."

* * *

Let us now return to Kant's text. Once Kant completes the sketch of the general context, he proceeds to focus on what is specifically at issue in the Transcendental Aesthetic.

The term "Transcendental Aesthetic" already indicates the issue in general. Kant takes "aesthetic" in its root sense, as pertaining to αἴσθησις (perception, sensation). So an aesthetic will be an investigation of sensibility or intuition. But Kant's aesthetic is to be a transcendental one. What does that mean? For now, let us take the definition Kant provides in the Introduction of the *Critique of Pure Reason*: "I entitle *transcendental* all knowledge occupied not so much with objects as with the mode of our knowledge of objects insofar as this mode of knowledge is to be possible apriori" (A11–12). That is to say, transcendental knowledge is knowledge *about* apriori knowledge of objects or, more specifically, about apriori synthetic knowledge of objects. Thus the Transcendental Aesthetic will deal with that apriori knowledge which is related to intuition, with that element of intuition by which some sort of apriori knowledge is made possible.

Kant proceeds to focus on this element by distinguishing different kinds of intuition. He speaks first of empirical intuition and defines it by introducing "sensation": "The effect of an object on the faculty of representation, insofar as we are affected by it, is sensation" (A19–20/B33–34). Thus sensation is what results from affection. Then Kant says: "That intuition which is in relation to the object through sensation is entitled empirical. The undetermined (unthought) object of an empirical intuition is entitled appearance" (A20/B34).

If we recall the general context, namely, that an object can be given to us only by affection, then it follows that all human intuition of objects must be empirical. The question is: can there be a kind of intuition that is not an intuition of objects? In order to show that there can be another kind, Kant proceeds to distinguish between two components of appearance: "That in the appearance which corresponds to sensation I term its matter; but that which brings it about that the manifold of appearance can be ordered in certain relations, I term the form of appearance" (A20/B34).

So form is that by virtue of which sensations can be ordered. This form is not itself sensation. Instead, it is pure, not something resulting from affection. Thus it must "lie ready for the sensations apriori in the mind and so must allow of being considered apart from all sensation" (A20/B34). This pure form of sensibility Kant calls "pure intuition."

Kant then identifies this element of pure intuition as the subject matter of the Transcendental Aesthetic: "The science of all principles of apriori sensibility I call transcendental aesthetic" (A21/B35). More specifically, the Transcendental Aesthetic requires two steps for its subject matter to be delimited, beginning with the following: "In the Transcendental Aesthetic we shall, therefore, first isolate sensibility by taking away from it everything the understanding thinks through its concepts, so that nothing may be left save empirical intuition" (A22/B36).

So sensibility is to be completely isolated from thought, from the understanding. This raises a very serious question: since thought is not just coordinate with sensibility and since it is required because of the very character of human intuition (its derivative, finite character), can sensibility be adequately understood in isolation from thought? In other words, is not a treatment of human intuition under such conditions as are imposed in the Transcendental Aesthetic necessarily abstract, partial, preliminary?

The second step in delimiting the subject matter of the Transcendental Aesthetic is a further separation. Everything in intuition that belongs to sensation is separated out, so all that remains is *pure* intuition.

Kant concludes by saying that the investigation will show there are two such pure forms of sensibility or pure intuitions: space and time. Note that these forms are linked by Kant to the derivative character of human intuition in contrast to divine, original intuition. Although Kant does not explain the link, we might suppose it results from some lack of order, some chaos, in the material element (sensation) on which human empirical intuition is built. In other words, for Kant it is because the material component lacks order that the formal, order-giving element of pure intuition is required. In any case, an original intuition by contrast would have no need for such forms, and in fact Kant says of God: "We are careful to remove the conditions of time and space from his intuition" (B71).

* * *

To show that space and time are pure intuitions, pure forms of sensibility, Kant considers each in turn and provides:

(A) a metaphysical exposition
(B) a transcendental exposition
(C) conclusions regarding space and time resulting from those expositions.

Space

(A) Metaphysical Exposition of Space

Kant presents the metaphysical exposition in §2. The exposition proper is preceded by three preliminary considerations.

First, Kant distinguishes between inner sense and outer sense. Outer sense is that by which we represent to ourselves objects as outside us. All such objects are represented as in space. Inner sense is that by which the mind intuits itself or its inner state. Everything belonging to this inner state is represented as in time. So space is linked to outer sense, time to inner sense. In fact, Kant says: "time cannot be outwardly intuited, any more than space can be intuited as something in us" (A23/B37).

The distinction Kant draws here is merely taken over from the modern post-Cartesian tradition and probably from Locke, who formulates it as a distinction between sensation and reflection (*Essay*, Book II, Chapter 2). In the course of the *Critique of Pure Reason*, however, this distinction will be radically rethought. Indeed, the rethinking already gets under way in the Transcendental Aesthetic. At A38, Kant refers to the position that the reality of objects of inner sense is "immediately evident through consciousness," whereas the reality of outer objects is not certain; such objects may be illusory. That is the Cartesian position, a grounding of philosophy on the self-certainty of the *cogito*. Against this, Kant argues that such a priority of inner sense cannot be maintained. Eventually, in the Analytic, he will show that even inner sense has a peculiar dependence on outer sense.

The second preliminary consideration is launched by Kant abruptly posing the question: "Then what are space and time?" He offers several possible answers: "Are they real beings? Are they only determinations or relations of things, yet such relations as would belong to things even if they were not intuited? Or are space and time such that they belong only to the form of intuition and therefore to the subjective constitution of our mind, apart from which they could not be ascribed to anything whatever?" (A23/B37–38).

Already we can anticipate that the last of these answers (space and time as forms of intuition) is the one Kant will undertake to establish. We need to see, however, just what Kant is excluding: what are the other answers to which he alludes? They are clearer in a corresponding statement in the Dissertation, posed there not as a question but as an assertion: "Space is not something objective and real, neither substance nor accident nor relation, but something subjective and ideal, issuing by a constant law from the nature of the mind" (§15).

Kant makes a similar assertion with respect to time. So he is excluding three views: space and time as (i) real substances, (ii) real accidents, and (iii) real relations. Let us consider these in turn.

(i) Space and time are not real substances.

That is, space and time are not containers in which all else is contained. Later in the Transcendental Aesthetic, Kant speaks openly of the nonsense to which this view leads. The upholders of the view "have to admit two eternal and infinite absurdities (space and time), which exist (yet without there being anything real) only in order to contain in themselves all that is real" (A39).

(ii) Space and time are not real accidents.

Especially important here is the historical background, namely, the Leibniz-Clarke Correspondence. That is an exchange of letters in 1715–16, the last phase of a long controversy between Leibniz and various Newtonians. The Correspondence consists of five letters by Leibniz and as many replies by Samuel Clarke as spokesman for Newton.

The question of space and time figures prominently in the debate. Newton's view as presented here is that space and time are accidents. Specifically, since space and time are infinite, they are accidents of the infinite substance. In other words, they are accidents of God. Or, as Clarke says in the fourth reply, they are *properties* of God. Even more specifically, the Newtonian view traced—but not made entirely explicit—in the Correspondence is that space and time constitute the "divine sensorium," that in and through which the intellect and will of God are present to the physical world so that God can perceive and guide it.

A faint vestige of this view of space and time can be found in Kant's Dissertation (§22). Kant refers there to space as "phenomenal omnipresence" and to time as "phenomenal eternity." Then Kant says, "We intuit all things in God." But in the *Critique of Pure Reason*, there is no remnant of this view at all.

(iii) Space and time are not real relations.

Here the Leibnizian view is in the background. According to Leibniz, space is the order of coexistence, and time the order of succession. Leibniz' fourth letter states: "Space is that order which renders bodies capable of being situated and by which they have a situation among themselves when they exist together, just as time is that order with respect to their successive position" (*The Leibniz-Clarke Correspondence*, ed. H. G. Alexander, Manchester University Press, 1956, p. 42).

Kant does not reject the general Leibnizian view of space and time as relational. But Kant does reject the view that they are *real* relations. Actually, Leibniz also rejected such a view, for he argued that no relations are real; all relations are representations. To use Kant's term, they are "ideal." The difference between Kant and Leibniz is that Leibniz defines this ideality in reference to the divine mind, whereas Kant defines it in reference to the human mind.

Kant's third preliminary consideration, before proceeding to the actual exposition, lays down exactly what is meant by a "metaphysical exposition." Kant says it is the exhibition of a concept as given apriori. In other words, it exhibits a concept as apriori and also shows the form in which it is given apriori. Specifically, something can be given either intuitively or conceptually, either as an intuition or as a concept. What Kant wants to show is that space and time are given intuitively. Thus they are pure intuitions rather than pure concepts. So the metaphysical exposition of space will show that space is apriori (arguments #1 and #2) and intuitive (arguments #3 and #4).

* * *

We come now to the actual metaphysical exposition of the concept of space. There are four arguments; the first two are meant to show that space is apriori. According to the definition given in the introduction to the exposition, that means space is independent of, not derived from, sense experience. Yet that is only the weaker sense. There is another, more crucial sense, and it is this latter one that is primarily operative here. According to this stronger sense, apriori means: prior to sense experience as a necessary condition for it. Clearly, the weaker sense is entailed by the stronger.

Argument #1.
    Actually, there are at least two distinguishable arguments here:
    (1) In order to be able to represent things as outside one another and alongside one another, the representation of space is presupposed. That is, in terms used by the Dissertation, I cannot conceive things as outside one another except by locating them in different places in space; so the representation of space is presupposed. The representation of the relations among things presupposes the representation of space. Therefore, the representation of space cannot be acquired empirically, by abstraction from the relations among things.

Note that the stronger sense of apriori is argued, and the weaker sense inferred from it. Also, in the background is the ontological understanding of space as relational—more specifically, the Leibnizian conception of space as "the order of coexistence."

(2) The second distinguishable argument establishes the same result as the first but does so more decisively by arguing that outer sense as such, and not merely certain things represented in it, presupposes the representation of space. The argument runs as follows: outer sense, the representing of objects as outside oneself, is possible only if sensations are *referred* to some region outside oneself. But such referral requires that the outside be already in view in some way. In other words, space as such must already be represented.

We need to ask regarding argument #1: what is the sense of "argument" here? What kind of argument is this? Ultimately, it is a transcendental argument, from a "given" to its transcendental ground. But more immediately, argument #1 seems to turn on a certain awareness of our representational powers, an awareness of what we can and cannot represent. That is to say, it turns on a certain presence to self, a presence of reason to itself, self-knowledge. But such self-knowledge would seem to have no place in the *Critique of Pure Reason*.

Argument #2.

It takes up the same issue, now in terms of a kind of "thought experiment": "We can never represent to ourselves the absence of space, although we can quite well think it as empty of objects" (A24/B38). This says: we can neither intuit nor think the absence of space, whereas we can think space as empty of objects. So the crucial difference is one of thinkability: we cannot think the absence of space, but we can think space without objects.

What does Kant mean in saying we cannot think the absence of space? What does this impossibility bring to light? What is it about this concept that renders it unthinkable? A clue is found in a footnote to the Preface in B (xxvi) where Kant contrasts knowing with thinking. He says: "But I can think whatever I please, provided only that I do not contradict myself." So the unthinkable concept, the concept of the absence of space, must be contradictory. Kant does not say what the contradiction is between absence and space, but we might well suppose it results from the character of space as that which makes possible presence and absence as such. That is, if presence and absence presuppose space as a condition of possibility, then it is contradictory to speak of the absence of space.

What precisely does this "thought experiment" establish? Kant says we can think space without objects. That is, such a thought is not contradictory, not logically impossible. But we cannot think the absence of space, which means we cannot think objects without space. That is contradictory. In other words, it is logically impossible for there to be objects without space. Therefore, the representation of space cannot be based on the representation of objects, that is, cannot be derived by abstraction from relations among objects. So what is strictly proven is that space is apriori in the weaker sense.

According to Kant, we can *think* space without objects. But note that he does not say we can *intuit* (hence have an experience of) space without objects, empty space. He leaves open the question of the intuition of space, because the discussion of that question requires the refinements that are to be developed in arguments #3 and #4.

Arguments #3 and #4.

What Kant wants to show in these two arguments is perhaps best illustrated by a curious matter he first discusses in a little work of 1768 called "Concerning the ultimate foundation of the differentiation of regions of space." In the *Prolegomena*, Kant explicitly relates this matter to the present problem. The matter is incongruent counterparts: for example, a hand and the mirror image of the other hand. In terms of the proportion and the relation of parts to one another and the size of the whole, the one palm and the mirror image of the other palm are identical. The same description must apply to both. Thus "There are in this case no internal differences which our understanding could determine by thinking alone" (*Pro*, p. 33).

The point is that the difference between them is not a conceptual difference. It is an intuitive difference, one we grasp not by thought but by intuition. Likewise, Kant wants to show that space as such is intuited rather than thought. In other words, space is fundamentally an intuition, not a concept. So argument #3 begins: "Space is not a discursive or, as we say, general concept of relations of things in general, but a pure intuition" (A24/B39). This does not mean we have no concept of space but only that intuition is primary and the concept is derived from it.

The argument will be clearer if we begin by thematizing the general difference between an intuition and a concept. Kant says of them: "The former relates immediately to the object and is single; the latter refers to it mediately by means of a feature several things may have in common" (A320/B377).

Let us now regard arguments #3 and #4 as constituting a single argument involving three steps:

(1) The initial step is expressed as follows: "We can represent to ourselves only one space; and if we speak of diverse spaces, we mean thereby only parts of one and the same unique space" (A25/B39). So space is one, single, as is required for intuition. Yet this does not suffice to show it is an intuition rather than a concept. For a concept is also, in some sense, single. It is a one applicable to many, a single feature many things have in common. Thus what really distinguishes an intuition from a concept is not that the former is one and the latter many,

but rather that they are different kinds of ones; they involve different kinds of one-many relations. So what is crucial is to show that the one-many relation in the case of space is radically different from the kind of one-many relation characteristic of a concept.

(2) Kant proceeds to draw the contrast. First, spaces are parts of space, parts contained within it, whereas the instances of a concept, the many to which it applies, are not parts of the concept.

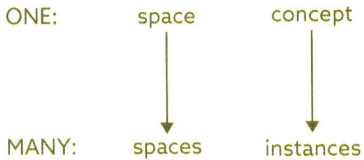

Furthermore, both cases involve a limiting of one side in order to attain the other. But the direction of the limitation is different. In the case of concepts, the *instance*, the individual thing, is limited in order to attain the concept. That is, the individual is taken in some one respect; the one respect is abstracted out. In the case of space, *space* is limited in order to attain spaces.

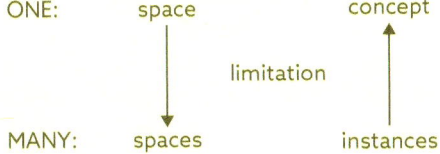

We can summarize the contrast as follows: the concept contains its instances *under* itself, space contains spaces *within* itself.

(3) Thus, it is established that space is not—fundamentally—a concept. It must then, in some sense, be an intuition. But in precisely what sense? From arguments #1 and #2, we know that it must be a pure (apriori) intuition. So Kant proceeds to treat space as an intuition by drawing out the difference between it and *empirical* intuition. The main point of the contrast is that an appearance, that which is intuited in empirical intuition, is always a composite. Accordingly, the whole does not precede the parts, whatever the precise part-whole relation may be. Instead, the parts are constituents out of which the whole is then composed. In the case of space, however, the whole is absolutely prior to the parts. More precisely, the parts "can be thought only as *in* it. Space is essentially one; the manifold in it and therefore the general concept of spaces depend solely on limitations" (A25/B39).

What is the precise sense of this priority? How can the whole absolutely precede its parts? Kant expresses this priority by saying that "Space is represented as an infinite *given* magnitude" (A25/B39). Clearly, he does not mean that space is an immense thing of unlimited extent. Space is not a kind of infinite container, for that could certainly not be given nor even represented as given. Rather, by saying that space is an "infinite *given* magnitude," Kant means it is the "extensiveness" which makes possible definite, quantitative extension: "The quantum wherein all quantity can be determined is, with regard to the number of parts, indeterminate and continuous; such are space and time" (*Kants handschriftlicher Nachlass*, vol. 5, no. 5846).

(B) Transcendental Exposition of the Concept of Space

By "transcendental exposition" Kant means "the explanation of a concept as a principle from which the possibility of other apriori synthetic knowledge can be understood" (A25/B40). So Kant's procedure is to exhibit a body of synthetic apriori knowledge and to argue that its possibility—already established by the fact of its existence—requires that space be a pure intuition.

The body of knowledge Kant presents is geometry. And thus he argues that geometrical judgments are synthetic apriori. To say they are *apriori* means that geometry is not an empirical science. This is evident in the fact that geometrical propositions are apodictic, that is, bound up with consciousness of their necessity. Such necessity could never be derived from experience. For example, that space has three dimensions is not an empirical generalization but something the geometrician asserts to be necessarily true. A more strictly geometrical example would be: if two parallel lines are cut by a transversal, the opposite interior angles are equal.

To say that geometrical judgments are *synthetic* means the predicate adds something beyond what is already contained in the subject. For example: "A straight line is the shortest distance between two points." If this were analytic, then it would be possible, by examining the subject-concept, to discover the predicate-concept in it. But, Kant argues, that is impossible, for the subject-concept is a matter of quality (straight) whereas the predicate is a matter of quantity (shortest distance).

Kant offers other examples (cf. A47/B65): "Two straight lines cannot enclose a space, and with them alone no figure is possible." "Given three straight lines, a figure is possible." Kant maintains that we cannot derive the predicate (possibility or impossibility of a figure) from the concepts of straight line and the numbers 2 or 3. In fact, what do we do with such propositions? We have recourse to intuition. We try to construct a figure corresponding to the concept.

So geometry, the science determining the properties of space, contains synthetic apriori knowledge. The question is: how can it do so? What is required for that possibility? In order for geometrical judgments to be *synthetic*, that is, to go beyond mere concepts, what is known must be given in intuition. Accordingly, space must be an intuition and not a concept. And in order for geometrical judgments to be *apriori*, space must be a *pure* intuition. Hence, Kant concludes that geometry as synthetic apriori knowledge is possible only if space is a pure intuition.

Although it is not his primary concern, Kant does thematize the general nature of mathematics (cf. Section V of the Introduction and especially the chapter on the "Discipline of pure reason" in the Doctrine of Method). Let us consider three propositions:

1. A triangle has three interior angles.
2. The sum of the interior angles of figure ABC (the triangle here drawn on the blackboard) = 180°.
3. The sum of the interior angles of any triangle = 180°.

Proposition 1 is analytic. (Analytic judgments do have a place in mathematics; they can connect different synthetic judgments and define concepts.)

Proposition 2 is aposteriori (empirical). We would establish it by taking a protractor and measuring. It is not a mathematical judgment at all.

Proposition 3 is a genuine mathematical judgment; it is apriori synthetic. What grounds the synthesis of subject and predicate in this proposition? In other words, how do we go about proving it? We do so by constructing a figure:

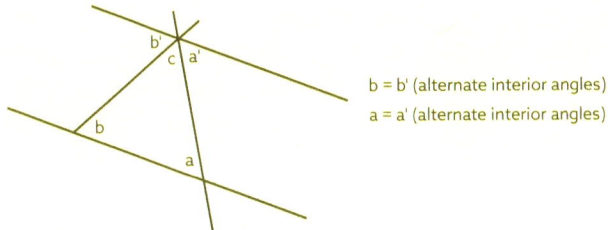

b = b' (alternate interior angles)
a = a' (alternate interior angles)

What we have done is to construct a figure corresponding to the subject-concept; that is, we have constructed the figure in such a way as to allow a summing of the interior angles. Through that construction, we validate the synthesis of the predicate with the subject.

From this example, we can understand Kant's general formulation: "Mathematical knowledge is knowledge gained by reason from the construction of concepts. To construct a concept means to exhibit apriori the intuition corresponding to the concept" (A713/B741). Kant adds: "The single figure we draw is empirical, and yet it serves to express the concept without impairing the universality of that concept. For in this empirical intuition we consider only the act whereby we construct the concept, and we abstract from the many determinations (for instance, the magnitude of the sides and of the angles), which are quite indifferent, as not altering the concept 'triangle'" (A713/B741).

Let me make three additional remarks concerning mathematics:

(1) We have seen that mathematics involves exhibiting the intuition corresponding to the concept. But what is the precise sense of this correspondence? That is, how does an intuition correspond to a concept? What in general is the relation between an intuition and a concept? *That* is the problem of the Transcendental Analytic. Therefore, the full meaning of mathematical construction cannot be developed in the framework of the Transcendental Aesthetic.

(2) To what extent is Kant's notion of mathematical knowledge as construction of concepts adequate outside of geometry? Is it even adequate for analytic geometry, in which geometrical constructions are replaced by algebraic operations? Let me mention only that Kant allows (in algebra) a kind of non-ostensive construction (as in geometry)—a "symbolic construction" (cf. A717). Also, Kant's general view of mathematics has been highly developed into one of the major schools of mathematical thought in this century by Brouwer and Heyting: Intuitionism.

(3) Kant remarks with respect to mathematical construction: "We can determine our concepts in apriori intuition inasmuch as we *create* for ourselves, in space and time, through a homogeneous synthesis, the objects themselves—these objects being viewed simply as quanta" (A723/B751). We should relate this to a matter that arose in our consideration of the Prefaces to the *Critique of Pure Reason*. As already cited, Kant says in the Preface to B that we can know apriori of things only what we ourselves place into them. In different terms, an apriori knowing of things, a knowing that is not dependent on affection, is possible only if we *create* what is known. Thus such knowledge is possible only if we create the thing in the very act of knowing it. Indeed, Kant says in reference to mathematics that the objects "are given through the very knowledge of them . . ." (A87–88/B120). This means, then, that with respect to things known in such knowing, our intuition is original, like divine intuition. Mathematical construction is precisely such a creating of the object in the very knowing of it. So Kant brings to light the *creativity* of mathematical thought.

(C) Conclusions as Regards Space

(1) "Space does not represent any property of things in themselves, nor does it represent them in their relation to one another. That is to say, space does not represent any determination that attaches to the objects themselves . . ." (A26/B42). So Kant is saying that space is not a determination of things in themselves. This conclusion follows from the apriori character of space. If space were a determination of things, it could not be represented prior to the representation of things and so could not be a condition of possibility of the representation of things.

Instead, it could be represented only empirically, through affection by things. As Kant expresses it: "For no determinations, whether absolute or relative, can be intuited prior to the existence of the things to which they belong, and none, therefore, can be intuited apriori" (A26/B42).

(2) The second conclusion is that space is the form of outer appearances, their subjective condition. This conclusion follows from the first one. Since space does not belong to things in themselves, it must belong (originate, have its ground) on the side of the subject. In other words, space is contributed to the appearances by the intuiting subject. In this sense, space is subjective.

Yet space is not something the subject *just happens* to contribute; it is something *necessary*. The intuition of space is a condition of the possibility of the intuition of things. In other words, space is the form in which appearances of outer sense *must* be intuited if they are to be intuited at all. So Kant expresses the conclusion as follows: "Space is nothing but the form of all appearances of outer sense. It is the subjective condition of sensibility, under which alone outer intuition is possible for us" (A26/B42).

(3) Kant summarizes his results by speaking of the "empirical reality" and "transcendental ideality" of space. Empirical reality is objective validity with respect to outer appearances. That is, all things, *considered as* objects of our sensible intuition, are side by side in space. Transcendental ideality has two senses, positive and negative. The negative sense is that with respect to things in themselves (things considered without regard to the constitution of our sensibility), space is nothing at all, has no objective validity. Space is not real in the sense that things in themselves are real. The positive sense is that space has its origin (ground) in the subject and so is ideal, but its ideality is a transcendental ideality. What does "transcendental ideality" mean here? Recall Kant's earlier discussion of "transcendental." The transcendental has to do with the possibility of apriori knowledge. So transcendental ideality is an ideality, something grounded in the subject, providing a basis for apriori synthetic knowledge (in this case, geometry).

It is then fitting that Kant contrasts space with another kind of representation which is also subjective, namely, sensations (for example, of color, sound, and heat). The difference is that sensations yield no apriori knowledge. And the reason, according to Kant, is that sensations have no ideality. That is, they do not originate from the subject but from the *affection* of the subject by something else. They originate in receptivity rather than in spontaneity, whereas we can know apriori of things only what we ourselves place into them, only what we produce out of our spontaneity.

Time

A. The Expositions of Time

The expositions of the concept of time are almost perfectly parallel to those of space. Kant presents almost the same arguments to show that time also is a pure intuition. Then he draws three conclusions with respect to time corresponding to those with respect to space:

> Time is not a determination of things in themselves.
> Time is the form of inner sense, that is, the subjective condition under which inner intuition (intuition of oneself and of one's inner state) is possible.
> Time is empirically real and transcendentally ideal.

There are, however, two points of difference between the treatments of space and time:

(1) There is a difference in the transcendental exposition, although the outcome of the treatment of time is not affected. Recall that a *transcendental* exposition proceeds by exhibiting a body of apriori synthetic knowledge and arguing that space (or time) must have a certain character in order to account for the possibility of this knowledge. In the case of space, Kant is emphatic, both in the *Critique of Pure Reason* and the *Prolegomena*, that this body of knowledge is geometry. In the case of time, however, he refers to various different bodies of apriori synthetic knowledge, presumably because it is not so clear just which knowledge is most appropriate. Specifically, Kant mentions three different possibilities, without extensively developing any of them.

(a) In the *Prolegomena*, the expositions of space and time are most nearly analogous: "Geometry is based on the pure intuition of space. Arithmetic achieves its concept of number by the successive addition of units in time" (*Pro*, p. 30). Just as geometry proceeds by construction in one form of pure intuition (space), so arithmetic proceeds by construction in the other (time). Therefore, arithmetic is an appropriate body of apriori synthetic knowledge to be exhibited by way of establishing that time is a pure intuition.

(b) Another possibility is mentioned under argument #3 in the metaphysical exposition of time in the *Critique of Pure Reason*. (Kant later indicates that #3 actually belongs to the transcendental exposition.) Kant argues that there are certain "axioms of time in general" which are synthetic apriori and which would accordingly not be possible if time were not a pure intuition. Examples of such axioms are that time has only one dimension and that different times are not simultaneous but successive.

(c) Under the heading "The transcendental exposition of the concept of time" in the *Critique of Pure Reason*, Kant refers to the body of apriori synthetic knowledge that is exhibited in the general doctrine of motion. His point is that the concept of alteration—hence, the concept of motion—presupposes the concept of time, so that such apriori synthetic knowledge about motion requires that time be a pure intuition.

(2) The second point of difference between the treatments of space and time in the *Critique of Pure Reason* does not concern mere variation in the way of exposition but rather is a difference in the matters themselves. We have seen that time is the form of inner sense, that is, of the intuition of ourselves and of our inner state. So time applies only to inner appearances and is not a determination of outer appearances. Kant notes that this is why, when we want to represent time in outer appearances, we must resort to a spatial analogy such as that of time as a line.

Nevertheless, having thus restricted time to inner appearances, Kant then maintains that, in another sense, time is the form of all appearances whatever: "But since all representations, whether they have for their objects outer things or not, belong, in themselves, as determinations of the mind, to our inner state, and since this inner state stands under the formal condition of inner intuition and so belongs to time, time is therefore an apriori condition of all appearances whatever. It is the immediate condition of inner appearances (of our souls) and thereby the mediate condition of outer appearances" (A34/B50).

This says that regardless of what is represent*ed* (state of one's soul or outer appearance), the represent*ing*, as belonging to our inner state, is in time. So time, at least mediately, is a necessary condition for whatever is represented. Thus *in some sense* time underlies even outer appearances, although the precise sense in which these are in time remains to be determined. At any rate, the result is that time underlies all objects of intuition; all appearances are, in some sense, in time. Time is a universal, all-inclusive, form of appearances. This result is of utmost importance for the Transcendental Analytic. There, time will come more and more to the center of the problematic. This will be possible precisely because time, in contrast to space, is the universal form of intuition.

B. The "General Observations" of §8

(1) We have seen that outer appearances involve the two pure forms, space and time, and also involve a matter, sensation. These are the components of appearance. Space and time, in Kant's conclusions, pertain to the object only as appearance, not to the things in themselves. So one component pertains to the thing only as appearance. But, even more evidently, sensations cannot be attributed to the thing in itself either, since they arise from affection through the senses and depend on the peculiar constitution of sense in the affected subject. Thus there is no element, neither form nor matter, in the appearance that can be attributed

to or be said to correspond to the thing in itself. Hence Kant says: "The things we intuit are not in themselves what we intuit them as being.... What objects may be in themselves, and apart from all this receptivity of our sensibility, remains completely unknown to us" (A42/B59).

In this connection, Kant explicitly relates his conclusions to a famous distinction, much debated in modern thought, between primary and secondary qualities. Galileo and Locke established a distinction between two kinds of qualities in objects of outer sense. The primary qualities are the "objective" ones, ones really belonging to a thing independently of our experience. They include extension, place, and shape, or as Kant says, "space with all that belongs to it" (*Pro*, p. 37). The secondary qualities are those that do not belong to the thing itself but only to its appearance; they arise merely from interaction between things and our senses. Thus secondary qualities have no existence outside of our representation. Examples are colors, tastes, smells.

Kant accepts this distinction of qualities. But he insists that it does not go far enough, and so he extends it. For him, primary qualities (everything pertaining to space) also belong only to appearances and not to the things in themselves. He says in the *Prolegomena*: "All the properties which constitute the intuition of a body belong merely to its appearance" (*Pro*, p. 37). Yet in insisting that primary qualities, like secondary ones, belong only to appearances, Kant is not simply abolishing the distinction. There is still a distinction in qualities, and for Kant what distinguishes the primary qualities is that they belong to a domain of transcendental ideality, in contrast to the secondary qualities. Accordingly, apriori synthetic knowledge is possible with respect to primary qualities: mathematical science of nature.

(2) We have seen that intuition presents only appearances. No component can be said to correspond to the things in themselves. This holds not only of outer appearances but also of that inner intuition by which we intuit ourselves and our inner state. With respect to the *form* of inner intuition, this restriction is clear: time pertains only to appearances and not to things in themselves. Yet this is not the fundamental sense of the restriction.

In general, something can be intuited only if one of two conditions holds. Either what is intuited is created in the very act of intuition, or what is intuited affects the "knower." In the latter case, it can be intuited only as it appears, only as appearance. If we apply this to the case of intuiting oneself, then the first alternative is that I create myself in the very act of intuiting myself. That is what Kant is referring to when he says: "if all that is manifold in the subject were given by the activity of the self, then inner intuition would be intellectual" (B68).

But that possibility is not open to human beings: the manifold of inner states is not *given* by the act of knowing it. Instead, the manifold precedes the act of knowing. In other terms, self-knowing is not original. Thus the intuition of the self (hence, self-knowledge) is possible only through affection, self-affection. In inner sense, therefore, the self intuits itself as it is affected by itself, as it appears to itself, not as it is.

So the disparity between the self in itself and the self as appearance does not result from the fact that the self as it appears is in time. On the contrary, it results from the dependence of intuition on affection. It results from the finitude of intuition. That is what is at the root of the character of self-intuition as appearance.

* * *

To conclude our considerations of the Transcendental Aesthetic, let me indicate two issues that go far beyond it and that lead to the Transcendental Logic.

(1) Kant's theory of self-affection places a severe restriction on self-knowledge. In inner intuition, the self knows itself only as appearance, not as it is in itself. This virtually amounts to a denial of self-knowledge, since all knowledge must ultimately relate to intuition. Such restriction then raises a difficult and far-reaching problem with regard to the very project of a critique. The problem is this: how is such a denial of self-knowledge to be reconciled with the necessity of a certain presence to self as the very condition of the possibility of a critique of reason to be carried out by reason?

We can highlight this tension—bordering on, but never quite becoming, contradiction—by setting side by side the theory of self-affection (denial of self-knowledge) and the following statement already cited from the Preface in A: "I have to deal with nothing save reason itself and its pure thinking; and to obtain complete knowledge of these, there is no need to go far afield, since I come upon them in my own self."

In different terms, the problem is that the critique is itself, as Kant says, a matter of self-knowledge. How then is a critique possible, if we grant this denial of self-knowledge to which it has already led? I suspect this is a problem amenable to no easy or very direct answer, either affirmative or negative. One could perhaps even read all of German Idealism as moving within the tension of this problem.

(2) I want to extend an issue touched on previously. The very concept of "pure intuition" harbors a curious tension. As intuition, it has the sense of something *given to* the subject, in contrast to the spontaneity of thought. On the other hand, as pure, it is something not derived from experience and hence is something *originated* by the subject rather than something given to the subject "from elsewhere." So a pure intuition would be something given which, however, originates in the subject. In other words, pure intuition would be given by the subject to itself. What is the character of this giving?

The Transcendental Aesthetic provides no answer, but let me anticipate. Eventually, Kant will describe a peculiar power that combines receptivity and spontaneity in an intrinsic way. So it is a power of spontaneous receptivity, a power of giving oneself something to intuit without that thing having to be present to one's senses. Kant will designate this power by the term "imagination." In the *Opus Posthumum*, Kant writes regarding space and time: "They are only given in the subject, that is, their representation is an act of the subject itself and a product of its imagination" (*Opus Posthumum*, tr. E. Förster and M. Rosen. Cambridge: Cambridge University Press, 1993, p. 185).

IV. The Transcendental Analytic

A. Introduction: The Idea of Transcendental Logic

The "Transcendental Doctrine of Elements" is divided into the Transcendental Aesthetic and the Transcendental Logic. We have seen that this division corresponds to a division of human knowing into two stems: intuition and understanding. Intuition is treated by the Aesthetic, and, specifically, the pure elements of intuition are treated by the *Transcendental* Aesthetic. Understanding or thought is to be treated by logic, and, specifically, the pure elements of understanding by *Transcendental* Logic. Yet it is necessary to delineate more precisely the concept of a transcendental logic, for its concern with the pure elements of thought does not suffice to distinguish it from all other types of logic. Consequently, Kant begins his Transcendental Logic with a detailed presentation of the *idea* of transcendental logic. First he lays out the concept of general logic:

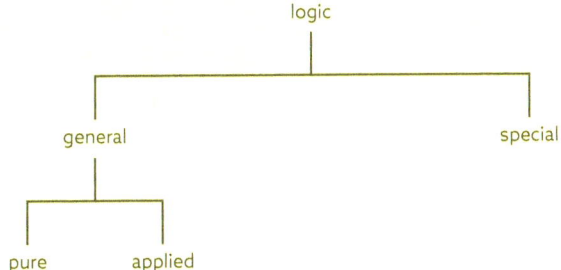

General logic (the logic of the general employment of the understanding) contains the absolutely necessary rules of thought, without regard to the particular object thought about. Special logic (the logic of the special employment of the understanding) contains rules for correct thinking with respect to a certain kind of object.

General logic then is divided into pure and applied. *Pure* general logic abstracts from all empirical conditions under which understanding is exercised (for example, as influenced by the senses, imagination, memory, habit, prejudice). This logic has nothing to do with empirical principles and does not borrow anything from psychology. This is the classic statement of a non-psychologistic theory of logic (cf. Husserl). *Applied* general logic deals with rules for the employment of understanding under the subjective empirical conditions taken up by psychology.

Thus pure general logic (formal logic) abstracts from all content of knowledge and deals only with the mere form of thought in general. The question then is: can there be another logic which remains non-empirical (general) but does not abstract entirely from content? In other words, can there be a logic which is general without being merely formal?

In order to sketch out the possibility of such a logic, Kant draws upon a result of the Transcendental Aesthetic: there are pure as well as empirical intuitions. So he proposes that a provisional distinction may analogously be drawn between pure and empirical thought of objects, that is, between a *pure* objective thought-content and an *empirical* objective thought-content.

Then there could be a logic dealing with a pure objective content. Such a logic would be general (non-empirical), since it would abstract from all empirical content. But it would not be merely formal, since it would not abstract from all objective content. In Kant's words: "This other logic, which should contain solely the rules of the pure thought of an object, would exclude only those modes of knowledge which have empirical content. It would also treat of the origin of the modes in which we know objects, insofar as that origin cannot be attributed to the objects" (A55/B80). Such a logic Kant calls "transcendental logic."

* * *

We need to take up two further issues regarding transcendental logic in general. First, note how Kant divides transcendental logic:

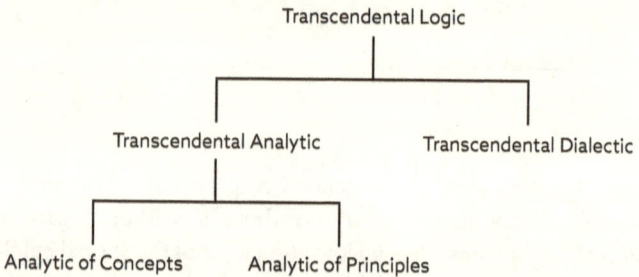

The Transcendental Analytic deals with the elements (concepts) of pure understanding and with the principles without which no object can be thought, thus the principles that govern the pure thought *of objects*. The Transcendental Dialectic is the critique of the dialectical illusion resulting from the misuse of these elements and principles by extending them beyond their legitimate domain of application.

The Analytic of Concepts investigates the possibility of pure concepts by searching for them in the understanding "as their birthplace." This requires a dissection (analysis) of the understanding. It is important to note that what is analyzed is the understanding, not concepts.

This articulation of the Transcendental Analytic is preliminary. One of the major tasks in interpreting the Analytic is to unfold the immense complications and problems broached by this apparently simple distinction between an Analytic of Concepts and an Analytic of Principles. The most profound structural complication is the transformation of this twofold articulation into a threefold one by way of the emergence, between these two divisions, of what amounts to a third division of the Analytic, the Schematism.

The second issue—regarding the Transcendental Logic in general—has to do with the way this logic isolates pure understanding, separates it out from knowledge as a whole, just as the Transcendental Aesthetic isolates pure intuition. In the Transcendental Logic, understanding is isolated from sensibility; in addition, within understanding, the pure elements (originating in understanding itself) are separated off from the elements originating in sensation. Kant contrasts the pure understanding (thus isolated, as the theme of the Transcendental Logic) with sensibility. According to him, pure understanding "is a unity, self-subsistent, self-sufficient, and is not to be increased by any additions from without. The sum of its knowledge thus constitutes a system, comprehended and determined by one idea" (A65/B90).

This self-sufficiency (systematic character) lies in the fact that pure understanding (more generally, thought) involves no receptivity; that is why it is "not to be increased by any additions from without." Instead, it is pure spontaneity. That distinguishes it from all intuition, even pure intuition. Yet here we must make an important distinction. Although thought does not involve any receptivity and is itself pure spontaneity, it does nevertheless have a certain dependence on intuition. Specifically, it is dependent on intuition, not *as* thought, but in order to be thought *of an object*, in order to have objective validity. In other words, if thought is not to be empty, its spontaneity must be exercised on what is provided by intuition. Though complete in itself, it has objective validity only when in service to intuition.

Thus it turns out that the transition from the Transcendental Aesthetic to the Transcendental Logic is not as straightforward as it might seem. Specifically, it does not suffice to define transcendental logic merely in terms of its orientation to pure rather than empirical thought. The complication is that general (that is, formal) logic can be described in the same terms: it, too, abstracts from everything empirical and thus deals only with *pure* thought. Hence, it is necessary to distinguish between formal logic and transcendental logic. Kant does so by distinguishing three different modes of thought, specifically in terms of two axes rather than the single axis (pure—empirical) used in the Transcendental Aesthetic.

	formal (abstracts from all content)	objective
pure (a priori)	formal ('pure general') logic	transcendetal logic
empirical (a posteriori)	X	special logic

B. Book I: Analytic of Concepts. Chapter I: Pure Concepts

Transcendental logic abstracts from all empirical content (is pure) but does not abstract from all content whatever (is not merely formal). It contains "the rules of the pure thought of an object." Kant will identify these rules as categories, pure concepts of the understanding. And so the full title of the first chapter of the Analytic of Concepts is "The clue to the discovery of all pure concepts of the understanding."

The major parts of this chapter are:

(1) the logical employment of the understanding (sections 1–2)
(2) the transcendental employment of the understanding (first part of section 3)
(3) the transition from the logical to the transcendental employment (last part of section 3).

Here it is already clear what "the clue" is, namely, the formal logical employment of the understanding or, in other words, traditional formal logic.

(1) The logical employment of the understanding.
Kant begins his analysis by reiterating the connection between understanding and concepts. The knowledge yielded by the understanding is a knowledge by means of concepts; it is discursive rather than intuitive. So the obvious questions are: what are concepts? And what is the character of knowledge by means of concepts? Section 1 is devoted primarily to answering these questions.

We can best understand Kant's answer if we begin with the definition of "concept" in his *Logic*: "a general representation or a representation of that which is common to many objects" (*Logic*, tr. R. S. Hartman and W. Schwarz, Indianapolis: Bobbs-Merrill, 1974, p. 96). So a concept is a one applicable to many, a one in which many agree. Yet concepts, unlike intuitions, are not simply *given*. Instead, they arise through the spontaneity of thought. Specifically, they arise through the activity of bringing a many under a one. This basic act of conceptualization Kant calls "reflection."

In his *Logic*, Kant treats this matter quite precisely. He begins by distinguishing between the matter and the form of concepts. The matter may be either made or given and may be given apriori or aposteriori. The form is always made. How does the form originate? Kant's answer is that it originates by reflection or, more precisely, by reflection together with two other accompanying acts, comparison and abstraction: "The logical acts of the understanding by which concepts are generated as to their form are: comparison, that is, the likening of representations to one another in relation to the unity of consciousness; reflection, that is, the consideration of how the various representations can be comprehended in one consciousness; and finally abstraction or the segregation of everything else by which given representations differ" (*Logic*, §6, p. 100).

It is important to see that what is central to the origination of concepts is reflection. The other two acts are subordinate. Comparison merely prepares for reflection, and abstraction, as Kant says, "only completes and encloses the concept within its definite limits," that is, only *fixes* what reflection has accomplished.

In the *Critique of Pure Reason*, this centrality of reflection is maintained, except there Kant usually (but cf. A85/B117) refers to this act as "function" rather than as "reflection": "Concepts rest on functions. By 'function' I mean the unity of the act of bringing various representations under one common representation" (A68/B93). So Kant is delimiting the meaning of concept (the concept of concept) by referring back to the subjective origin, the act of reflection. This is a particular case of a regressive movement occurring throughout the various phases of the critical project, the movement expressed, for example, in the notion of the "Copernican revolution." It is the movement from the object (or at least from its formal elements) back to its transcendental origin or ground. At the specific level, one may suppose that concepts bear the stamp of this origin. Furthermore, granted the centrality and character of reflection, we may say that a concept is not just a common element on the same "level" as the things that have it in common but rather is a one as *unifying* the many. The one-many structure of a concept is essential, as also is its active character, its unifying.

We come now to the other question: what is the character of knowledge by means of concepts? In other words, how does the understanding make use of concepts so as to know? According to Kant: "The only use the understanding can make of these concepts is to *judge* by means of them" (A68/B93). So the understanding makes use of concepts for judging. Knowing by means of concepts is judging. In fact, Kant goes on to say: "We can reduce all acts of the understanding to judgments, and the understanding may therefore be represented as a faculty of judging" (A69/B94). Then the question becomes: what is judging and how are concepts made use of in judging?

Kant's answer is that judgment is a *mediate* knowledge of an object, that is, a representation of a representation of an object. (Recall that concepts are never immediately related to objects; only intuitions are.) Kant explains this mediate knowing by reference to an example: the judgment that "all bodies are divisible."

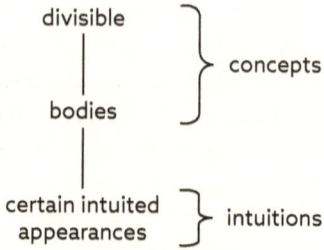

The point is that the concept of "bodies" unifies certain intuited appearances, that is, provides a "one" under which various appearances are unified. The concept of "bodies" is then unified with other concepts under the concept of "divisible." So to judge means to come to know something by bringing it under a higher representation in which it is united with other things. Kant says elsewhere: "Judgment in general is the faculty of thinking the particular as contained under the universal" (*CJ*, p. 179). In the *Critique of Pure Reason*, the discussion of judging concludes as follows: "Accordingly, all judgments are functions of unity among our representations; instead of an immediate representation, a *higher* representation, which comprises the immediate representation and various others, is used in knowing the object" (A69/B93–94).

This raises a very important and difficult question: why is it necessary, at least for human beings, to come to know things in this way? In other words, why does human knowing involve thought, understanding, judgment, in contrast to divine knowing, which would be only intuition and would involve no thought?

A very general answer has already been suggested in the Transcendental Aesthetic: thought is required because of the derivative character of human intuition, its dependence on affection. Kant alludes to the same answer by stating, as we have just heard, that "instead of an immediate representation, a higher representation . . . is used in knowing the object." This suggests that the recourse to a higher representation (concept) is required because the immediate representation (intuition) is *insufficient* for knowing the object.

But then the question arises: what is this insufficiency in human intuition? And just how does the recourse to thought compensate for it?

Since conceptualizing is primarily a matter of unifying, we may suppose that the insufficiency in human intuition consists in a lack of unity. In other words, the insufficiency lies in the fact that the "given" is fragmentary, manifold, in need of unity. Concepts would then provide the unity intuition lacks. But they would do so in a roundabout way; rather than simply providing a singular unity to the intuited, they bring it under a *higher* unity.

Clearly, a whole complex of problems is lurking here—problems we are hardly even in a position to formulate adequately at this point. Let me mention only two problems, in rough formulation. First, how is the fragmentary character of intuition to be critically established? Second, even granted the lack of unity in intuition, how is it to be established that this lack is a need for unity, that unity is required for knowledge? For now, we will just have to carry these questions along—unanswered and hardly even formulated.

Let us return to the development in Kant's text. Granted the general character of understanding as providing unity, the question is then: what are the specific modes of unity the understanding provides? Kant's answer is that within the purely logical employment of the understanding, that is, without regard to content, these modes are the same as the modes of unity in judgment, since understanding is the faculty of judging. In turn, these modes of unity in judgment, that is, the moments of the unifying activity operative in judgment, are represented in the traditional logical table of judgments:

I. <u>quantity</u>

universal	[All men are human]
particular	[Some men are human]
singular	[Socrates is human]

II. <u>quality</u>

affirmative	[The soul is mortal]
negative	[The soul is not mortal]
infinite	[The soul is non-mortal]

III. <u>relation</u>

categorical	[All men are human]
hypothetical	[If all men are human, then the moon is made of green cheese]
disjunctive	[either all men are human or the moon is made of green cheese]

IV. <u>modality</u>

problematic	[The moon can be made of green cheese—it is possible]
assertoric	[The moon is made of green cheese]
apodeictic	[The moon must be made of green cheese—it is necessary]

(2) The transcendental employment of the understanding (categories).

We have seen that transcendental logic does not abstract from all content, from all relation to objects, but only from all *empirical* content. Thus it considers the understanding in its pure, non-empirical relation *to objects*. In general, the understanding can relate to objects only mediately, only through intuition, and it can have a *pure* relation to objects only through *pure* intuition. This means, then, that transcendental logic considers understanding in its relation to pure intuition.

We need to note that here, almost at the beginning, the isolation of understanding from intuition already becomes questionable. And the very principle by which the Transcendental Logic was distinguished from the Transcendental Aesthetic is also brought into question. Thereby we gain a first glimpse of a structural transformation by which the Transcendental Analytic will prove to deal not merely with understanding in distinction from intuition and the Transcendental Aesthetic, but rather with both understanding and intuition.

This transformation is intrinsically connected to another one I have mentioned: the transformation of a twofold division of the Transcendental Analytic into a threefold division.

In any case, the immediate question is this: how can understanding be related to pure intuition, granted that Transcendental Logic considers the understanding in this relation? Kant's answer is that it can do so only by exercising its spontaneity on the material (the content) provided by pure intuition, that is, only by providing concepts under which this material is unified. Thus Kant says that the manifold of pure intuition provides the "material for the concepts of pure understanding" (A77/B102). Let us note that it is by no means clear in what sense pure intuition constitutes a material—we will return to this problem later.

Kant continues: "In the absence of this material, the concepts of pure understanding would be without any content, therefore entirely empty. . . . But the spontaneity of our thought requires that this manifold first be gone through in a certain way, taken up, and connected, in order that knowledge be produced from it. This act I name synthesis" (A77/B102). Accordingly, it is through the act of synthesis that understanding comes into relation with pure intuition and hence into *pure* relation to objects.

What is synthesis? Kant says: "By synthesis, in its most general sense, I understand the act of putting different representations together and of grasping what is manifold in them in one act of knowledge" (A77/B103). So synthesis is the act of bringing a manifold to unity. In other words, "synthesis" designates at a more general level what in formal logic Kant calls "reflection." Kant stresses the crucial role of synthesis in human knowledge; it is "what first gives rise to knowledge" (A77/B103). Because of this role, it will quickly move to the center of Kant's problematic: "It is to synthesis, therefore, that we must first direct our attention, if we would determine the origin of our knowledge" (A78/B103).

The next step Kant takes is crucial. He identifies *imagination* as the power by which synthesis is carried out: "Synthesis in general, as we will hereafter see, is the mere result of the power of imagination, a blind but indispensable function of the soul, without which we would have no knowledge whatever, but of which we are scarcely ever conscious" (A78/B103). Thus Kant is introducing a third power alongside intuition and understanding or, rather, *between* intuition and understanding. The transformation of the twofold into a threefold structure has begun.

So then, contrary to what we might have surmised initially, it is not the understanding that produces the synthesis of the pure manifold. What, then, is the role of the understanding? Kant says: "To bring this synthesis *to concepts* is a function belonging to the understanding, and it is through this function of the understanding that we first obtain knowledge properly so called" (A78/B103).

Understanding brings the synthesis to concepts. Understanding adds the conceptual component, which, as Kant stresses, is an essential ingredient in knowledge proper. But what is this conceptual component? Kant continues the passage just cited: "Pure synthesis, represented in general, gives us the pure concepts of the understanding" (A78/B104). This says that the understanding represents in concepts the unity instituted in the manifold by the synthesis performed by imagination. That is, the conceptual component (categories, pure concepts) are representations of those forms of unity instituted by imagination in the manifold.

In summary: the theme of transcendental logic, namely, the pure relation of the understanding to objects, involves three basic elements.

(a) (pure) intuition—which supplies the pure manifold
(b) imagination—which carries out the synthesis of this manifold
(c) (pure) understanding itself—through which we think, that is, represent conceptually, those modes of unity that are actually instituted in the pure manifold by the synthesis performed by the imagination. These concepts of pure synthesis are the pure concepts of the understanding, the categories.

(3) In dealing with Chapter I of the Analytic of Concepts, we have discussed two of the three major themes, namely, the logical and the transcendental employments of the understanding. We turn now to the third major theme: the *transition* from the logical to the transcendental employment.

Kant's account has shown that the understanding, in both kinds of employment, has the same function, namely, giving unity: "The same function which gives unity to the various representations in a judgment also gives unity to the mere synthesis of various representations in an intuition; and this unity, in its most general expression, we entitle the pure concept of the understanding" (A79/B104).

The point is that both in judgment and in supplying concepts of the synthesis of the pure manifold, understanding is performing the same general function—giving unity. Recall that reflection and synthesis have the same one over many structure. Hence the modes of unity, the moments of unifying activity, are analogous in the two cases. That is why there can be a transition from the logical employment of the understanding to the transcendental employment, that is, from the table of judgments to the table of categories. In other words, that is why the logical table of judgments provides "the clue to the discovery of all pure concepts of the understanding."

Kant's way of making this transition has proved controversial. The frequent criticism is that Kant has not actually derived his list of categories but has instead simply taken it over from the traditional logical table of judgments. But the matter is perhaps not so simple. Attend closely to the title of the chapter: *Vom dem Leitfaden der Entdeckung aller reinen Verstandesbegriffe*, "On the clue to the discovery of all pure concepts of the understanding." Kant does not speak here of derivation (*Ableitung*) or deduction or determination (*Bestimmung*). Instead, here we have a discovering, an uncovering, of the categories—or of the general framework of the categories. But a discovering, unlike a derivation or determination, can leave many things vague, indefinite, still to be determined. We might say that a discovering first discloses something as a whole, so that it can subsequently be determined in all its particulars and its rights and lawfulness deduced.

In this connection, note that the next chapter (the Transcendental Deduction) makes virtually no reference to the list of categories. Instead, the Transcendental Deduction demonstrates the necessity and function of categories as such and as a whole, not of this specific list of categories. Indeed, it is only in the "Analytic of Principles" that the individual categories are actually worked out and determined in their transcendental functions.

So if we wanted to look for the "real derivation" of the categories, we would need to look in the "Analytic of Principles." But perhaps, instead of rushing ahead so precipitously, we would do better to keep in view the various interrelated, yet subtly distinct ways that the problem of categories is taken up. Thus we need to distinguish:

(a) the discovery of the categories as a whole—Chapter I of the Analytic of Concepts
(b) the deduction of the categories as a whole—Chapter II of the Analytic of Concepts
(c) the determination of the categories in particular—the Analytic of Principles.

We would then need to pay attention to the limits of the discovering in Chapter I, the limits serving to distinguish it from deduction and determination. Those limits are constituted by those of the basic analogy, the one on which Kant bases the transition from the table of judgments to the table of categories: both judgment in general and the synthesis of the pure manifold involve the same function, the same giving of unity. The limit of the analogy lies in the structural difference between these two ways of giving unity.

In judgment, thought supplies the concept, or at least its form, and brings the manifold under the concept. So the structure of judgment is twofold: there is the level of the many, either intuited in the case of a singular judgment or already thought in the case of a general judgment, and there is the level of the one, the higher concept under which the many are thought in the judgment.

On the other hand, in pure synthesis, thought supplies the concept but does not itself bring the manifold under that concept. So the structure here is threefold. There is the level of the manifold (pure intuition), the level of the one (the concept supplied by pure thought), and there is also the synthesis itself (the bringing of the manifold under a one by imagination).

In this difference between a twofold and threefold structure, we see the limit of the basic analogy between judgment and pure synthesis and hence the limit of the discovering in Chapter I. That discovering can have disclosed *only* what remains invariant in this transition from the twofold to the threefold structure.

Yet we still need to consider Kant's most outrageous remark: "In this treatise, I purposely omit the definitions of the categories, although I may be in possession of them" (A82–83/B108). This remark serves to emphasize how general and indefinite the table of categories is at the level of the "discovering." But Kant says he is omitting definitions not only here but in the entire treatise. What is transpiring? Is Kant simply being perverse in omitting the definitions of the categories, thus violating the most elementary rule of sound thinking, and then suggesting he does possess those definitions?

We need to glance ahead to a passage in A omitted in B. Kant refers to his earlier omission of the definitions and then says: "It was no evasion but an important prudential maxim not to embark upon the task of definition. . . . But we now perceive that the ground of this precaution lies still deeper. We realize that we are unable to define them even if we wished" (A241). So, remarkably, the categories cannot be defined! What sort of concepts are they, then? One thing is certain: it is not self-evident what would constitute a derivation or determination of such curious concepts.

* * *

Kant and the history of transcendental philosophy.

Toward the end of the Chapter I of the "Analytic of Concepts" (in §12), Kant discusses the "transcendental philosophy of the ancients." He deals specifically with the scholastic transcendental determinations and relates them to his table of categories. What is the relation between Kant's transcendental philosophy and that of the ancients? In other words, how is Kant's transcendental philosophy related to the history of transcendental philosophy, especially to the treatment of the transcendental determinations in scholasticism on the basis laid down by Aristotle?

(1) Aristotle. The basis for the medieval discussion of the transcendentals is found in *Metaphysics* Γ. Aristotle takes up the question of the relation between

being and one, and these turn out to be coextensive, or, as the Scholastics will say, being and unity are "convertible": "'one existent man' adds nothing to 'existent man,' so that obviously the addition in these cases means the same thing, and unity [oneness] is nothing other than being" (*Metaphysics*, 1003b).

This statement needs to be connected with two other developments in Aristotle. First, Aristotle shows that being is not a genus. Being does not designate any *class* of things. That is, being has universal extension. It applies to everything. Thus it *transcends* all division into classes. Furthermore, being does not even designate the *highest* genus, from which we could proceed by division from genus to species. Instead, being completely *transcends* this very way of dividing, since there can be no difference outside being by which being could be divided. Thus, in scholasticism, "being" will be called a *transcendental* determination, and the same with whatever is convertible with being.

Second, such determinations are fundamentally different than those involved in Aristotle's articulation of being in terms of categories such as substance, quality, quantity, relation. A transcendental determination differs from a categorial determination. According to Aristotle's example, a categorial determination such as "white" adds something to that of which it is predicated: "white house" says more than "house"; it adds a further determination. But "one house" says no more than "house." Therefore, categorial determinations, in contrast to transcendental ones, designate genera and are not convertible with being.

(2) Thomas Aquinas. He elaborates the doctrine of the transcendentals especially in *De Veritate*. Aquinas works out several other transcendentals: being (*ens*), one (*unum*), thing (*res*), something (*aliquid*), true (*verum*), good (*bonum*). All of these are convertible, considered with respect to their applicability, their extension. They are all universally applicable. Then how do transcendentals differ among themselves? What kind of division of being is this? In response to this question, there is one decisive development. It occurs in Question 5 of Part I of the *Summa Theologiae*. Aquinas is discussing the relation between being and goodness and says: "Goodness and being are really the same and differ only in idea." The development is that the "division" of being into transcendentals, that is, the constitution of the transcendentals, is referred back to *ratio*, reason.

Here we can look ahead to Kant: certain fundamental determinations, "categories," will be referred entirely to reason, considered to be grounded in reason.

(3) John Duns Scotus. He develops the doctrine of the transcendentals even more thematically. Scotus defines metaphysics as the science of the transcendentals and makes precise the concept of transcendental: "Whatever is not contained under any genus is transcendental. Hence, not to have any predicate above it

except 'being' pertains to the very notion of a transcendental" (*Philosophical Writings*, tr. Allan Walter. Indianapolis: Bobbs-Merrill, 1962, p. 4).

Scotus extends the scope of the transcendental determinations to include "disjunctive attributes":

> "Being" possesses not only attributes which are coextensive with it, such as "one," "true," and "good," but also attributes which are opposed to each another such as "possible-or-necessary," "act-or-potency," and suchlike.... It is not necessary, then, that a transcendental as transcendental be predicated of every being, unless it is coextensive with the first of the transcendentals, namely, "being." (*Philosophical Writings*, p. 4)

This development is important because it will allow Kant to treat as transcendental not only unity and the like but also such disjunctive determinations as substance-accident, cause-effect, and possible-actual-necessary.

For Scotus, the very articulation of being incorporates the issue of the transcendentals. Thus he distinguishes three forms of being as follows:

(a) *ens reale*: substance and accident
(b) *ens rationis*: purely mental beings such as mythical beasts
(c) *ens formale*: the transcendentals.

(4) Ockham. He extends the scope of *ens formale* (transcendental being) until it comes to encompass most of what was previously considered *ens reale*. Specifically, for him all categories except substance and quality have transcendental being.

(5) Leibniz. Here this development comes to a kind of completion. The only *ens reale* is substance, interpreted as monad; all other determinations, all accidental categories, have *ens formale*, that is, are grounded in *ratio* as divine reason.

(6) Kant. As in Leibniz, all categorial determinations (quantity, quality, relation) are referred back to reason as their ground. But the reason which grounds is now taken as finite human reason rather than divine reason. And Kant takes the final step beyond Leibniz: even substance is an *ens formale*, is grounded in *ratio*.

Kant thus treats categorial determinations not as categories but as transcendentals, that is, as determinations applicable singly or disjunctively to every being, insofar as being = object of experience. These are determinations transcending all empirical differences among objects, hence transcending all division into genera and species. Here we can see the appropriateness of Kant's use of "transcendental": transcendental knowledge = knowledge of our modes of apriori knowledge = knowledge of those elements making apriori knowledge possible = knowledge of the categories functioning as transcendentals. Therefore, transcendental knowledge = knowledge of transcendentals.

If the categories take over the function of the transcendentals, then what becomes of the scholastic transcendentals? That is the question Kant takes up in §12. He shows that the determinations *unum, verum, bonum* are simply the three categories of quantity in the form they take when applied not to things, but to our knowledge of things. Thus to the extent that they are legitimately applicable, the scholastic transcendentals form a special case of the Kantian categories.

* * *

As a conclusion to our reading of Chapter I, let me outline a certain textual strategy. Specifically, I want to set two texts side by side. The first is one we have looked at rather closely: "instead of an immediate representation, a *higher* representation, which comprises the immediate representation and various others, is used in knowing the object."

This text occurs in Kant's consideration of "knowing by concepts." The point is that we supplement the insufficiency of intuition by having recourse to conceptualization and judgment. In other words, given the insufficiency of a direct knowing of things, we have recourse to an indirect way of knowing them by bringing them under a higher unity. An analogous recourse has also been sketched at the transcendental level: a lack at the level of pure intuition must be supplemented by pure thought. So within the very conditions of the possibility of experience, there is operative a certain supplementary recourse to thought.

Let us set beside this text one from a Platonic dialogue, *Phaedo*. The specific text occurs in the section in which Socrates tells his own history, how he had pursued direct investigations of φύσις in various ways and how these investigations had repeatedly failed. As a result, Socrates tells Cebes, he eventually set out on a "second sailing," a δεύτερος πλοῦς:

> Well, then, after these, since I had renounced this looking into beings, it seemed to me that I had to be on my guard so as not to suffer the very thing those people do who behold and look at the sun during an eclipse. For surely some of them have their eyes destroyed unless they look at the sun's image in water or in some other such thing. I thought this over and feared that my soul would be blinded if I looked at things with my eyes and attempted to grasp them by each of the senses. So it seemed to me that I should have recourse to λόγοι and look in them for the truth of beings. (*Phaedo*, 99 d–e)

The general connection is clear: both the Kantian text and the Platonic speak of the need of recourse to indirection, that of thought or of λόγοι. That is, both speak of a supplementary recourse to indirection. The connection becomes more substantive if we make some simple substitutions. In Kant's text, substitute "reason" for "thought," which can easily be justified on the basis of other Kantian texts. In Plato's text, substitute "reason" for λόγοι, λόγος, which merely reproduces the metaphysical transformation/translation of λόγος into the Latin *ratio* and then into "reason." If these substitutions are made, then both texts speak of the same supplementary recourse.

C. Book I: Analytic of Concepts. Chapter II: The Transcendental Deduction

Before we begin considering the Transcendental Deduction, we should note Kant's statements regarding the great difficulty of the matters at issue. He says that these "matters are by their very nature deeply veiled," and he speaks of "the inevitable difficulty of the undertaking" (A88–89/B121). Or again, he speaks of the Transcendental Deduction as being "a matter of such extreme difficulty, compelling us to penetrate so deeply into first grounds of the possibility of our knowledge in general" (A98).

We may expect that here Kant's "incorruptible clarity" will consist not in any easy intelligibility but rather in an endeavor not to introduce a sham clarity where the matter itself is intrinsically obscure and veiled. I suggest we too need to take care not to introduce a sham clarity. That is, we need to be attentive to the deeply veiled nature of matter at issue. We need to practice here a kind of reticence.

* * *

Because of the difficulty of the Transcendental Deduction, Kant does not begin immediately with the deduction proper. Instead, he begins with an introductory section explaining what in general constitutes a transcendental deduction (Section 1: "The principles of any transcendental deduction"). Furthermore, after this introductory section, Kant still defers the deduction proper. On account of its difficulty, Kant prefaces it with still another section, meant to "prepare" the reader (Section 2: "The apriori grounds of the possibility of experience"). Only in Section 3 do we finally arrive at the deduction proper.

I will work with the version of the deduction in A. In B, the deduction was entirely rewritten. Kant says it was for the sake of "a more intelligible exposition." Kant insists that the B version alters "absolutely nothing in the fundamentals," although he admits that in B certain things not absolutely essential were omitted. I will follow primarily the A version, if for no other reason than that it is, by Kant's own testimony, more complete. Yet I will also use the B version to clarify certain issues. Of course, we will need to be very careful here, in view of the possibility—argued by many—that there may be a basic discrepancy between the two versions. That, however, is not the sort of thing that can be decided in advance.

(1) Section 1 of the Transcendental Deduction.

This section is called "The Principles of any Transcendental Deduction" and is divided in two parts, §13 and §14, devoted respectively to (a) the general task and (b) the elaboration of that task.

(a) The general task of the Transcendental Deduction (§13).

Kant's discussion of the general character of a transcendental deduction is couched in juridical terms. A deduction has to do with the question of right (*quid juris*) in distinction from the question of fact (*quid facti*). The deduction will be a proof of the right, the legal claim, of certain concepts. Thus the question of the deduction is: what right do certain concepts have to be employed?

We can see why Kant speaks here in juridical terms if we recall how he described the *Critique of Pure Reason* itself in the Preface to A, namely, as "a tribunal which will assure to reason its lawful claims and dismiss all groundless pretensions" (A xi). In the *Critique of Pure Reason*, pure reason is placed on trial and its rights and lawful claims determined. In general, what sort of claim does pure reason make? It lays claim to knowledge independent of all experience, most notably in "special metaphysics," where the claim is made to purely rational knowledge of God, the soul, and the world. So, in Kant's terminology, reason lays claim to apriori synthetic knowledge. That is the claim to be decided in the *Critique of Pure Reason*.

In general, there are two ways something could be known apriori: through pure intuition or through pure concepts. The right of the first way has been decided in the Transcendental Aesthetic. So it is the other claim that has to be settled in the Transcendental Logic: the claim to know things apriori through concepts or, in other words, the claim to possess concepts which, without being derived from things, nevertheless apply to things. In order to settle this claim, it must be shown how such pure objective concepts are possible. That is the task of the Transcendental Deduction, a task defined by Kant as "the explanation of the manner in which concepts can relate apriori to objects" (A85/B117).

(b) Elaboration of the task of the Transcendental Deduction (§14).

According to Kant, there are only two ways a representation and an object can be connected: either the object makes the representation possible or the representation makes the object possible. In the first case, the relation is empirical, and the representation is an empirical representation, not an apriori one. So apriori representation must be the other case; it must be such as to make the object possible. Therefore, the specific question is: how do pure concepts make possible the object of experience? Kant excludes one alternative: they do not make the object possible in the sense of producing it, bringing it into existence. Rather, to begin with a general formulation, they make the object possible *as* an object. They make possible its character as an object; they constitute its objectivity, and so, more generally, they first make it possible for there to be objects. Kant expresses this as follows:

> The question now arises whether apriori concepts do not also serve as antecedent conditions under which alone anything can be, if not intuited, yet thought as object in general. In that case, all empirical knowledge of objects would necessarily conform to such concepts, because only as thus presupposing them is anything possible as an object of experience. Now all experience does indeed contain, in addition to the intuition of the senses through which something is given, a concept of an object as being thereby given, that is, as appearing. (A93/B125–26)

This passage says that pure concepts make it possible for appearances to be experienced not merely as appearances, but as appearances *of something*, of an object. This is a preliminary formulation. We will see later how Kant returns to this question of the object in Section 2 and how he works out there the character of this making-possible.

For now, his focus is the general solution to the problem of the Transcendental Deduction, and he asks: how is it possible for concepts to relate apriori to objects? He answers: "They relate of necessity and apriori to objects of experience for the reason that only by means of them can any object of experience be thought" (A93/B126). That means certain concepts relate apriori to objects because these concepts are conditions for the possibility of the objects *as* objects.

So the task of the Transcendental Deduction is to work out this conditioning in its full range, that is, to show, both from the side of thought and from the side of intuition, why such conditioning is required.

(2) Section 2 of the Transcendental Deduction.

This section is called "The Apriori Grounds of the Possibility of Experience." It develops the principal themes that enter into the Transcendental Deduction. It remains preparatory insofar as it develops these themes somewhat independently, in contrast to Section 3, where Kant will weave them together in the Deduction proper. The three main themes are: (a) synthesis, (b) the transcendental object, and (c) transcendental apperception.

(a) Synthesis.

We have seen in general that a synthesis, carried out by the imagination, is necessary if there is to be a connection between pure understanding (pure concepts) and objects. Since it is precisely such a connection that is at issue in the Transcendental Deduction, the problem of synthesis will be central. Thus Kant begins Section 2 with a more specific account of the character of synthesis (A97–104). According to this account, there is not just a single synthesis but rather three syntheses or, more precisely, a threefold synthesis, a synthesis involving three moments. (At least this is the schema with which Kant begins; it eventually is transformed.) Furthermore, this synthesis takes place at two different levels, the transcendental and the empirical.

At the transcendental level, the manifold to be synthesized is the *pure* manifold of space and time, the manifold of pure intuition. This synthesis is accomplished by imagination in its transcendental employment or, as Kant usually puts it, by "transcendental imagination." It is the synthesis by which the unity represented in the categories is instituted.

There is also an empirical synthesis. Here the sense manifold, the disordered array of sensations, is directly synthesized. The synthesis is accomplished by imagination in its empirical employment or, again as Kant usually puts it, by "empirical imagination." It is important to keep in mind that in this account, Kant deals primarily with *empirical* synthesis and touches on pure synthesis largely by extrapolation. He does this despite the fact that his major concern is the pure synthesis. This indicates that even here, his considerations remain preliminary. And we must be careful to keep constantly in mind the distinction between the two levels and to avoid assuming there is a perfect analogy between them.

Let us consider each moment of the synthesis:

(i) Synthesis of apprehension in intuition.

At the empirical level, this is simply the act in which a manifold of sensations is "run through and held together," that is, apprehended, collected, gathered up, as a manifold. Kant explicitly observes that the synthesis of apprehension is also exercised apriori—"in respect of representations which are not empirical."

Although it is designated as a synthesis *in* intuition, this does not mean it is carried out *by* intuition. It is *in* intuition only as being "directed immediately upon intuition," that is, applied to the manifold of intuition. But the *agent* of synthesis is imagination. Kant is explicit later; referring to imagination, he says: "Its action when immediately directed upon perceptions, I entitle apprehension" (A120).

Kant says about the *pure* synthesis of apprehension: "For without it we would never have apriori the representations either of space or of time" (A99). This statement has profound consequences. It says that the intuition of space and time, that is, pure intuition, is not simply prior to the activity of imagination, as the Transcendental Aesthetic would lead us to believe. Pure intuition, the pure manifold, is not simply an already constituted "material" on which the imagination operates. Rather, it is first fully constituted as pure intuition *through* the activity of imagination. That is most clearly expressed in a footnote in B: "In the Aesthetic, I have treated this unity [that corresponding to the forms of space and time] as belonging merely to sensibility, simply in order to emphasize that it precedes any concept, although, as a matter of fact, it presupposes a synthesis which does not belong to the senses but through which all concepts of space and time first become possible" (B160).

(ii) Synthesis of reproduction in imagination.

At the simplest level, this is the activity by which we keep before our mind what has been given but is no longer given. It is the activity by which we keep in mind certain things previously given by continually reproducing them through imagination.

Kant insists that such reproduction is essential to experience. This means simply that in order to have experience, we must retain the successive phases of the experience rather than let each phase drop out when we pass to the next.

In fact, such synthesis of reproduction is even necessary in order for there to be a synthesis of apprehension: I can run through and hold together a manifold of sensations only if the previously given sensations are reproduced along with the presently given ones. Thus Kant says: "The synthesis of apprehension is inseparably bound up with the synthesis of reproduction" (A102).

So through reproduction *and* apprehension, a manifold is composed or formed into a certain coherent unity. Such forming, however, does not occur at random. Not just any previous intuition is reproduced and synthesized, in just any way, with the present intuition. Instead, the reproduction follows certain laws, and the manifold is accordingly formed in a certain definite way. How is it formed? Into what form is it brought by imagination? Kant says: "Imagination has to bring the manifold of intuition into the form of an image" (A120). So reproduction and apprehension have to be carried out in such a way that the manifold is composed as an image, is brought into the form of an image. It is in this regard that Kant says "imagination is a necessary ingredient of perception itself" (A121, footnote).

All of this concerns the synthesis at the empirical level. What about the corresponding transcendental function of imagination? At this point, Kant does little more than indicate that there is such a transcendental synthesis and that it grounds the possibility of the empirical synthesis of reproduction.

(iii) Synthesis of recognition in a concept.

This synthesis refers to the act in which what has been composed by the imagination through apprehension and reproduction is grasped (represented, thought) in its essential unity by being brought under a concept. Here we could speak of recognizing an image as the image *of* something.

Kant's treatment here is very brief, and much is left undecided. He says nothing about the transcendental synthesis corresponding to this empirical synthesis of recognition. And it is not even clear in what sense he can legitimately refer to a *synthesis* of recognition. For recognition is not, strictly speaking, a part or phase of the synthesis performed by imagination. It is, at most, a kind of completion of that synthesis, a kind of conceptual ratification of the unity already constituted pre-conceptually. Furthermore, this "synthesis" of recognition is not even performed by the imagination but by the understanding, and this too sets it apart from the imaginative synthesis. We might say it is a second-order synthesis, one connecting the outcome of the imaginative synthesis with the correlative concepts of the understanding.

(b) The transcendental object.

This is one of the most difficult themes to interpret. Within the Transcendental Deduction, consideration of the transcendental object is limited almost exclusively to two short passages in Section 2 (A104–5, 109). The term, although not the issue, drops out almost entirely in B. On the other hand, the term and the issue are taken up again in the last chapter of the Analytic ("Phenomena and Noumena") and worked out at a more fundamental level. So our present interpretation, limited to the Transcendental Deduction, can at best be merely provisional.

The theme of the transcendental object is related to an issue Kant raised in the last part of Section 1: how pure concepts (categories) make possible the object of experience. The task that remained was to determine the character of this making-possible. In order to undertake it, Kant proposes to clarify what is meant by "object" or, specifically, by an "object of representations." He begins: "We have stated above that appearances are themselves nothing but sensible representations, which, as such and in themselves, must not be taken as objects capable of existing outside our power of representation. What, then is to be understood when we speak of an object corresponding to, and consequently also distinct from, our knowledge?" (A104).

So appearances alone as supplied by intuition do not constitute objects. Appearances lack objectivity, lack the character of standing over against our knowledge. The problem then is: how can there be objects? How is an object constituted? Or, to reformulate it: what is the "objectifying function" by which appearances are referred to an object, that is, constituted as appearances *of* an object?

We might suppose that the objectifying function is a matter of referral, the referral of appearances to an object, a connecting of appearances with the object.

Strictly speaking, however, that is not possible. For the object is not given; only appearances are given. It is not as though we intuit appearances as well as objects and, having both before us, then refer one to the other. According to Kant: "It is easily seen that the object must be thought only as something in general = x, since outside our knowledge we have nothing we could set over against this knowledge as corresponding to it" (A104).

Since the object is not given, it can enter into the structure of experience only as something thought, something posited by thought. As what is it posited? As having what specific determinations? Kant is saying that it is not posited as having any specific determinations, since there are no specific objective determinations given, which it could then be posited as corresponding to. Instead, it is thought (posited) only as something in general = x. It is thought as an object in general, as having only those determinations anything must have in order to be an object in the most general sense.

The object thus posited is the transcendental object. At least Kant identifies it as such provisionally: "But these appearances are not things in themselves; they are only representations, which in turn have their object—an object which cannot itself be intuited by us and which may therefore be named the non-empirical, that is, transcendental object = x. The pure concept of this transcendental object, which in reality throughout all our knowledge is always one and the same, is what can alone confer on all our empirical concepts in general a relation to an object, that is, objective reality" (A109).

We could say that since the object is not given, it can only be posited as object in general, as transcendental object. Appearances would then in some way be "referred" to this object. So the objectifying function would involve two components: first, a positing of the transcendental object and, second, a referral of appearances to this object. Let us consider these components more closely.

The transcendental object is simply an object in general, the totality of those determinations that belong to any object whatever and that define the very sense of object. The crucial point is that these determinations are *forms of unity*. Thus Kant speaks of "that unity which constitutes the concept of an object" (A105). More specifically, they are precisely those forms of unity represented by the categories. So Kant says that the categories "are fundamental concepts by which we think objects in general for appearances" (A111). Pure thought, pure understanding, is the thinking of the transcendental object, the thinking in which the transcendental object is posited.

We could also express this issue in terms of form-matter. Pure understanding represents (posits) the objective form for the matter of appearances. This is the form under which the matter of appearances must be brought, the form by which the matter must be informed, in order to be objectified, that is, constituted as the appearance *of* an object. So the transcendental object = objective form.

We come now to the second objectifying function, the referral of appearances to the transcendental object. The expression of the issue in terms of form-matter makes it easier to understand the character of the referral. In a sense, it is not a referral at all but rather an informing, a unifying, of appearances: "Now we find that our thought of the relation of all knowledge to its object carries with it an element of necessity; the object is viewed as that which prevents our modes of knowledge from being haphazard or arbitrary and which determines them apriori in some definite fashion. For insofar as they are to relate to an object, they must necessarily agree with one another; that is, they must possess that unity which constitutes the concept of an object" (A104).

Taken with our other conclusions thus far, this passage says that for appearances to be related to an object requires them to possess that unity, those forms of unity, thought in the transcendental object, that is, in the categories. Otherwise worded, appearances must be *made to embody* that unity. The manifold of intuition must be synthesized in such a way as to embody the unity thought in the categories: "It is only when we have thus *produced* synthetic unity in the manifold of intuition that we are in a position to say we know the object" (A105). Or, as Kant puts it in the B version of the Transcendental Deduction: "An object is that in the concept of which the manifold of a given intuition is united. Now all unification of representations demands unity of consciousness in the synthesis of them. Consequently, it is the unity of consciousness that alone constitutes the relation of representations to an object . . ." (B137). Here we find the entire issue linked up to the further issue of the unity of consciousness, that is, linked to apperception.

(c) Transcendental Apperception.

As we have seen, the referral of appearances to the transcendental object is accomplished by instituting in the appearances those forms of unity which are thought in the categories. So the total structure is the positing by thought of objective unity and the synthesis by imagination of the intuitive manifold in such a way as to produce that unity in the manifold. It is precisely this structure that is at issue in the third principal theme of the Deduction. The third theme is transcendental apperception. And the issue is the unity, the coherence, of the two moments of the structure. In other words, the issue is the relation between thought (understanding) and imagination.

I will attempt to recompose Kant's analysis and give it a coherence it does not have in Kant's text. In smoothing it out, I realize I may well be in a sense impoverishing it, suppressing certain directions and possibilities Kant neither worked out nor brought into full correspondence with the major direction. On the other hand, we are perhaps best able to recognize and retrieve these possibilities precisely when, having recomposed the major, explicit development, we then re-read Kant's text.

I will recompose the analysis in seven steps.

(1) We need to notice the exact context in which transcendental apperception is introduced. In order for there to be an experience of objects, a two-sided objectification is necessary, as we have seen: the positing of the transcendental object and the instituting of the corresponding unity in the manifold of intuition. It is in this context that Kant says: "All necessity, without exception, is grounded in a transcendental condition. Accordingly, there must be a transcendental ground of the unity of consciousness in the synthesis of the manifold of all our intuitions, and consequently also of the concepts of objects in general, and so of all objects of experience, a ground without which it would be impossible to think any object for our intuitions. For this object is no more than that something, the concept of which expresses such a necessity of synthesis" (A106).

So the question becomes: what is the transcendental ground of that unity posed as the transcendental object and instituted in the imaginative synthesis? Or, more specifically: what is the transcendental ground of the requirement that there be unity in the manifold and of the unity thus required? Kant answers: "The original and transcendental condition is none other than transcendental apperception" (A106).

(2) What is the character of this condition? Kant writes: "There can be in us no modes of knowledge, no connection or unity of one mode of knowledge with another, without that unity of consciousness which precedes all data of intuition and by relation to which a representation of objects is alone possible. This pure, original, unchangeable consciousness I shall name transcendental apperception" (A107).

Here several characteristics are closely related.

(i) Transcendental apperception is the "unity of consciousness" in the sense of that unity which consciousness *is*. It is that "one consciousness" to which experience is related. It is "the thoroughgoing identity of the self in all possible representations" (A116). Or we might say: it is that self-identical self which is the subject of all representations, the subject of experience.

(ii) Transcendental apperception is "*pure* consciousness." It is prior to everything empirical. What it primarily grounds is *pure* thought and *pure* synthesis.

(iii) Transcendental apperception is original. Like original, divine intuition, it is not dependent on sensibility, receptivity. It is prior to the empirical order.

(iv) Transcendental apperception is unchangeable. It is prior to the order of intuition and time. It is that unity to which even temporal manifoldness is referred back.

So Kant summarizes: "The abiding and unchanging 'I' (pure apperception) forms the correlate of all our representations insofar as it is to be at all possible that we could become conscious of them" (A123). In different terms, transcendental apperception is that I to which Kant refers in his famous statement about the "I think": "It must be possible for the 'I think' to accompany all my representations" (B131).

(3) Yet transcendental apperception is not merely an enduring I standing behind its manifold representations. The I does not possess its representations the same way a substance possesses its accidents. We can see this in the statement just cited: "It must be possible for the 'I think' to accompany all my representations." The point is that this statement alludes to an *activity* in the relation between the I and its representations. The statement means in effect that it must be possible to *refer* all representations back to an I to which they belong. Furthermore, this referral is itself accomplished by the I. In other words, it is a self-referral in which the I represents itself as having certain representations. This is expressed and elaborated in the B version. Following the introduction of the "I think," Kant says: "But this representation is an act of spontaneity; that is, it cannot be regarded as belonging to sensibility. I call it pure apperception, to distinguish it from empirical apperception, or again, original apperception, because it is that self-consciousness which while generating the representation 'I think' (a representation which must be capable of accompanying all other representations and which in all consciousness is one and the same) cannot itself be accompanied by any further representation" (B132).

Note first that Kant says the generating of the representation "I think," that is, the referral of representations to the I of the "I think," "cannot itself be accompanied by any further representation." The point is that the referral of representations to the I is not accomplished by some further I to which a further reference would then be called for. Instead, the I itself refers representations to itself. That is why Kant can say apperception is what generates the representation "I think," that is, carries out the referral of representations back to the I, even though he has previously identified apperception as the I.

Thus apperception is both the I to which representations are referred and the I which refers them. Apperception is both the I which is represented as the subject of representations and the I which does that representing. And this I is one and the same. That is, apperception is the self-representing I. Accordingly, the identity of the I is not the mere passive persistence of a substratum for representations; instead, it is also "consciousness of the identity of the self" (A108).

Apperception is intrinsically also consciousness of oneself *as* original apperception. It is not a mere static, passive oneness, but rather is the spontaneous unification of self-consciousness. Hence apperception is self-consciousness. Or, more precisely, it is the *possibility* of self-consciousness, since what is required is only that it be *possible* for the "I think" to accompany all my representations, not that it actually do so.

(4) Recall that transcendental apperception was introduced as ground, specifically as the transcendental ground of the requirement of unity and of the unity required for the possibility of the experience of objects. Kant expresses the way it functions as ground: "As *my* representations (even if I am not conscious of them as such) they must conform to the condition under which alone they *can* stand together in one universal self-consciousness, because otherwise they would not all without exception belong to me" (B132). This says that my representations would not be mine unless they could stand together in one universal self-consciousness (that is, all be referred back to one and the same I) and that that is possible only if those representations are so unified as to conform to the unity of self-consciousness. Accordingly, "The original and necessary consciousness of the identity of the self is thus at the same time a consciousness of an equally necessary unity of the synthesis of all appearances according to concepts, that is, according to rules, which . . . determine an object for their intuition, that is, the concept of something wherein they are necessarily interconnected" (A108).

The point is that representations can be mine, can stand in one self-consciousness, only if they are brought to unity, that is, given the forms of unity corresponding to apperception itself. Thus transcendental apperception grounds both the requirement of unity and the forms of unity thus required.

(5) Kant states: "The principle of apperception is the highest principle in the whole sphere of human knowledge" (B105). We have seen how this is so: apperception is the ground of the requirement for unity and of the unity required; therefore, the principle expressing this grounding is the highest principle. Nevertheless, Kant continues, this principle is "an identical and therefore analytic proposition" (B135). Why is this highest principle merely analytic? Kant explains: it is analytic because "it says no more than that all my representations in any given intuition must be subject to that condition under which alone I can ascribe them to the identical self as my representations and so can comprehend them as synthetically combined in one apperception through the general expression 'I think'" (B138).

The principle of apperception merely says that my representations must conform to the conditions required for them to be my representations. Accordingly, it is an analytic proposition.

(6) We arrive now at a crucial development. The merely analytic principle of apperception is linked up with the fundamental synthesis performed on the pure manifold by transcendental imagination, and this synthesis is the ground of the possibility of all synthetic judgments. Thus Kant distinguishes here between analytic unity (that of mere apperception) and synthetic unity (that instituted in the manifold). How exactly are these two unities related?

We have seen already that apperception (analytic unity) is the transcendental ground of the imaginative synthesis (synthetic unity). But the point now to be made is that apperception, too, requires the imaginative synthesis, is dependent on it. In other words, synthesis is required for self-consciousness. Kant says that the analytic principle "reveals the necessity of a synthesis of the manifold given in intuition, without which the thoroughgoing identity of self-consciousness cannot be thought" (B133). He continues: "Therefore, only insofar as I can unite a manifold of given representations in one consciousness is it possible for me to represent to myself the identity of consciousness throughout these representations. That is, the analytic unity of apperception is possible only under the presupposition of a certain synthetic unity" (B133).

Kant is even more explicit on the next page: "Synthetic unity of the manifold of intuitions, as generated apriori, is thus the ground of the identity of apperception itself, which precedes apriori all my determinate thought" (B134). In addition, in A, he refers to the synthesis of imagination as "prior to apperception" (A118). So, in one sense, transcendental apperception is the ground of the imaginative synthesis, but in another sense, the imaginative synthesis grounds apperception. More specifically, transcendental apperception grounds the requirement of unity in the manifold and the form of unity thus required, and in this sense it is the ground of the synthesis. But apperception does not *perform* the synthesis and thus does not in the full sense ground the actually accomplished unity in the manifold. Instead, that unity is instituted by imagination. So to the extent that apperception is dependent for its own actualization on actual unification, it is dependent (grounded) on imagination.

Thus we can say as regards transcendental apperception and transcendental imagination: each requires (is grounded by) the other, even though the sense of requirement and of ground is different in each case. We can perhaps best express this situation by saying that they belong together and constitute a structured totality.

(7) From the outset of his discussion, Kant contrasts transcendental apperception with empirical apperception, inner sense. The point of the contrast is that the self as presented in inner sense is, like everything given in intuition, merely appearance. Inner sense "represents to consciousness even our own selves only as we appear to ourselves, not as we are in ourselves" (B152–53).

The contrast raises a question: granted that in empirical apperception I represent myself merely as appearance, how do I represent myself in transcendental apperception? What kind of self-representation occurs in transcendental apperception? Kant answers: "On the other hand, in the transcendental synthesis of the manifold of representations in general and therefore in the synthetic original unity of apperception, I am conscious of myself not as I appear to myself, nor as I am in myself, but only that I am. This representation is a thinking, not an intuiting" (B157).

Notice what Kant is excluding here. In transcendental apperception, I am not conscious of myself as I am in myself. That is, transcendental apperception is not consciousness of the self in itself. Furthermore, I am not conscious of myself as I appear to myself, as appearance. In transcendental apperception, there is no appearing, no intuition of self. So transcendental apperception is a thinking in which I am conscious only that I am.

But what kind of thinking is this? If we go back to something we noted earlier, at step 3, then we may now say that transcendental apperception is a thinking in which the "I think" gets attached to my representations, that is, a thinking in which my representations are explicitly referred back to myself as subject, back to the I to which those representations already belong. Here we can begin to see how apperception depends on the imaginative synthesis. The point is that the actual referral can be accomplished (that is, the I can posit itself as subject of its representations) only on the basis already provided by the imaginative synthesis whereby the manifold is brought to the unity which, prescribed by apperception, makes it mine. In other words, actual referral of my representations to the I can occur only if those representations are already mine, already given the unity required for them to be mine. This then means that transcendental apperception is simply that thinking by which is posited the I to which representations have already been attached by means of the imaginative synthesis.

So what kind of *thinking* is transcendental apperception? It is a *positing* of self, a self-positing. That is why Kant says: in transcendental apperception I am conscious only that I am.

Let me conclude our discussion of Kant's preparation for the Deduction proper with a historical note. One could easily write the history of German Idealism in terms of the peculiar interdependence of apperception and imagination, especially if this interdependence is formulated as one between self-consciousness and the synthesis by which objects are brought forth over against consciousness. In Fichte, it becomes the problem of the non-I. The interdependence is expressed accordingly: the I can posit itself as determinate, finite I only by bringing forth through the imagination a non-I. In Schelling, the non-I is taken to be simply the I itself. And so the non-I is not only a transcendental condition of self-consciousness but actually serves to reflect the I back to itself in the manner of a dark mirror in which the I sees itself. All of this prepares the way for Hegel's concept of spirit. Spirit must undergo estrangement, loss of self in otherness, in order to be given back to itself from that otherness and achieve full presence to itself in absolute knowledge.

(3) Section 3 of the Transcendental Deduction.

This section is called "The Relation of the Understanding to Objects in General, and the Possibility of Knowing Them Apriori." After all the preparation, it contains the Deduction proper. Yet before we take it up, we need to recall again just what a Transcendental Deduction is; we need to recall those formulations of the task of the Deduction given by Kant in Section 1. In addition, we need to see how the developments in Section 2 provide a basis for another, more fundamental formulation.

In its first formulation, the task is to settle a question of right as regards certain concepts. A decision is to be made regarding the right with which pure concepts—concepts not derived from experience—can be applied to objects of experience, can have objective validity.

In its second formulation, the task is to show how pure concepts make possible the objects of experience, how they provide conditions for the possibility of objects of experience. This is directly connected with the first formulation: a concept that is not derived from objects can rightfully apply to them only if it is such as to make objects possible, only if it is a condition of their possibility.

We can now extend the above to a third formulation. The analysis of the transcendental object has indicated how pure concepts can make objects of experience possible, namely, by governing the very constitution of them as objects, by governing the constitution of appearances as objective, as appearances *of* an object. Appearances are simply what is given in intuition. So pure concepts can make objects possible and hence have objective validity only if *thought* is so linked to *intuition* as to be able to govern the objectification of the intuitive manifold. In other words, the fundamental issue in the Deduction is the connection between thought (understanding) and intuition (sensibility), since on this connection is based the character of pure concepts as making objects possible, as possessing objective validity. Near the end of the Deduction, Kant indicates that precisely this connection is ultimately the issue: "This is all that we were called upon to establish in the transcendental deduction of the categories, namely, to render comprehensible this relation of understanding to sensibility and, by means of sensibility, to all objects of experience" (A128).

We need to add one other point, especially prominent in Section 2, namely: *imagination* is integral to this connection, inasmuch as it mediates between thought and intuition. We may then say that the fundamental issue in the Transcendental Deduction concerns the interconnections among understanding, imagination, and intuition. So, in a third formulation, the task of the Deduction is to exhibit the interconnections among these three powers. The task is to show how they are woven together in the total fabric of experience. That is precisely what Kant does in the Deduction proper.

So we arrive finally at the Deduction itself. What it amounts to is Kant simply tracing out the interconnections among the three terms, the three powers. In general, these interconnections can be shown starting with either extreme term. So there will be two Deductions given:

(a) Deduction from above (A116–19): from apperception to imagination to intuition.
(b) Deduction from below (A120–25): in the opposite direction.

These directionalities, however, do not yet provide the full structure of the two ways of Deduction. There is also another element involved in the structure, namely, the distinction between the pure (transcendental) employment of the powers and their empirical employment. In fact, the first two paragraphs of Section 3 are primarily devoted to formulating this distinction.

How does the distinction bear on the structure of the two ways? When Kant speaks of proceeding "from below," he means both that he will start from intuition and that he will start with *empirical* rather than transcendental intuition. By contrast, the Deduction "from above" begins with *transcendental* rather than empirical apperception.

There are accordingly six terms involved in the structure of the Transcendental Deduction:

Empirical understanding	Pure understanding (apperception)
Empirical imagination	Pure imagination
Empirical intuition	Pure intuition

Most of the interconnections among these have already been sketched out in Section 2. Kant needs now merely to make explicit, and retrace as a whole, what the previous analyses have developed.

(a) The Deduction from above.

This deduction actually adds very little to what was already prepared. It begins with transcendental apperception. All representations, in order to be *my* representations, must be capable of belonging to my one consciousness. That means the manifold of intuition must be unified in the way prescribed by (appropriate to) the unity of transcendental apperception. In other words, the appropriate forms of unity must be instituted in the manifold through synthesis.

This synthesis prescribed by apperception cannot be performed by apperception (pure thought), however. Instead, it requires imagination. It is a synthesis by transcendental imagination or, as Kant now says, by "the *productive* synthesis of the imagination," in contrast to a re-productive, empirical synthesis.

Through this productive synthesis, the manifold of intuition is given that unity which is necessary in order for it to belong to the I and hence constitute experience. More precisely, Kant says that the transcendental synthesis "is directed exclusively to the apriori combination of the manifold" (A118). Now, the apriori combination of the manifold must be a synthesis of that manifold with respect to its apriori elements and only derivatively with respect to its empirical elements. So, it is fundamentally a synthesis of the formal manifold, the manifold of pure intuition (space and time) and only derivatively of the empirical content falling under these forms.

We have seen in the Transcendental Aesthetic that time has a certain priority over space; time is the universal form of intuition, whereas space is the form only of outer intuition. As a result, time is primary in the transcendental synthesis. That is, the synthesis is primarily a unification with respect to the manifold of *time* and is the productive synthesis of time, the constitution of time.

The determinations through which time is thus constituted Kant calls "transcendental schemata." The working out of this dimension of the critical problem is the next major stage in the Analytic.

We can now see why Kant places an observation regarding time at the beginning of Section 2 and insists that this observation is quite fundamental for the Deduction: "Whatever the origin of our representations, they must all, as modifications of the mind, belong to inner sense. All our knowledge is thus finally subject to time, the formal condition of inner sense. In time, they must all be ordered, connected, and brought into relation. This is a general observation which, throughout what follows, must be borne in mind as being quite fundamental" (A98–99).

(b) The Deduction from below.

It begins with appearances as given in empirical intuition. Kant stresses the fragmentary character of the given and the resultant need for synthesis: "Since every appearance contains a manifold and since different perceptions therefore occur in the mind separately and singly, a combination of them, such as they cannot have in sense itself, is demanded. There must therefore exist in us an active faculty for the synthesis of this manifold. I call this faculty imagination" (A120).

Note especially how Kant describes the fragmentary character: intuitions (perceptions) occur in the mind separately and singly; there is a manifold of these separate and single elements. Let us relate this to an earlier statement. Speaking of impressions (sensations), Kant said: "for, each representation, insofar as it is contained in a single moment, can never be anything but absolute unity" (A99). So at the level of the intuitively given, there is a manifold of sensations, and each sensation is an absolute unity, a unit, occurring separately without any relation whatever to any other units. The manifold consequently is a sheer plurality, totally lacking all unification among the units that make it up.

It could be asked: how is this fragmentary character of the given to be established? On what basis? Certainly, there is no immediate evidence for such radical fragmentation. In any actual object of experience, synthesis has always already done its work. So, what is the basis? Kant gives no direct answer. It is often supposed that he simply took this over as something self-evident from his predecessors, especially the British Empiricists. It has also been suggested that he regarded this fragmentary character as a consequence of the finitude of human intuition, specifically a consequence of the dependence of human intuition on affection. Yet it is by no means clear that affection must yield such atomistic sensory units. The *Critique* itself might suggest that Kant came to his position through a "regressive reflection," that is, a reflection which would begin with the object and then reflectively reverse (undo) the work of synthesis. But, among other problems, such reflection would require that presence of reason to itself of which Kant spoke in the Preface as methodologically necessary but the possibility of which has, to say the least, not been vindicated by the *Critique* thus far. Clearly, neither inner sense nor transcendental apperception constitutes such a self-presence.

In any case, granted the fragmentation, a synthesis that would repair it is needed. The synthesis is, in the first instance, the work of the empirical imagination. Empirical imagination synthesizes the manifold of intuition and brings it "into the form of an image" (A120).

This forming, the synthesis of apprehension and synthesis of reproduction, cannot be carried out arbitrarily; it must be lawful. More precisely, it is lawful in two different ways, that is, on two different levels. First, there is a lawfulness (order, regularity) with respect to the empirical content; certain intuitions are connected only with certain others. "The reproduction of the intuitions must, therefore, conform to a rule, in accordance with which a representation connects in the imagination with some one representation in preference to another. This subjective and empirical ground of reproduction according to rules is what is called the association of representations" (A121).

So this empirical lawfulness makes the forming be an association of representations. But there must be a further, transcendental lawfulness underlying the empirical one: "Now if this unity of association had not also an objective ground which makes it impossible that appearances should be apprehended by the imagination otherwise than under the condition of a possible synthetic unity of this apprehension, it would be entirely accidental that appearances should fit into a connected whole of human knowledge" (A121). This says that there must be a lawfulness; the way intuitions get connected must render them subject to the unity of apperception, that is, render them capable of belonging all together in one consciousness. The character appearances have by virtue of this lawfulness is the "affinity of appearances" (A123).

This lawfulness (affinity) is ultimately grounded in transcendental apperception. It grounds both the demand for unity and the forms of unity demanded. But, although grounded (prescribed) by transcendental apperception, these forms of unity must be instituted by transcendental (productive) imagination. And therefore, as we approach the end of the Deduction proper, what comes especially into focus is the mediating role of pure imagination:

> A pure imagination, which conditions all apriori knowledge, is thus one of the fundamental powers of the human soul. By its means we bring the manifold of intuition, on the one side, into connection with the condition of the necessary unity of pure apperception on the other. The two extremes, namely, sensibility and understanding, must stand in necessary connection with each other through the mediation of this transcendental function of imagination, because otherwise sensibility, though indeed yielding appearances, would supply no objects of empirical knowledge and consequently no experience. (A124)

* * *

Let me make brief concluding comments on the Transcendental Deduction. First, note the path taken by the deduction from above in distinction to the path of the deduction from below. The path of the deduction from above is down from pure understanding (transcendental apperception) to pure imagination and then to pure intuition. The deduction from below moves up from empirical intuition to empirical imagination to transcendental apperception and then down to pure imagination. The deduction from above remains entirely on the transcendental level. The deduction from below plays out for the most part on the empirical level but does then pass to the transcendental. Both forms of the deduction move through the three faculties and weave them together; by moving in two directions, the weaving, the interconnection, is more firmly established. Now, as already mentioned, the interconnection of understanding and intuition through the mediation of the imagination is exactly what the deduction was supposed to accomplish. The interconnection is what justifies the application of the categories or, in other words, shows how the categories make possible the objects of experience. So Kant says, as already cited: "This is all that we were called upon to establish in the transcendental deduction of the categories, namely, to render comprehensible this relation of understanding to sensibility."

D. Book II: Analytic of Principles. Chapter I: Schematism

The two Books of the Transcendental Analytic are the "Analytic of Concepts" and the "Analytic of Principles." But Kant also gives Book II another title, "Doctrine of Judgment," and claims that this title more accurately indicates the task to be undertaken.

To understand this latter title, we need to consider a point made near the end of the Transcendental Deduction, at A126. Kant reviews the various definitions of the understanding that have emerged: spontaneity, power of thought, faculty of concepts or of judgment. He notes that all these "definitions" actually say the same. Then he adds still another definition: faculty (power, *Vermögen*) of rules. According to Kant, this definition comes closest to the essential nature of the understanding. In general, we can see why. Those pure concepts serving as conditions of the possibility of objects of experience function precisely as rules of unification. That is to say, they are rules according to which the imagination brings the manifold to synthetic unity. In the Introduction to Book II, Kant makes the following connection between judgment and the understanding as the faculty of rules: "If understanding in general is to be viewed as the faculty of rules, judgment will be the faculty of subsuming under rules, that is, of distinguishing whether something does or does not stand under a given rule" (A132/B171).

So the task of the Transcendental Doctrine of Judgment is to determine the specific applicability of the categories as rules, to specify apriori the instances to which these rules are to be applied.

The Doctrine of Judgment consists of two parts:

(1) Schematism of the Pure Concepts of the Understanding. This part will deal with the "sensible condition" required for all application of pure concepts.
(2) System of the Principles of Pure Understanding. This will deal with the synthetic judgments resulting from the application of pure concepts.

(1) Schematism.

The problem is that in order for something to be subsumed under a concept, it must be homogeneous with that concept, must have something in common with the concept. In the case of empirical concepts, this need for homogeneity is easily met. There is homogeneity between things and concepts because concepts are derived by abstractive reflection from the things. But in the case of pure concepts, the situation is different; they are *not* derived from appearances. Thus the required homogeneity between the pure concept and appearances is problematic.

In general, what is necessary in order to solve this problem is a third thing, a mediating factor homogeneous with the category (and so must be intellectual) and also homogeneous with the appearance (and so must be sensible). This third thing is the transcendental schema, which is a transcendental determination of time. It is a determination of time in terms of the rule expressed in the corresponding category. It is the category in the form of a ruling of time, a rule for time-determination.

So the transcendental schema is homogeneous with the category: "it is universal and rests on an apriori rule" (A138/B178). We can even say it *is* the rule, but *as* ruling time. And the transcendental schema is also homogeneous with appearances, because time is the universal pure intuition, presupposed by all appearances. Time is the pure manifold presupposed by every empirical manifold.

Thus the general problem of the subsumption of appearances under categories is solved, in a way already more or less worked out in the Transcendental Deduction. The subsumption of appearances under a category is possible by means of a transcendental determination of time. The transcendental schemata thus mediate the subsumption. Furthermore, as we would expect from the Transcendental Deduction, Kant says that the schema is a product of imagination. The remainder of the chapter on the schematism simply elaborates this general solution.

Kant proceeds to explain the meaning of schema by discussing some examples (A140–42/B179–81). These deal primarily with the relation between schema and image. Perhaps the best example offered is a mathematical one, the example of a triangle. When I prove something about triangles, I use an image, a triangle drawn on paper. But an image is never adequate to (congruent with) the concept of triangle in general. The image is too definite. By proving something about an image of a triangle, I could never prove anything about triangles in general. Accordingly, what my proof concerns, what I am directed toward in my proof is *not* a particular image. Instead, it is *that which governs* all images of triangles. And that is what Kant calls a "schema." Thus he says: "This representation of a universal procedure of imagination in providing an image for a concept, I entitle the schema of this concept" (A140/B179–80).

Kant also extends this analysis to empirical concepts. No individual dog is adequate to the concept of dog in general. How is subsumption then possible? It is so by means of a schema, and in this case the schema is "a rule according to which my imagination can delineate the figure of a four-footed animal in a general manner, without limitation to any single determinate figure" (A141/B180).

Finally, Kant extends the consideration to schemata of pure concepts, and that is of course the real issue. Here a decisive difference occurs. By their very nature, pure concepts (categories) have no images, in the sense in which there are images of triangles or of dogs. So to what do transcendental schemata link the categories? They link the categories to a *pure image*, to what Kant calls the pure image "of all objects of the senses in general" (A142/B182), namely, time. And by linking the categories to time, schemata thereby link categories to all appearances, of which time is the universal form, the pure image. Accordingly, in an extended sense, all things are images of the categories.

Transcendental schemata (transcendental determinations of time) are capable of mediation because as *transcendental determinations*, they are homogeneous with categories (they *are* the categories under their aspect of rules of time-determination), and, as determinations *of time*, they are homogenous with appearances (since time is the universal form of appearances). Thus there are transcendental schemata corresponding to the various categories. The general correspondence is:

> Quantity—generation of time itself (time-series)
> Quality—filling of time (time-content)
> Relation—connection according to a rule of time-determination (time-order)
> Modality—time itself as correlate of the determination of whether and how an object belongs to time (scope of time).

Kant summarizes: "The schemata are thus nothing but apriori determinations of time in accordance with rules. These rules relate, in the order of the categories, to the time-series, the time-content, the time-order, and lastly to the scope of time in respect of all possible objects" (A145/B184).

What in general is accomplished by the doctrine of the schematism? It exhibits the schemata as the sole conditions under which categories have a relation to objects, that is, as the "sensible condition" governing the subsumption under categories, governing the applicability of the categories apriori. In turn, this means the categories have no objective employment beyond the domain marked out by this sensible condition, that is, beyond the bounds of possible experience. Accordingly, pure thought has objective employment only in providing rules for time-determination or, in other words, only in its relation to the transcendental imagination.

E. Book II: Analytic of Principles. Chapter II: Principles

Chapter I (Schematism) of the "Analytic of Principles" has dealt with that general sensible condition to which thought is subject. Chapter II ("The System of All Principles of Pure Understanding") will now present the synthetic apriori judgments possible under that condition: "Our task now is to exhibit, in systematic connection, the judgments which the understanding, under this critical provision, actually achieves apriori" (A148/B187).

Chapter II is divided into three sections:

> Section 1 concerns the highest principle of all analytic judgments.
> Section 2 concerns the highest principle of all synthetic judgments. It is from this principle that the entire system of principles flows.

Section 3 is a presentation of the system of principles, with discussion of individual principles.

Section 1: The Highest Principle of All Analytic Judgments.

Kant presents the principle of contradiction as a sufficient principle of all analytic judgments. The principle of contradiction suffices for determining the truth of an analytic judgment. For example, "Man is rational" is true because its opposite would involve a contradiction. Beyond the sphere of analytic judgments, however, the principle of contradiction is not a sufficient criterion of truth but only a negative condition. That is, if a judgment involves a contradiction, it is false, but freedom from contradiction does not guarantee truth.

Important here is Kant's negative intent. He is *restricting* the principle of contradiction in opposition to Wolff, for example, who regarded it as the highest principle of all knowledge. The crucial point is that for Kant, the principle of contradiction is not the highest principle of the rational knowledge *of objects* but only of that knowledge which involves nothing but the clarification of concepts. More precisely, the principle of contradiction is not the highest principle of rational knowledge because rational knowledge in the highest sense requires that reason be subjected to a sensible condition, whereas any such bond of reason to sensibility is entirely lacking in the mere principle of contradiction. That is why Kant takes such pains to show that a condition of time does not belong in the statement of the principle of contradiction.

Section 2: The Highest Principle of All Synthetic Judgments.

Formally regarded, a synthetic judgment is one in which the predicate cannot be found by analysis of the subject; the predicate goes beyond the subject. In such cases, something is then required for synthesis of the two concepts, a third thing in some way connecting them. What is this third thing? Kant says it is an object. That is, in synthetic judgments, the predicate can be connected to the subject only by a "passage" through the object thought in the subject. For instance, "The cow is black": the third thing is the actual cow thought in the subject-concept, the object to which I can refer in actual experience.

This character of synthetic judgments is important for Kant's concept of judgment in general. A synthetic judgment is not merely a relation between two concepts but rather is a synthesis of them by passage through the object thought in the subject-concept. The passage through the object is essential to the structure of the judging.

This essentiality forms the background against which Kant, in the B Deduction, makes his famous remark about judgment: "I have never been able to accept the interpretation logicians give of judgment in general. It is, they declare, the representation of a relation between two concepts. . . . I need only point out that this definition does not determine in what the asserted relation consists" (B140–41).

These logicians understand the essence of judgment from the point of view of mere analytic judgments and hence leave out of account that passage through the object which is an essential moment, and not just some added feature, of synthetic judgments. Should not synthetic judgments instead provide the point of view for understanding the essence of judgment?

In general, synthetic judgments require a passage through the object. More precisely, their truth (objective validity) can be grounded only by reference to the object thought in the subject-concept. In cases of aposteriori judgment, it is clear enough how such reference and grounding can be accomplished, namely, by experience. But how is this reference possible in cases of apriori judgment? How can such judgments involve a reference to the object, and hence, a grounding, since as apriori they are independent of experience? The answer is that they can do so not in relation to actual objects, but only with respect to the *possibility* of objects. That is to say, such judgments refer to the possibility of the objects of experience and thereby refer to all actual objects of experience.

What must be the character of this "reference" of a judgment to the possibility of the objects of experience? Answer: the judgment must state one of the conditions constituting such possibility, must state some condition required for the very possibility of objects of experience. Such a condition would necessarily hold for all actual objects of experience, and such a judgment would be true for them. Furthermore, the truth of such conditions, their objective validity, would be establishable independently of all actual experience of objects.

It is possible for us to form judgments stating conditions of possibility of objects of experience only insofar as these conditions are in some way revealed to us. But how is that possible? How could conditions of possibility of objects ever be revealed to us independently of all experience of objects? There is only one possible way, namely, the way indicated in Kant's "Copernican revolution." Kant now expresses this way as follows: "We then assert that the conditions of the possibility of experience in general are likewise conditions of the possibility of the objects of experience and that for this reason they have objective validity in a synthetic apriori judgment" (A158/B197).

So, independently of experience, we can form judgments stating conditions of the possibility of *objects* of experience because these conditions are identical with the conditions of the possibility of *experience as such*, and these latter can be determined independently of experience. Then what are these conditions? They all derive from a single condition: the unity required by apperception must be instituted in the manifold of intuition. That is to say, the manifold of intuition must be brought under a certain necessary synthetic unity. From this condition, as condition for the possibility not only of experience but especially of the objects of experience, all synthetic apriori judgments flow. Thus Kant says: "The highest principle of all synthetic judgments is therefore this: every object stands under the necessary conditions of the synthetic unity of the manifold of intuition in a possible experience" (A158/B197).

Section 3. Systematic Presentation of All the Synthetic Principles of Pure Understanding.

There is an introductory part, leading up to the considerations of the individual principles, and we need to note two points about it:

(a) Note especially the reference to "system" in the title of the chapter as a whole: "The System of All Principles." The reference to system is repeated in the title of this Section 3: "Systematic Presentation." What is the sense of system here? How is it that principles constitute a system? They do so by the fact that they are all specifications of one and the same highest principle, namely, that "highest principle of all synthetic judgments" presented in Section 2. Furthermore, this unity of principles corresponds to and is grounded on the unity of apperception as the fundamental unity, of which the categories are specifications. So, that there is a *system* of principles is grounded in the unity of apperception.

(b) The titles of both the chapter and the section include the phrase "Principles of pure understanding," *Grundsätze des reinen Verstandes*. The genitive here is ambiguous. It may be taken either subjectively or objectively. In the objective sense, the principles would *govern* pure understanding, the way we speak of the principles (laws) of gravitation. In the subjective sense, the principles would be *grounded in*, would originate from, pure understanding. But Kant leaves no doubt as to which sense is meant. Section 3 begins: "That there should be principles at all is entirely due to the pure understanding. Not only is it the faculty of rules in respect of that which happens, but is itself the source of principles according to which everything that can be presented to us as an object must conform to rules" (A158–59/B197–98). So the sense of the genitive is subjective: pure understanding is the *source* of the principles. It not only supplies the rules but also—as standing under the sensible condition (schematism)—prescribes the subsumption of objects under those rules, that is, originates the principles.

But what are the principles principles of in the objective sense of the genitive? They are principles of the totality of appearances, or, as Kant says near the end of the A Deduction, they are principles of nature: "Thus the understanding is something more than a power of formulating rules through the comparison of appearances; it is itself the lawgiver of nature" (A126). This then means that laws of nature in the usual sense as dealt with in natural science are grounded in the principles of pure understanding; those laws are only specifications or applications with respect to special regions of appearances. Kant explains the general connection: "The laws of nature, indeed, one and all, without exception, stand under higher principles of understanding. They simply apply the latter to special cases of appearances. These principles alone supply the concept which contains the condition, and as it were the exponent, of a rule in general. What experience gives is the instance which stands under the rule" (A159/B198).

Kant develops this issue in *Metaphysical Foundations of Natural Science* (tr. J. Ellington, Indianapolis: Bobbs-Merrill, 1970, pp. 5–6). There Kant distinguishes between:

(a) a transcendental metaphysics of nature, which makes no reference to any empirical determinations of appearances.
(b) a special metaphysics of nature, which introduces the empirical concept of a specific kind of thing, namely, body or matter. But beyond this specifying concept, no further empirical elements are introduced. In other words, this metaphysics of nature takes the empirical concept of matter and works out the corresponding possible apriori synthetic knowledge.
(c) a mathematical system of nature, which incorporates the apriori intuition corresponding to concepts of natural things (cf. Newton's *Principia*). This is the empirical part of natural science, whereas the transcendental and the special metaphysics of nature form the pure part.

In the *Critique*, Kant introduces four sets of principles corresponding to four sets of categories:

Quantity—axioms of intuition
Quality—anticipations of perception
Relation—analogies of experience
Modality—postulates of empirical thought in general.

He proposes a classification of these into two groups:

(a) the mathematical principles (axioms and anticipations) concern "the mere intuition of an appearance in general" (B110). These principles prescribe that certain characters must belong to every appearance as intuited.
(b) the dynamical principles (analogies and postulates) concern "existence," or, in a more complete expression, they are concerned with "the existence of these objects, in their relation either to each other or to the understanding" (B110).

(i) Axioms of intuition.

In B, Kant provides a new statement of the principle of the axioms of intuition and also adds a new proof of the principle. For the most part, the B version approaches the issue more directly. According to the new statement, Kant says, referring to the axioms: "Their principle is: all intuitions are extensive magnitudes" (B202).

Before we consider the proof of this principle, we should refer back to the relevant schema. The schema of magnitude (*quantitas*) is number, that is, the representation of the successive addition of homogeneous units. More precisely: "The schema of magnitude is the generation (synthesis) of time itself in the successive apprehension of an object" (A145/B184). This statement raises two questions. First, why does Kant speak of the schema not of quantity (*Quantität*) as in the table of categories but of magnitude (*Größe*) in the sense of *quantitas*? Second, how can the schema be the generation of time? Is not time, as pure intuition, in some respect, if not entirely, prior to synthesis? These two questions and hence the meaning and import of the schema are explained in the course of the proof of the principle.

Kant speaks of magnitude as *quantitas* because he wants to distinguish this from another sense of magnitude, which he calls *quantum*. What is *quantitas*? In other words, what is the sense of quantity which is thought in the category and which, as schematized, takes the form of number? Kant says that *quantitas* is what we refer to when we answer the question: "What is the magnitude of a thing?" So, *quantitas* is a measure, that is, a determinate totality of many units, a totality of some unit taken many times.

Granted that quantity as category means *quantitas*, we see that there is only *one* category of quantity and that the three terms listed under quantity (unity, plurality, totality) are not categories but only the moments which, in their interconnection, define *quantitas*.

What is the other sense of quantity or magnitude? What does *quantum* mean? To answer, we need to recall a matter we considered in the Transcendental Aesthetic. Kant said that space is essentially one and that individual spaces are derived from it by limitation. In other words, with respect to space, the whole precedes the parts. That is precisely the opposite of what holds with respect to *quantitas*, where the parts precede the whole and the whole is a mere aggregate of homogeneous parts. Furthermore, Kant said that "space is represented as an infinite *given* magnitude." We saw that this could not mean space is an "infinite container"; instead, space is the "extensiveness" which makes possible any definite quantitative extension. Space (and likewise time), so regarded, is a *quantum*. It is the extensive, the sizeable, the measurable, which is presupposed by all determinate extension, size, measure.

In effect, what the "proof" says is that the possibility of experience requires the transition from *quantum* to *quantitas*. According to Kant, appearances "cannot be apprehended, that is, taken up into empirical consciousness, except through that synthesis of the manifold whereby the representations of determinate space or time are generated" (A162/B202). That is, if we are to apprehend appearances, a determinate space and time must be represented, namely, the space and time "occupied" by that appearance. Such a determinate representation requires infinite space and time to be divided into parts and put together out of these parts in a determinate way, so as to generate determinate limits, namely, the spatial and temporal limits of the appearance. But this amounts to applying to *quanta* (pure space and time) the concepts of unity, plurality, and totality, or, in other words, it means applying the category of quantity as *quantitas*.

Therefore, it may be affirmed as a principle that every appearance must embody what results from such application and must then be an extensive magnitude.

This section is called "axioms of intuition," yet in fact it is not about the axioms, but about their principle. What are the actual axioms of intuition? They are the axioms of mathematics, especially of geometry. What the principle does is to ground these axioms, ground their application, and hence the application of mathematics, to appearances: "This transcendental principle of the mathematics of appearances greatly enlarges our apriori knowledge. For it alone can make pure mathematics, in its complete precision, applicable to objects of experience" (A165/B206).

In summary, the principle of the axioms of intuition is the synthetic judgment resulting from the application of the category of quantity (as *quantitas*) to pure intuition (space and time as *quanta*). In this problematic, we can distinguish four elements:

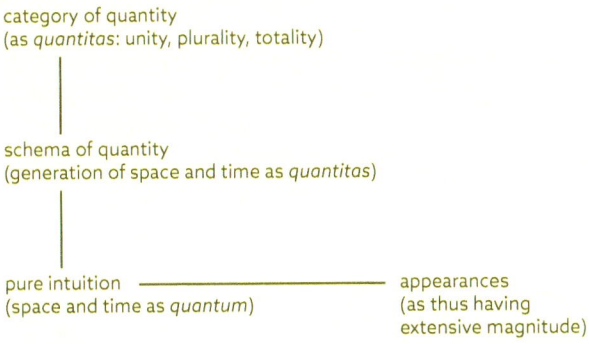

If we generalize, we can see here the basic structure of the problematic of the Transcendental Analytic and in fact the structure of the entire first half of the *Critique of Pure Reason*. The Transcendental Analytic involves three main elements:

(a) categories = *rules* considered in general, independently of that to which they are to be applied
(b) schemata = rules *as* rules for pure intuition, that is, as *ruling* pure intuition and thereby ruling appearances
(c) principles = expression of the character of appearances as thus *ruled*.

So categories, schemata, and principles, the three elements of the Transcendental Analytic, pertain respectively to rules, ruling, ruled. The fourth element, pure intuition, belongs to the Transcendental Aesthetic. Yet, precisely because pure intuition is an element within this total structure, the treatment of it in isolation in the Transcendental Aesthetic is incomplete and abstract and thus only preliminary.

In the chapter on the schematism, Kant treats schemata primarily as transcendental determinations of *time*. He presents time as that pure image which is to be ruled by categories through schemata. We see now, however, by considering the axioms, that at least some categories serve as rules for both kinds of pure intuition—for space as well as time. That means at least some schemata are transcendental determinations of time *and* space. Although Kant does not develop this issue in the chapter on the schematism, he indicates it at one point. When he says that time is the pure image of all objects, he adds: "The pure image of all magnitudes (*quantorum*) for outer sense is space" (A142/B182).

(ii) Anticipations of Perception.

In A, Kant begins the proof of the principle of the anticipations with some remarks regarding anticipation in general. The remarks are intended to make us notice that there is something strange in this title, "*Anticipations* of Perception." Kant says all synthetic apriori knowledge may be entitled anticipation. That means all such knowing is a knowing which anticipates the object known, a knowing in which the object is known prior to its being given. So all the principles are principles of anticipations. Why, then, is one particular principle singled out and specifically designated as a principle of anticipation? Presumably, it is because this one principle of the anticipations *of perception* has to do with anticipation in some exceptional sense.

To say perception is to say sensation. But sensation is precisely that which, in general, cannot be anticipated. Sensations constitute the material element, which must be given. They correspond to that aspect of the object knowable only empirically and not apriori, thus not by anticipation. Having granted all this, Kant then says: "If, however, there is in every sensation, as sensation in general (that is, without a particular sensation having to be given), something that can be known apriori, this will, in a quite special sense, deserve to be named anticipation" (A167/B209).

What is it about sensation that can be anticipated? That is what the principle expresses: "The principle which anticipates all perceptions as such is the following: in all appearances, sensation and the real which corresponds to it in the object (*realitas phaenomenon*) have an intensive magnitude, that is, a degree" (A167). So what can be anticipated regarding sensations is that they have intensive magnitude.

We turn now to the proof of the principle. In B, everything following the statement of the principle comes under the heading of "Proof." More precisely in terms of content, the proof runs to the end of A168/B210. Next comes a discussion of the implications of the principle, especially for physics and mathematics. Then, in the last paragraph, Kant returns to the principle itself and summarizes the proof.

We will concentrate on the proof proper. But in order to know how to do so, we need to understand what "proof" means here. Kant gives a hint when he speaks of a proof "from the subjective sources of the possibility of knowledge of an object in general" (A149/B188). We can understand this in terms of our sketch of the structure of the Transcendental Analytic. The principles express the character appearances must have by virtue of the application of the categories, that is, by virtue of the application of a rule to pure intuition and thereby to appearances or, in other words, by virtue of the ruling of the rule. Therefore, to prove a principle from subjective sources means to carry out a regress and to do so in such a way as to clarify the ruled by way of the regress

> from the ruled = that character of appearances expressed in the principle
> to the ruling = schema
> to the rule = category.

We begin with the ruled or, more precisely, with that character of appearances expressed in the principle. This character is intensive magnitude. According to the principle, this character belongs precisely to that element in appearances that corresponds to sensation and even (according to the A version) belongs to sensation itself. What exactly is intensive magnitude? In the first place, it is to be contrasted with extensive magnitude. The sense of the contrast derives from the fact that intensive magnitude is a magnitude *of sensation*: "Apprehension by means merely of sensation occupies only an instant, if, that is, I do not take into account the succession of different sensations. Since sensation is that element in the appearance the apprehension of which does not involve a successive synthesis proceeding from parts to the whole representation, it has no extensive magnitude" (A167/B209).

So intensive magnitude is not the magnitude of a whole built up from parts. Apprehension of sensation and of its intensive magnitude involves no progression from parts to whole. That means the whole, the unity, is immediately grasped rather than built up. Thus Kant defines as follows: "A magnitude which is apprehended only as unity and in which multiplicity can be represented only through approximation to negation = zero, I entitle an intensive magnitude" (A168/B210). For example, a loud tone is not apprehended as the sum of several softer tones. Its magnitude is one of degree (louder or softer).

We come now to a crucial point: although apprehension of sensations with their intensive magnitude is instantaneous and does not involve a successive synthesis from parts to whole, this does not mean it involves no synthesis whatever. That is, the apprehension of sensation is not a mere receiving. Instead, Kant says: "This magnitude is generated in the act of apprehension" (A166/B208). So even in the instantaneous apprehension of sensation, a synthetic activity is already operative. From that character of sensation expressed in the principle, we are referred back to a synthetic activity generating it; we are referred back from the ruled to a ruling, from a principle to a schema.

The schema corresponding to the principle of the anticipations of perception is the filling of time. That is the synthesis of sensation with the representation of time, the synthesis of sensation with time. So the ruling, the synthetic activity involved in the very apprehension of sensation, is a specific transcendental determining of time, a filling of time to some degree. Because of this ruling of time, what is eventually ruled, the appearance, exhibits the intensive magnitude expressed in the principle.

Yet if we are to understand the character of this ruling more precisely, we must make further regress to the rule, namely, the category of quality, with its subdivisions of reality, negation, limitation. What does quality have to do with the filling of time and with intensive magnitude? And where do reality, negation, and limitation fit in here?

In order to answer, we need to begin by clarifying the meaning of "reality" (*Realität*). "Reality" does not mean "actuality" (*Wirklichkeit*) or "existence" (*Dasein*). If it did, reality would be included under modality, not under quality. Kant equates "reality" with *realitas* (derived from Latin *res*, "thing"). In fact, Kant uses "reality" in precisely the sense given to *realitas* by Wolff and Baumgarten. Accordingly, reality or the real is that which belongs to *what* a thing (*res*) is, that which belongs to the *essence* of something, whether or not that thing exists. Recall that in the Transcendental Deduction, Kant speaks of proving the "objective reality" of pure concepts. He does not mean proving that the concepts objectively exist but proving that they belong to objects, that they are among those characters that constitute the objectivity of the object.

So it is now clear why reality has to do with quality: it is, in a sense, the same as quality. We might say it is the "positive moment" in the full structure of quality. It is also clear why reality has to do with sensation, why, as Kant repeatedly says, reality "corresponds" to sensation. It corresponds because sensation is precisely what provides the material content of appearances, their what-content, their quality, or in other words, their reality.

What about the other subdivisions: negation and limitation? Kant says that just as reality corresponds to sensation, what corresponds to the absence of sensation is negation. The opposition between reality and negation "rests on the distinction of one and the same time as filled and as empty" (A143/B182). So reality corresponds to sensation. Negation corresponds to empty time, that is, time as pure intuition. Thus the filling of time (the synthesis of sensation with time) is a synthesis of reality and negation: "There consequently exists a relation and connection between reality and negation, or rather a transition from the one to the other, which makes every reality representable as a quantum" (A143/B182–83). This synthesis of reality and negation yields limitation, which corresponds to a determinate intensive magnitude of sensation in an instant of time.

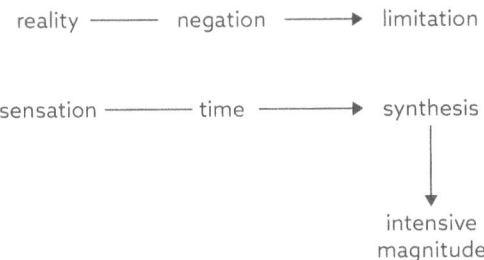

So again, as with quantity, we see that we do not have here three categories. Quality is the category. Reality, negation, and limitation are not categories but are simply elaborations of the meaning of the one category; they are its *moments*.

Let me make two comments on the Anticipations. First, a deepening of the problematic can be discerned in view of the fact that the ruling may be regarded in two ways. As we have already discussed, the ruling consists in the application of the category of quality to time. Ruling is in this sense a transcendental determining of time, the prescribing of a way of filling time, namely: time is to be filled to some degree. A generation of degree, which is conceptually represented in the category, is imposed on the manifold of time. So regarded, the synthesis is purely apriori; the category rules time and *only thereby* is carried over to appearances, since time is their form. Absolutely no empirical elements are involved. This would be a synthesis prior to any *given* elements, a synthesis already accomplished prior to all sensation. That is how we have regarded the ruling thus far. But there is another way. The need for it is evident in the definition of the schema: synthesis of *sensation* and time. Here the ruling is not merely a transcendental determining of time, but rather is a determining of a connection between time and sensation in general. It is still apriori inasmuch as the ruling is not determined by any empirical elements, by any particular sensation that may happen to be given. But it does prescribe and institute the connection between time and sensation in general.

In this latter regard, the transcendental synthesis is such as also to open onto the empirical synthesis; that is, the transcendental synthesis is at once the synthetic connecting of the transcendental synthesis and the *empirical* synthesis. Presumably that is why Kant speaks at B208 of a transition and synthesis between empirical consciousness and apriori consciousness. So Kant finally treats the unity of the transcendental synthesis and the empirical synthesis.

The second comment is that since, as we have just said, the apriori synthesis connects the transcendental and the empirical synthesis, so this gathering surpasses the one exhibited in the Transcendental Deduction. It is not merely a gathering up of intuition, imagination, and thought on two separate levels, transcendental and empirical, as for the most part occurs in the Deduction, but is a gathering of the levels themselves. This gathering of apriori and empirical is then presupposed in the analogies, since there the apriori (the pure intuition) is ruled by means of a ruling of the empirical in general: for example, by causality as image of and as constituting temporal succession.

(iii) Analogies of experience.

The analogies result from an application of the category of relation. In A, Kant says, "The general principle of the analogies is: all appearances are, as regards their existence, subject apriori to rules determining their relation to each other in one time" (A176–77). In B, the principle is restated as follows: "Experience is possible only through the representation of a necessary connection of perceptions" (B218).

The proof of this general principle proceeds directly from the "subjective sources." In fact, it proceeds from the highest source, namely, transcendental apperception. I will articulate the proof into three main steps:

(1) Transcendental apperception requires the unity of all appearances in time. Appearances must be so related that they all belong together in *one* time, correlative to the oneness of transcendental apperception. The question then arises: what is required for this unity of appearances in time?

(2) It might seem that nothing is required beyond what the Transcendental Aesthetic already provided. If time is the form of all intuition, and if time is one whole as quantum, as pure intuition, then it would seem that all appearances fall in this one time. But that answer is too facile. We need to ask in just what sense appearances fall in time as a result of time being the form of all intuition. What is the precise sense of things being *in* time? To answer, recall the Aesthetic: time is the form only of inner sense and is the form of outer sense only *mediately*, only by the fact that the *representations* of outer appearances belong, *as representations*, to inner sense. Because these representations are in inner sense, they are in time. So, strictly speaking, what is in time are the *representations* of outer appearances, not those appearances themselves.

What about the being in time of our representation of things? What about this time order? It is quite accidental, arbitrary. The order in which we represent things does not necessarily correspond to any temporal order in the appearances themselves, that is, to any objective time-order. As Kant says: "Perceptions come together only in accidental order. . . . But since experience is a knowledge of objects through perceptions, the relation involved in the existence of the manifold has to be represented in experience not as it comes to be constructed in time but as it exists objectively in time" (B219).

(3) So the character of time as a form of intuition does not suffice to constitute the kind of unity of appearances in time required for there to be an experience of objects, that is, for there to be a unity of objectivity correlative to the unity of transcendental apperception. Therefore, this unity must be instituted. Certain general relations of appearances in time must be instituted. In other words, certain universal rules of time-determination must be applied to appearances.

That is the proof, but before we consider the individual analogies, we must take up some preliminary matters. First, Kant says that there are "three orders of time," that is, three respects in which there can be relations of appearances in time. These are duration, succession, and coexistence. So there will be three rules for the relations of appearances in time, one rule for each mode of time. The three rules are the categories of relation:

substance—duration
cause—succession
community—coexistence.

More precisely, these rules, as rules for time-determination, are the *schemata* corresponding to the categories of relation. So Kant defines this schema as follows: "The schema of relation is the connecting of perceptions with one another at all times according to a rule of time-determination" (A145/B184). The corresponding principles (the analogies of experience) then express the character appearances must exhibit as a result of the ruling of the rules. These principles are the individual analogies of experience.

Kant contrasts these principles with the previous (mathematical) principles. The analogies do not pertain to the intuition of appearances, either with respect to the form (axioms of intuition) or with respect to the matter (anticipations of perception). The analogies do not define properties of a single appearance but instead pertain to the existence of appearances in their relation to one another. Kant also brings out the difference by saying that the first two are constitutive principles and govern the constitution of the intuited appearances; the analogies are regulative, not constitutive.

Kant then elaborates the general character of the analogies by explaining why he calls them "analogies." Mathematical analogy (proportion) expresses the equality of two quantitative relations, such that if three members are given, the fourth can be determined ($2 : 4 :: 3 : x$). Philosophical analogy differs because it expresses the equality of two qualitative, rather than quantitative, relations. As a result, if three members of a philosophical analogy are given, we can determine apriori only the *relation* to a fourth (that a fourth member exists) but cannot determine apriori what that fourth member is. For example, we know that effect : cause :: melting of wax : x. We cannot say apriori what x is, but we know there must be such a cause preceding the melting.

(1) The first analogy of experience: the principle of the permanence of substance.

The principle is stated in A as follows: "All appearances contain the permanent (substance) as the object itself and the transitory as its mere determination, that is, as a way in which the object exists" (A182). The proof proceeds in three main steps:

(a) Time is the substratum for all succession and coexistence. That is, changes in appearances are *in* time, but time itself cannot change. "For time is that in which, and as a determination of which, succession or coexistence can alone be represented" (B225).

(b) Kant continues: "Time cannot by itself be perceived" (A182/B225). That is to say, time is not an object of empirical intuition; it is the form of all intuition but is not itself empirically intuited.

(c) Kant concludes: "Consequently, there must be found in the objects of perception, that is, in the appearances, a substratum which represents time in general; and all change or coexistence must, in being apprehended, be perceived in this substratum and through a relation of the appearances to it" (A182/B225). That is, time is substratum; but time is not perceived. So, there must be a substratum that *is* perceived, that stands in for time, "represents time in general." Such a substratum, however, is just what is called *substance*. Therefore, in all appearances, there is a substance as permanent substratum, substratum of permanence.

(2) The second analogy of experience. In general, the analogies concern those relations among appearances in time that must be instituted if experience of objects is to be possible. Strictly speaking, however, what is expressed in the first analogy is not an instituted relation among appearances in time but rather a precondition for any such relation, namely, permanence. As Kant says, substance is among the categories of relation "rather as the condition of relations than as itself containing a relation" (A187/B230). So it is only in the second and third analogies that the instituted relations among appearances are expressed. More precisely, these analogies express the character of the relations that must exist among appearances in order for there to be objective temporal succession and coexistence.

The second analogy is called "The Principle of Succession in Time in Accordance with the Law of Causality." In B, the analogy is stated as follows: "All alterations take place in conformity with the law of the connection of cause and effect" (B232).

Kant provides an extended treatment of this analogy. The extent of the treatment is indicative of the importance the problem of causality had in the development of Kant's thought. He famously declared in the *Prolegomena* (*Pro*, p. 8) that he was awakened from his dogmatic slumbers by the Humean attack on the concept of causality and that he generalized from the problem of causality to the problem of how it is possible for any pure concepts to apply to objects of experience (the problem of apriori synthetic judgments).

There are three main steps in the proof. I will treat them only briefly, since the proof is merely a more specific form of the proof of the general principle of the analogies.

(a) As we have seen, transcendental apperception prescribes unity to all appearances in time; that is the subjective source. One kind of temporal relation by which appearances can be unified is the relation of succession in time. What is required for there to be such relations of succession among appearances?

(b) In a sense, such succession is already provided by the fact that time is the form of inner intuition: we intuit appearances successively. This, however, is a succession of our *representations* of appearances, not of the appearances themselves, not of the appearances as appearances of objects distinct from our mere acts of representation. This already present succession is a subjective succession, and there is no guarantee it corresponds to any objective succession, a succession in the objects.

For example, I see the front and then the back of a house. I have a representation of the front succeeded by a representation of the back. But we obviously would not say this succession in representation corresponds to any objective succession. The back of the house does not succeed the front. There is no relation of succession between the front and back.

Consider a different example: I see a ship move downstream. Here is a subjective succession of representations. But in this case there is also an objective succession. There is a succession in the object itself. Indeed, the subjective succession is governed by the objective one; I cannot simply reverse the order of the succession of my representations as I could in the case of the house.

(c) So an objective succession is required and must be *instituted*. This could be accomplished if each appearance were assigned to some definite position in time, so that the order of succession would be determined independently of how I might intuit the appearances. What would such an assigning of appearances to definite positions in time involve? Presumably I would need to have time somehow before me in order to assign appearances to their temporal positions.

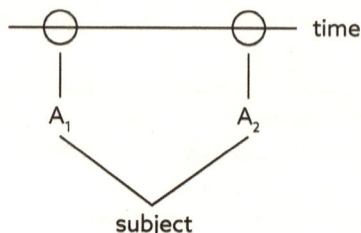

But I obviously do not have time spread out before me in any such manner. I do not "hover" above time; instead, I intuit *in* time. So how, then, is it possible to institute objective succession? According to Kant: "Since absolute time is not an object of perception, this determination of position cannot be derived from the relation of appearances to it. On the contrary, the appearances must determine for one another their position in time and make their time-order a necessary order" (A200/B245).

This says the establishing of objective succession does not take place by a direct assignment of appearances to definite positions in time. Objective temporal succession cannot be instituted directly. Instead, some general connection instituted among appearances themselves must determine their position in time and hence their objective order of succession. So what is that general connection? Kant says: "Only that which is the cause of another, or of its determinations, determines the position of the other in time" (A212/B259). So the general connection is causality, the connection of appearances as cause and effect.

More precisely, the establishing of the time position and of an objective succession of appearances is accomplished through the ruling of a rule, namely, the rule prescribing a connection of appearances as cause and effect. In this precise form, Kant outlines the proof at the end of the entire section on the analogies: "Time is not viewed as that wherein experience immediately determines a position for every existence. Such determination is impossible, inasmuch as absolute time is not an object of perception with which appearances could be confronted. What determines for each appearance its position in time is the rule of the understanding through which alone the existence of appearances can acquire synthetic unity as regards relations of time" (A215/B262).

Thus the second analogy ("All alterations take place in conformity with the law of the connection of cause and effect.") expresses the ruling of the rule over appearances, a ruling required for objective temporal succession. That is to say, it expresses the character of the relations that must exist among appearances in order for there to be objective temporal succession.

(3) Third analogy: Principle of Coexistence, in Accordance with the Law of Reciprocity or Community.

The statement of the analogy in A is: "All substances, insofar as they coexist, stand in thoroughgoing community, that is, in mutual interaction" (A211).

In B: "All substances, insofar as they can be perceived to coexist in space, are in thoroughgoing reciprocity" (B256). This principle involves the same issue as that of the second analogy, except it treats of temporal coexistence (simultaneity) rather than succession. The question at issue is: what is the character of the relations that must exist among appearances in order for there to be objective temporal coexistence?

Kant's procedure in dealing with this question corresponds almost exactly with his way of proving the second analogy. The establishing of simultaneity among appearances cannot be accomplished by an *assignment* of appearances to the same position in time, because "time itself cannot be perceived." Instead, there must be instituted a connection among the appearances themselves which determines that they occupy the same position in time or, in other words, which determines their objective simultaneity.

What is required is mutual causation. Each substance must contain the cause of certain determinations in the other. Thus simultaneity is possible only the basis of community, mutual interaction, reciprocity.

Before we leave the analogies, recall one of the matters we dealt with in the Transcendental Deduction. We saw that for the possibility of *objects* of experience, it is necessary that appearances be "supplied" with an object. There must be an "objectification" by which appearances are referred beyond the mere subjective sphere of intuition and are taken as appearances of an object standing "over against" the subject. We saw that the categories supply the concept of such an object. At the center of the discussion of the second analogy, Kant again raises this question of objectivity. He speaks of "mere representations, that is, inner determinations of our mind in this or that relation of time. How, then, does it come about that we posit an object for these representations and so, in addition to their subjective reality, as modifications, ascribe to them some mysterious kind of objective reality?" (A197/B242).

In effect, what Kant proceeds to say is that precisely through the institution of objective time-relations among appearances, these appearances are given their specifically objective character, that is, are "constituted" as over against the subject, independent of the subject's particular acts of intuition. Thus the connections among appearances expressed in the analogies (specifically, causality and community) are the ground of the objective character of the objects of experience.

(iv) Postulates of Empirical Thought.

The postulates differ from all the other principles. They do not express any character of appearances, either singly or in their relations, resulting from the ruling of a rule. The characters they express—corresponding to the categories of possibility, actuality, necessity—are not something "added" to the concept of the object. Instead, these characters concern only the relation of the object to the subject, that is, to the faculty of knowledge: "No additional determinations are thereby thought in the object itself; the question is only how the object, together with all its determinations, is related to the understanding and its empirical employment, to empirical judgment, and to reason in its application to experience" (A219/B266).

The postulates express connections between subject and object that are established, posited, by the subject. The postulates are just an explanation of the concepts of possibility, actuality, and necessity *in their empirical employment*, that is, insofar as they pertain to objects of experience.

The statement of the three principles is the same in A and B:

1. That which agrees with the formal conditions of experience, that is, with the conditions of intuition and of concepts, is possible.
2. That which is bound up with the material conditions of experience, that is, with sensation, is actual.
3. That which in its connection with the actual is determined in accordance with universal conditions of experience, is (exists as) necessary. (A218/B265–66)

I will make two comments on the individual principles. First, the actuality or existence of an object requires perception; it requires that the object be given either directly or else as necessarily connected with something given in perception. This means in general that existence is not a determination of objects but only of the relation of objects to a subject. In other words, existence is the kind of relation objects have to a subject in those cases in which the object is materially given, either directly or indirectly. This, then, means that being or existence is not a *real* predicate; to predicate being or existence of something is not to say *what* that something is, what belongs to its concept. Existence could never be discovered by analyzing the concept of a thing, however complete that concept might be, not even if it is the concept of God.

Second, as regards possibility, the important point is that possibility is not (versus Kant's immediate predecessors) identical with non-contradiction: "It is indeed a necessary logical condition that a concept of the possible must not contain any contradiction; but this is not by any means sufficient to determine the objective reality of the concept, that is, the possibility of such an object as is thought through the concept" (A220/B268). So for an object to be possible requires not only that its concept be free of contradiction but also that it agree with the formal conditions of experience. This development of the concept of possibility—such that possibility is not merely conceptual but involves reference to the conditions of experience—will be of fundamental importance in the Dialectic. Many of the basic issues there will have to do with possibility, such as the possibility of God or of freedom.

F. Conclusion of the Analytic and Glance Ahead to the Dialectic

Immediately following the chapter on the System of Principles, Kant writes: "We have now not merely explored the territory of pure understanding and carefully surveyed every part of it but have also measured its extent and assigned to everything in it its rightful place" (A235/B295). Kant's topology of pure understanding has determined the possibilities and limits of reason in this form, that is, reason in the form of understanding. It is precisely such determination that constitutes critique.

At the beginning of the last chapter of the Transcendental Analytic, Kant uses a metaphor to describe the domain of pure understanding, the domain which has been measured by the Analytic. The description continues the passage just cited:

> This domain is an island, enclosed by nature itself within unalterable limits. It is the land of truth—enchanting name!—surrounded by a wide and stormy ocean, the native home of illusion, where many fog banks and many swiftly melting icebergs give the deceptive appearance of farther shores, deluding the adventurous seafarer ever anew with empty hopes and engaging him in enterprises he can never abandon and yet is unable to carry to completion. Before we venture on this sea, to explore it in all directions and to obtain assurance whether there is any basis for such hopes, it will be well to begin by casting a glance upon the map of the land we are about the leave. (A235–36/B295)

This glance cast back over the land traversed by the Analytic is especially revelatory in three respects:

(1) We find here a statement of the basic outcome of the Transcendental Analytic, that is, a statement regarding the limits within which pure understanding has its rights.
(2) We glimpse Kant's development of a fundamental distinction which becomes especially problematic in view of this outcome: the distinction between phenomena and noumena. This in turn leads to an important extension of the basic outcome of the Analytic.
(3) We gain a glance ahead with a preview of that wide and stormy ocean onto which the Transcendental Deduction will carry us.

(1) Outcome of the Analytic.

The outcome is the establishing of the limits of pure understanding. In order to give a precise statement of these limits, Kant introduces a distinction between two kinds of employment of concepts. Transcendental employment is the application to things in general and in themselves. Empirical employment is the application merely to appearances, to objects of possible experience.

The point of the distinction is that only the empirical employment is legitimate, regardless of the kind of concept. That is clear enough in the case of empirical concepts, since they are abstracted from appearances, and also for mathematical concepts, since they refer to pure intuition, the form of appearances. But why is it the case with pure concepts of the understanding, categories? Why do they allow only empirical employment? Kant says: "But the categories have this peculiar feature, that only in virtue of the general condition of sensibility can they possess a determinate meaning and relation to an object" (A244). This means a category can have objective reality (legitimate application to objects) only if it is brought under a sensible condition, that is, schematized. In turn, for a category to be schematized means that it serves as a rule for a ruling through that schema, a ruling of pure intuition and thereby a ruling of appearances.

Category (rule)
Schema (ruling)
Pure Intuition (ruled)—Appearances (thereby ruled)

So how can a category apply to an object? By serving as a rule by which an object is ruled. But the only objects so ruled are appearances. Therefore, the categories allow only empirical employment. In a general formulation: pure understanding is limited to empirical employment because of its bond to the general sensible condition, that is, because it is bound to a ruling of time and hence to imagination and intuition.

(2) Phenomena and noumena.

The development of this distinction takes into consideration many different issues. The relations among these issues are in some cases quite complex, hence the complexity of the corresponding pages in the *Critique of Pure Reason*. For example, Kant carries along simultaneously two somewhat different contrasts: sensible versus intellectual intuition and real versus logical use of the intellect (Dissertation). Through his considerations, he illuminates both distinctions. He does so, however, only at the cost of great complexity in the text. In B, he drastically revised this section and omitted many of the issues taken up in A. I will not attempt to lay out all these various issues but only what seems to be the central movement, which I will articulate in nine steps.

(i) One of the ways Kant introduces the distinction is by reference back to his Dissertation. He speaks of the division of objects into phenomena and noumena as a division into the sensible world and the intelligible world. Recall the title of the Dissertation: "On the form and principles of the sensible and the intelligible worlds." Sensible versus intelligible would be the most straightforward form of the distinction between phenomena and noumena. Accordingly:

Phenomena = sensible world: domain known by the understanding in its empirical employment, that is, by understanding operating under the sensible conditions brought to light through the Transcendental Analytic.

Noumena = intelligible world: domain known by pure understanding, by pure thought independent of all sensible conditions. The Dissertation called this the "real use" of the intellect.

(ii) The problem with this first form of the distinction is evident. The basic outcome of the Transcendental Analytic is that there can be no knowledge of things by pure understanding, no "real use" of the intellect. So the ground of the distinction between phenomena and noumena cannot be the distinction between two ways we could know things—through schematized thought and through pure thought—for we do not know objects at all through pure unschematized thought.

Kant develops this issue, not just straightforwardly, but in relation to another issue, that of the transcendental object. The main point is that in our knowledge, a pure thought is indeed operative. But this pure thought is simply the positing of the transcendental object, which must be added to appearances in order to render them objective. And this transcendental object is not a thing in itself outside the sphere of the subject; it is not a purely intellectual thing itself. On the contrary, the transcendental object is "a correlate of the unity of apperception" and "can serve only for the unity of the manifold in sensible intuition" (A250). In other words, the pure thought of the transcendental object is not a pure knowing of some special object of understanding in contrast to objects of sensible experience. Instead, it is merely a moment within the structure of sensible knowing. Thus Kant says: "Just for this reason, the categories represent no special object, given to the understanding alone, but only serve to determine the transcendental object, which is the concept of something in general, through that which is given in sensibility, in order thereby to know appearances empirically, under concepts of objects" (A251).

(iii) Nevertheless, in sensible knowing, in experience, we take appearances to be appearances *of something*. We do not simply remain with phenomena but regard noumena, things in themselves, to be behind the phenomena. Yet we have no means of knowing such things, neither pure thought (real use of the intellect) nor intellectual intuition (divine knowing). But if we have no experience of noumena by which we could be led to take phenomena as related to noumena, then our taking them as so related cannot be anything but our *adding* the noumena to the phenomena. That is, all that we know are phenomena. We do not know noumena or even the distinction between noumena and phenomena. None of this is "given" to our knowing. We simply add the noumena behind the phenomena, and in this adding we constitute, at the same time, the very distinction between phenomena and noumena.

So what is the ground of the distinction? The answer is the subject. And that raises two further questions with which all the remaining steps are concerned. First, what is the character of this "adding" and of what is added? Second, why do we make the addition?

(iv) The adding is an act of pure thought, and what is added is simply the concept of something in general. That is, the noumenon—in the only way it can enter the sphere of our experience—is something thought, something simply *posited* by thought: "There thus results the concept of a noumenon. It is not indeed in any way positive, and is not a determinate knowledge of anything, but signifies only the thought of something in general, in which I abstract from everything that belongs to the form of sensible intuition" (A252).

This is what Kant refers to in B as the noumenon in the *negative* sense: a thing insofar as it is not an object of our sensible intuition but instead is thought in abstraction from our mode of intuition. Kant distinguishes this from the inadmissible *positive* sense of noumenon: the object of a non-sensible (intellectual) intuition—of which, however, we cannot conceive even the possibility.

(v) The noumenon is something thought, but it is thought as being beyond the mere thought. It is posited as being more than a mere fiction, as being something beyond our experience and as independent of whether we think it or not. In this precise sense, it can be said that pure thought, pure categories, can extend beyond experience: "The categories accordingly extend further than sensible intuition, since they think objects in general, without regard to the special mode (sensibility) in which they may be given" (A254/B309).

(vi) How is the noumenon, so regarded, related to the transcendental object? In a sense, they are the same; Kant says of both that they are the indeterminate thought of something in general. But, on the other hand, he says explicitly that they are not simply identical. The basic difference is that the noumenon is the thought of something in general in abstraction from our sensible mode of intuition. The transcendental object is "the object of a sensible intuition in general" (A253). That means the transcendental object is the object in general which is added by thought to appearances such that they are made to embody the unity it prescribes; it is an object thought *for* sensible appearances. The noumenon is an object thought as *beyond* all sensible appearances.

This duality is most clearly indicated in a statement from the Appendix on the Concepts of Reflection: "Consequently what we do is to think something in general; and while on the one hand we determine it in sensible fashion, on the other hand we distinguish from this mode of intuiting it the universal object represented *in abstracto*" (A289/B345–46).

(vii) Why do we make this addition? Why do we posit in thought a noumenon behind the phenomenon? Better formulated: what is accomplished by this addition? Having in effect posed that question, Kant answers: "Sensibility (and its field, that of appearances) is itself limited by the understanding in such fashion that it does not have to do with things in themselves but only with the mode in which, owing to our subjective constitution, they appear" (A251). Or again: "The concept of a noumenon is necessary to prevent sensible intuition from being extended to things in themselves and thus to limit the objective validity of sensible knowledge" (A254/B310). And most importantly: "What our understanding acquires through this concept of a noumenon is a negative extension. That is to say, the understanding is not limited through sensibility; on the contrary, it itself limits sensibility by applying the term 'noumenon' to things in themselves (things not regarded as appearances)" (A256/B312).

The point is that by the positing of the noumenon beyond the phenomenon, understanding limits sensibility. That is, the understanding marks out those limits proper to human intuition by virtue of its sensible, receptive character. This same point is elaborated in the Appendix. To admit noumena in the negative sense amounts to saying "that our kind of intuition does not extend to all things but only to objects of our senses, that consequently its objective validity is limited, and that a place therefore remains open for some other kind of intuition and so for things as its objects. . . . The concept of the noumenon is, therefore, not the concept of an object but is instead a problem unavoidably bound up with the limitation of our sensibility, namely, the problem as to whether there may not be objects entirely disengaged from any such kind of intuition" (A286–87/B342–44).

So the adding of the noumenon is a way the understanding limits sensibility. It is the way the understanding restrains human intuition, and hence sensible knowing in general, within the compass of its finitude.

(viii) Let us combine this result with the previous one, which was that the understanding is limited by sensibility. That is, the understanding can have objective validity only by subjection to a sensible condition, only by serving as a rule for a ruling of the sensible. But now we see: understanding, as pure thought of something in general, as positing of the noumenon, restrains sensibility within those limits proper to sensibility as finite intuition. Therefore, in sensible knowing, there is a mutual limiting operative between understanding and sensibility.

(ix) Finally, recall that the distinction between phenomena and noumena was at first simply taken over. On the basis of subsequent developments, however, it can be brought under a radical reflection. So the last chapter of the Analytic is in this respect a return to the beginning of the *Critique of Pure Reason*. What was merely taken for granted at the beginning, merely posited at the level of philosophical reflection, namely, the noumenon and the distinction between phenomenon and noumenon, is now regarded as posited at the level of knowing consciousness.

The main structuration is as follows. Within sensible knowing, a pure unschematized thought is operative. This thought is a positing of the object in general. But in the structure of this positing, there is a duality. The object in general is simultaneously posited in two "directions": as transcendental object prescribing unity for appearances, thus as correlative to apperception, and as noumenon beyond appearances. To the question of why thought posits the noumenon, one may answer that it is in order to set the limits of sensibility. But why does thought (reason) set these limits? What is it about reason that sends it on the task of limiting sensibility? Can it be said that the *Critique of Pure Reason* itself is, in the end, a re-enactment, at the reflective level, of this limiting?

(3) Preview of the Transcendental Dialectic.

In relation to the chapter on phenomena and noumena, we gain a preview of the Dialectic in two regards:

(i) At the end of the first part of that chapter, after Kant has shown the necessity for restricting concepts and principles of pure understanding to their empirical employment, he says, referring to the understanding: "its principles are merely rules for the exposition of appearances; and the proud name of an ontology that presumptuously claims to supply, in systematic doctrinal form, synthetic apriori knowledge of things in general (such as the principle of causality) must therefore give place to the modest title of a mere Analytic of Pure Understanding" (A247/B303).

So Kant proposes to replace ontology with such an Analytic. But ontology is just the name for *metaphysica generalis*, the first part of metaphysics, dealing with being qua being. Thus Kant is presenting the Transcendental Analytic as that form general metaphysics takes once the critical demand is put into effect. In other words, the Transcendental Analytic is a critical general metaphysics, a critical theory of being qua being.

But in what way is it so? It is a theory of being qua being carried out in reference to finite subjectivity, whereby being is interpreted as objectivity correlative to finite subjectivity. That is, it presents those determinations, categories, belonging to objects qua objects. Granted that the Transcendental Analytic corresponds to general metaphysics, it is to be expected that the Transcendental Dialectic will correspond to special metaphysics. Indeed, that is so. The three main parts of the Dialectic deal respectively with the subject matter of the three areas of special metaphysics: soul, world, God.

There is, however, one crucial difference compared with the Analytic. What the Dialectic accomplishes is not simply a critical version of the traditional disciplines, but *in a sense* a destruction of them. A major problem in interpreting the Dialectic is to determine the precise sense of this destruction.

(ii) It has become clear that a mutual limiting between thought and sensibility is operative in sensible knowing. The problem with which the Transcendental Dialectic will deal, namely, dialectical illusion, arises when this mutual limiting is disrupted, when thought exceeds its sensible condition and sensibility is extended beyond the limits proper to it as finite intuition. Thus we see the general relation between the Analytic and Dialectic. Both deal with the relation between thought and intuition—the Analytic with the proper relation (resulting in knowledge), the Dialectic with the improper relation (resulting in illusion).

The transition from the Analytic to the Dialectic is a leaving behind of the isle that is the land of truth and a venturing forth on the wide and stormy ocean. Everything depends on deciphering the deceptive appearances of farther shores, so as not to suffer the fate awaiting an overly adventurous seafarer.[1]

---

[1] The entire second semester of the course on the *Critique of Pure Reason* was devoted to the Dialectic. Those lectures form the basis of Sallis' already published book, *The Gathering of Reason* (Athens: Ohio University Press, 1980; second edition Albany: SUNY Press, 2005), which will constitute Vol. I/3 of the Collected Writings.—Ed.

V. Conclusion to the Course

Let us conclude. We began with four general formulations of the critical problem, four initial views of the whole. After sketching these, we proceeded to our detailed textual work, proposing that eventually such work would allow us to regain, through the parts, those views of the whole with which we began. This "synthetic return" would allow us to vindicate, fill out, correct, and refine the initial formulations.

So let us consider at least briefly how our reading has touched on those initial formulations, so that we might, as far as possible, carry out the synthetic return. I will begin with the second formulation: the critical problem as one of synthetic apriori judgments, that is, the problem of how apriori synthetic judgments are possible. At the outset, Kant indicated in general how they could be possible. This indication occurred in the context of his so-called Copernican revolution. Such judgments would be possible if objects must *conform* to the subject, to the mind.

It could be said that the entire *Critique* thus far has been devoted to showing that objects must conform to the subject, that is, devoted to demonstrating precisely such conformity as would render apriori synthetic judgments possible. And it has done this at two levels, corresponding to the Aesthetic and Analytic:

  (a) at the level of intuition, the *Critique* shows that objects must conform to the forms of space and time and accordingly that apriori synthetic judgments are possible in mathematics
  (b) at the level of thought, that is, the level of the connection between thought and intuition, the *Critique* shows that objects must conform to the categories, that the categories thus have objective validity, and accordingly that apriori synthetic judgments involving the categories are possible, such as the judgment that every object has a cause.

In the third formulation, the critical problem is one of objectivity. In our reading, we have seen this developed in the theory of the transcendental object. There the issue is the objectification of appearances; that is, what we are given in *intuition* is referred, by means of the synthesis performed by *imagination*, to an object posited by *thought*. It could be said that the theory of the transcendental object merely retraces from the side of the object that same interconnection traced out more generally by the Transcendental Deduction as such, namely, the interconnections among the three faculties of thought, imagination, and intuition. Thus we see something of the generality of this problem, and hence we can understand the appropriateness of characterizing the critical problem as such in terms of objectivity.

Our reading has hardly touched at all on the first formulation: the critical problem as one of the unity of reason, the problem of resolving the conflict of reason with itself. This problem is not openly broached until the Transcendental Dialectic. Let me mention only one point. According to Kant's prefatory formulation, the conflict of reason with itself is not strictly speaking a matter of *pure* reason but is linked in some way to sensibility. More specifically, it is provoked by reason's relating to sensibility in a certain, perverse way. Our reading has shown that, in general, reason (thought) can be related to sensibility only through the mediation of the imagination. This suggests that imagination plays a decisive role in the disruption of the unity of reason, in the setting of reason against itself. Yet to demonstrate it would require a great deal of textual and interpretive work, beginning with a careful reading of the Transcendental Dialectic. But even that would not suffice, for the entire Dialectic, excluding the passages summarizing the Analytic, mentions imagination *only once*. Clearly, such a demonstration would require some "hermeneutical archaeology."

According to the fourth formulation, the critical problem is one of gathering. How has our reading touched upon this? In the Transcendental Deduction, the general issue, the cynosure of all the main themes, may be expressed as the issue of the twofold production of unity. More precisely, the issue is the production, in the intuitive manifold, of those forms of unity posited by pure thought in its positing of the transcendental object. But this is precisely a *gathering* in the sense originally introduced: a positing of unity *and* a synthesizing of the relevant manifold into that unity. In addition, Kant has expounded this gathering to be precisely that by which appearances are constituted as objects. It is a gathering by which objects are brought forth into presence, a productive or poetic gathering, a gathering into presence. Here, most of all, we find the archaic sense of reason still latently present in Kant's thought, namely, reason as λόγος in its early Greek sense.

Part Two.
Kant's Practical Philosophy

Lecture course presented at Duquesne University
Fall 1976

I. The Problem of Practical Philosophy

A. The situation.

Let us begin with a statement by Emmanuel Levinas, the very first lines of his book *Totality and Infinity*: "Everyone will readily agree that it is of the highest importance to know whether we are not duped by morality." This ready agreement and Levinas' appeal to it betray a sense that morality has become suspect as perhaps never since the Greeks, suspect not just in this or that particular but as a whole.

Yet if morality is thus suspect, then practical philosophy—especially if understood as reflection on morality—is questionable in the highest degree. According to Nietzsche: "In all 'science of morals' so far, one thing was lacking, strange as it may sound: the problem of morality itself; what was lacking was any suspicion that there was something problematic here" (*Beyond Good and Evil*, §186).

Since Nietzsche, it has become ever more difficult to suppress this problematic character of morality. That has made utterly questionable our traditional understanding of what constitutes a "science of morals" or practical philosophy.

The above is one side of the situation from out of which we shall take up Kant's practical philosophy and attempt a thoughtful dialogue with it. But there is another side. We see it in American Pragmatism, most sharply in Dewey's Instrumentalism, where thought is regarded as essentially problem-solving, as a means of adjusting to the environment, or in other words, as totally in service to praxis. This side is more radically expressed in Marxism. In the last of the *Theses on Feuerbach*, Marx said: "The philosophers have only *interpreted* the world differently; the point is to *change* it." Here is an unprecedented emphasis on praxis and a demand that thought be brought back into relation with it. In this regard, philosophy has almost exclusively become practical philosophy.

Thus, on the one hand, practical philosophy is more urgently demanded than ever, while on the other, it has become questionable as never before. This tension is an important element in the situation from out of which we will attempt our dialogue with Kant's practical philosophy.

B. Kant's practical writings.

Our main text is the *Critique of Practical Reason*, supplemented by *Foundations of the Metaphysics of Morals*. In order to gain an initial orientation and to formulate some questions, let us begin with the terms of the title of the former, in this order: reason, practical, critique.

(1) Reason. In the *Critique of Pure Reason*, "reason" is used primarily in contrast to the understanding. In this context, reason takes the form of dialectical reason, that is, *pure* thought in contrast to *schematized* thought, thought essentially linked up to experience. Dialectical reason exceeds all limits of experience, all limits of the understanding, and presumes to yield knowledge of the soul, world, and God. This alleged knowing, however, harbors dialectical illusion, as is most evident in the antinomies, where reason comes into open conflict with itself. The task of the *Critique of Pure Reason* and specifically of the Transcendental Dialectic is to restrain human knowing from these flights of pure reason, to bring reason back within the limits where it can assume its proper, legitimate employment.

With regard to our project, it is crucial that for Kant the proper employment of reason is primarily practical. Thus the critical philosophy wants to divert reason from its speculative employment onto the path of a practical employment.

But what is reason per se, regardless of whether it is employed dialectically or practically? A statement near the end of the *Critique of Pure Reason* draws the essential contrast: "By reason I here understand the whole higher faculty of knowledge and am therefore contrasting the rational with the empirical" (A835/B863). At this level, reason coincides with thought as such, in opposition to intuition, the capacity by which something is *given* to the subject. Reason is the spontaneity of the subject, in contrast to its receptivity. Reason is the power of positing, in contrast to the power of receiving, being affected.

Another aspect is visible if we situate the problem of reason historically. In Plato's *Phaedo* (99 d–e), Socrates is facing death. He looks back into his past and tells how he came to practice philosophy as he does. When a young man, he was enthusiastic about investigating nature, looking into the causes of coming to be and passing away, but was led to insoluble problems. Next he turned to Anaxagoras' writings on νοῦς but here too was disappointed. Finally, Socrates says, he set out on a "second sailing" in search of causes and had recourse to λόγοι in order to find in them the truth of beings. So Socrates' way was to have recourse to λόγοι rather than remain immersed in the immediate and particular.

We can regard such recourse as accomplishing two things. First, it makes possible the *universality* of theoretical knowledge, in contrast to merely looking at the particular. That is, it makes possible a knowing in which the immediate and particular are gathered under universal concepts and principles. Second, such recourse sets the knower at a distance from the immediate and particular, frees him from total involvement. That is, it brings about a *detachment* of the knowing subject.

In the course of the tradition, λόγος is translated as *ratio*, "reason," *Vernunft*. Man's character as having λόγος (ζῷον λόγον ἔχον) gets "translated" into his character as "rational animal." Thus what Socrates described as "having recourse to λόγοι" is taken over as that of which man is capable because he is rational, as that which is granted to man by reason. Hence it may be said that through reason two things are granted to man: universal, theoretical knowledge and detachment from the immediate.

(2) Practical. These two human endowments correspond to Kant's distinction between theoretical (speculative) reason and practical reason. Specifically, practical reason has to do with the subject's detachment, his freedom. Kant says in the *Critique of Pure Reason*: "By 'the practical' I mean everything that is possible through freedom" (A800/B828). Now, there can be such detachment not only in theoretical knowing but also in human action, praxis. It is to such detachment in praxis that practical reason pertains. In other words, practical reason is that by which man can be detached, free in action, self-determining rather than determined to action by the way he is pathologically affected by things ("pathological" taken not as abnormal but as passive, as acted upon).

(3) Critique. So what is a *critique* of practical reason? Its task is simply to exhibit this practical function of reason: "This critique concerns itself only with whether and how reason can be practical, that is, how it can directly determine the will" (*CPr*, p. 47). More fully, the *Critique of Practical Reason* (1788) needs to be distinguished from other practical writings of Kant's, the *Foundations of the Metaphysics of Morals* (1785) and the *Metaphysics of Morals* (1797).

The *Metaphysics of Morals* is pure moral philosophy proper, pure ethics. It is divided into a theory of justice and a theory of virtue. It works out concepts of various types of law (for example, public versus private law) and various elements of duty (for example, to oneself and to others). This is to be distinguished from the empirical side of practical philosophy, which constitutes practical anthropology. The *Critique of Practical Reason* provides the foundation for the *Metaphysics of Morals*.

A complication lies in the fact that Kant also published a book entitled *Foundations of the Metaphysics of Morals*. It does not simply present the same matter as the *Critique of Practical Reason*. Kant says that in a sense, it is presupposed by the *Critique*. The sense is this: the *Foundations* begins with common knowledge of morality on which people more or less agree, pre-philosophically, and makes a transition to philosophical knowledge of morality and finally to the level of the *Critique* itself.

C. Questions.

Let us formulate some questions, ones we will take as directive for our interpretation of the Kantian text, although we may eventually find it necessary to revise them. We have characterized practical reason in two respects: as reason, it is a power of positing (it has a positing-character); as practical, it is that through which man can be detached and free in action, rather than be pathologically determined (it has a detaching-character). Our four questions pertain to these two characters.

(1) What form does the positing take in the case of practical reason? The *Critique of Pure Reason* has shown that in the case of theoretical reason, reason posits *ideas* (of soul, world, God). So what does practical reason posit? What are its "postulates" in the broadest sense?

(2) What form does the detaching of the subject take? That is to say, how, by what means, does reason detach the subject from sheer determination by pathological affection? In other words, how does such *self*-detachment take place?

(3) Both of these questions join up in a third, which we will take as our central question: how do the two characters of practical reason (as positing and detaching) belong together? How is their unity to be understood? In what way is the positing, in the form it assumes in the case of practical reason, a self-detaching, and vice versa, the self-detaching a positing?

(4) Finally, how does practical reason belong together with theoretical reason? How is their unity to be understood? Kant himself formulates this question and insists on its importance. Near the end of the Preface to the *Foundations*, he says: "I require of a critical examination of a pure practical reason, if it is to be complete, that the unity of practical reason with the speculative be subject to presentation under a common principle, because in the final analysis there can be but one and the same reason which must be differentiated only in application" (*FM*, p. 8).

II. The Preface of the *Critique of Practical Reason*

WE TURN NOW to our principal text, the *Critique of Practical Reason*, and specifically to the Preface. Here Kant is preparing for the *Critique* in several ways. We can distinguish four distinct aims here. They can be indicated by saying that the Preface is:

(1) retrospective: Kant refers back to those results of the first *Critique* that are most crucial for the second
(2) prospective: Kant introduces the main issues to be treated in the second *Critique*
(3) polemical: Kant answers various critics who had reviewed the *Critique of Pure Reason* and the *Foundations of the Metaphysics of Morals*
(4) methodological: Kant offers some general remarks regarding procedure.

(1) Retrospective.

The Preface begins retrospectively: Kant refers to the parallelism with the *Critique of Pure Reason* and explains why the title of the new *Critique* is not what one would expect on the basis of the parallelism. What is the relevant parallelism? It is *not* one between pure reason and practical reason. Rather, both *Critiques* treat *pure* reason, the first in its speculative, theoretical employment, the second in its practical employment. In view of this parallelism, the two titles should be *Critique of Pure Speculative Reason* and *Critique of Pure Practical Reason*. In fact, these are the titles mentioned in an announcement of the future publication of the second edition of the *Critique of Pure Reason*, an announcement in the *Allgemeine Literaturzeitung* in November 1786.

At that time, Kant envisaged the second *Critique* as a mere appendix to the second edition of the first *Critique*. The announcement said: "To the critique of pure speculative reason contained in the first edition, in the second there will be appended a critique of pure practical reason." In the end, Kant called the second critique *Critique of Practical Reason* rather than *Critique of Pure Practical Reason*. Why? He said: "Its task is merely to show that there is a pure practical reason, and in order to do so it critically examines reason's entire practical faculty" (*CPr*, p. 3). This second *Critique* examines practical reason as such, hence its restricted title. But it makes this examination precisely in order to show that there is a pure practical reason; accordingly, its concern is still, as in the first *Critique*, *pure* reason.

Yet we might ask: once it is shown that there is a practical employment of pure reason, would it not then be necessary to examine such pure practical reason the way the *Critique of Pure Reason* examined pure speculative reason in the Transcendental Dialectic, namely, so as to determine whether it overreaches its limits and thus invalidates itself? And would not the parallel title be needed at least for such an investigation?

Kant's answer is that such an investigation is unnecessary: "If this critique succeeds in its task, there is no need to examine the pure faculty itself to see whether it, like speculative reason, presumptuously overreaches itself. For if pure reason is actually practical, it will show its reality and that of its concepts in action, and all disputations aiming to prove its impossibility will be in vain" (*CPr*, p. 3).

At this point, Kant does not indicate what form this showing of it in action will take. That can be done only in the development of the actual *Critique*.

In the second paragraph, Kant introduces the central concept of the *Critique of Practical Reason*, namely, freedom: "With the pure practical faculty of reason, transcendental freedom is also established" (*CPr*, p. 3). The rest of the paragraph is a reference back to the relevant results of the *Critique of Pure Reason*. We need to examine those results in some detail; they concern (a) the distinction between noumenon and phenomenon, and (b) resolution of the third Antimony.

(a) Noumenon and phenomenon.

The basis of the distinction is the sensible character of human intuition. Specifically, all knowing requires intuition, requires that the object be *given*. Human intuition is sensible, and the object can be given only as it affects us, only in terms of the effects it produces in us. So the object is not given as it is in itself but only as it affects us. This is the first level at which the distinction opens up. There is a thing in itself, the noumenon, the intelligible, over against the effects through which it announces itself to us.

There is a further level, for these effects do not yet constitute the phenomenon. Rather, they are merely sensations. In order for there to be experience, a knowledge of objects, these sensations must be taken up and synthesized by the subject and thereby brought into the form of an object. That is the work of understanding and imagination. The object thus constituted is the phenomenon, the appearance. It is the object as it *appears* in human experience, to be distinguished from the noumenon, the object as it is in itself.

(b) Third antinomy.

Kant deals with antinomies in the second of the three main parts of the Transcendental Dialectic of the *Critique of Pure Reason*. Antinomies arise in connection with rational cosmology, that is, in the attempt at purely rational knowledge of the world as a whole. Rational cosmology is an attempt to answer by reason alone such questions as whether the world has a first cause, a beginning in time, and limits in space. Kant shows that in each such question, reason is able to arrive by valid argumentation at contradictorily opposed conclusions, a thesis and its antithesis. Thus reason is caught in self-contradiction or in blind one-sidedness.

The third antinomy pertains to causality. If we begin with a phenomenon and follow the regressive series of causes, regressing repeatedly from effect to cause, is it possible to arrive at a first member, itself uncaused, or is the series infinite? A first member, an uncaused cause, would be an absolutely spontaneous action, that is, an act of freedom. Kant defines the transcendental concept of freedom as: "the power of beginning a state spontaneously" (A445/B473). So Kant expresses the antinomy as follows: "Thesis: causality in accordance with laws of nature is not the only causality from which the appearances of the world can one and all be derived. To explain these appearances, it is necessary to assume that there is also another causality, that of freedom. Antithesis: there is no freedom; everything in the world takes place solely in accordance with laws of nature" (A445/B473).

Kant shows that a resolution of this antinomy is possible; it is possible for both terms to be true. How? How can an effect be regarded as resulting both from causality by nature (hence, the effect of an infinitely extendable series) and from causality by freedom? Kant's answer is that it is possible insofar as we distinguish between phenomenon and noumenon. Specifically, an effect, a phenomenon, can be regarded in two different ways. Considered simply as a phenomenon, it belongs to an unlimited causal series and so is subject to natural causality. But it may also be regarded as corresponding to a noumenon which is the cause of what appears in the appearance, that is, as having a noumenal cause entirely outside the series. As outside all such phenomenal series, this noumenal cause *can* be a free cause.

Furthermore, not only can a single *event* be referred both to causality by nature and to causality by freedom, but also a single *agent* can be regarded as embodying both kinds of causality. That is possible insofar as the noumenal (intelligible) causality posited outside the entire series of appearances may belong to an agent that is also a phenomenon. That is to say, an agent may have both an intelligible character by which it exercises causality by freedom and a phenomenal character by which its causality is that of nature.

In the *Critique of Pure Reason*, Kant refers especially to this intelligible condition *in man*: "He is thus to himself, on the one hand, phenomenon, and on the other hand, in respect of certain faculties the action of which cannot be ascribed to the receptivity of sensibility, a purely intelligible object. We entitle these faculties understanding and reason" (A546/B574).

So the intelligible character in man is his character as *reason* (in the broader sense, inclusive of understanding). It is then reason which renders man intelligible, constitutes his intelligible condition, renders him a free agent. Here we come upon what we called the "detaching" character of reason.

What precisely does Kant establish in resolving the third antinomy? He does *not* prove the actuality of freedom, that freedom actually exists. He does not even prove the possibility of freedom in the non-formal sense of possibility ("real possibility") defined in the Postulates of the *Critique of Practical Reason*. All he proves is that freedom is *logically* possible, that there is no necessary contradiction between the assertion of freedom and of natural causality: "For speculative reason, the concept of freedom was problematic but not impossible; that is to say, speculative reason could think of freedom without contradiction, but it could not assure any objective reality to it. Reason showed freedom to be conceivable only in order that its supposed impossibility might not endanger the very being of reason and plunge it into an abyss of skepticism" (*CPr*, p. 3).

Why would the impossibility of freedom "endanger the very being of reason"? It is because man's character as rational and his character as free agent coincide; and so the denial of freedom is ultimately the denial of reason itself. Thus it is skepticism.

(2) Prospective. I will highlight four points.

(a) The most important result to be established in the *Critique of Practical Reason* is the actuality of freedom. On what basis? Kant says of freedom: "This idea is revealed by the moral law" (*CPr*, p. 4).

(b) The concept of freedom is the "keystone" of the entire system, in the sense that the establishing of the actuality of freedom carries over to other ideas: "All other concepts (those of God and immortality) which, as mere ideas, are unsupported by anything in speculative reason, now attach themselves to the concept of freedom and gain, with it and through it, stability and objective reality" (*CPr*, p. 3).

Kant stresses that the ideas of God and of immortality have a different status from that of freedom. Although we have no insight into freedom, we know it as the condition of the moral law, so that the fact of the moral law requires an immediate affirmation of freedom. With the other two ideas, the affirmation is not immediate (we will discuss its precise character later).

(c) The affirmation of freedom, God, and immortality in the framework of practical reason should not be regarded as an extension of theoretical knowledge: "Reason is not thereby extended in its theoretical knowledge" (CPr, p. 4). What is most important is that Kant explains the distinction between theoretical and practical affirmation by way of the concept of *need*. In theoretical knowing, affirmation serves a particular kind of need; in practical knowing, it serves another kind. The point is that the affirmation of the ideas of freedom, God, and immortality is such as to serve needs of a practical kind. This reference of affirmation back to needs (interests) will be important in trying to answer the fourth question we raised, the one concerning the relation between speculative and practical reason.

(d) Finally, let us connect this prospective sketch with the more basic issue in the resolution of the third antinomy. The resolution amounts to a diverting of reason from the positing of a first member in the causal series to a positing of a first member completely outside the series, the positing of an *intelligible* causality. Consider specifically the case of man. The diverting is this: reason comes to *posit* the human agent as *detached*, and so here we have "positing" and "detachment," the two characters of reason, brought explicitly together for the first time. Now, the posited intelligible causality is just reason itself, as Kant says and we have already noted. Accordingly, the resolution of the third antinomy involves reason positing itself as detached, reason's self-positing. In the Critique of Pure Reason, the mere *logical possibility* of such self-positing was established. In the Critique of Practical Reason, its *actuality* will be established on the basis of the moral law.

(3) Polemical.

Kant's polemics in the Preface are responding both to general criticisms and to quite specific ones.

The first general criticism was levelled by those who boasted to possess the kind of knowledge Kant claimed to have proved impossible: for example, knowledge of things in themselves. The famous Garve-Feder review of the Critique of Pure Reason attacked Kant for being a subjective idealist. Kant's response was to publish the Prolegomena. In the Critique of Practical Reason, Kant's rejoinder to such criticism drips with irony:

> Those who boast of such elevated knowledge should not hold it back but present it for public testing and acclaim. They wish to prove; very well, let them prove, and the critical philosophy will lay down its weapons before them as victors. "Why standing still? They would refuse. And yet 'tis in their power to be happy" [Kant is quoting the Satires of Horace]. Since they do not actually

wish to prove, presumably because they cannot, we must again take up these weapons.... (*CPr*, p. 5)

The second general criticism stemmed from those who refused to believe ethics required so subtle a foundation as Kant had supplied. For example, G. A. Tittel, "Über Herrn Kants Moralreform," charged that Kant simply used incomprehensible language in order to make old things look like new discoveries. Kant answers in a footnote (*CPr*, p. 8) by saying that his intention is not to introduce a new discovery, a new principle of morality, as though up until the present the entire world has been ignorant of duty. Kant is merely seeking a new formula.

Besides these general criticisms, four specific ones are addressed by Kant:

There is inconsistency involved in denying the extension of the categories to the supersensible in the field of speculative reason while affirming such extension for practical reason. This criticism was stated by H. A. Pistoris in his review of the *Foundations*. Kant described this critic as "truth-loving and acute and therefore worthy of respect" (*CPr*, p. 9). Kant's response in the Preface: "Only a detailed critique of practical reason can set aside all these misconceptions" (*CPr*, p. 7). This problem is then his chief concern in the Second Section of Chapter I of the Analytic.

There is circularity in the relationship of freedom and the moral law. J. F. Flatt, in his review of the *Foundations*, argued that each was used to prove the other. Kant answers in a footnote: "Though freedom is certainly the *ratio essendi* of the moral law, the latter is *ratio cognoscendi* of freedom" (*CPr*, p. 4). That is, freedom is required for the very possibility of there *being* a moral law, yet we *know* of freedom only *through* the moral law. This answer is elaborated in the First Section of Chapter I of the Analytic.

Pistoris also charged that "the concept of the good was not established before the moral principle" (*CPr*, p. 9). Kant admits this and defends his position in Chapter II of the Analytic.

Johann Feder criticized what he called the "alleged discovery" that there can be no apriori knowledge at all. Kant answers that there is no danger that such a discovery will be made. "It would be like proving by reason that there is no such thing as reason" (*CPr*, p. 12).

(4) Methodological.

We find in the Preface three important methodological statements. The first concerns parts and wholes. Kant says that in an investigation such as the one about to be launched, it is essential to begin with the parts, specifically with, as much as is possible, an exact and complete delineation of parts. Then it is necessary "to see all those parts in their reciprocal interrelation, in the light of their derivation from the concept of the whole and as united in a pure rational faculty.... Those who are loath to engage in the first of these inquiries and who do not consider acquiring this acquaintance worth the trouble will not reach the second stage, the synoptic view, which is a synthetic return to that which was previously given only analytically" (*CPr*, p. 10).

Kant is saying that most of his critics fail to reach the level of this "synoptic view," the level of a synthetic return to the parts in light of an idea of the whole. They fail to reach this because they do not first work through the parts in a complete and disciplined way. The methodological implication for us is that we must first gain thorough acquaintance with the parts, the details, and only then, in a synthetic return, can we really gain an adequate grasp of the whole. That is, we can understand Kant "in general" only by first understanding him "in detail."

Note that this idea of the whole, which comes explicitly into play in the synthetic return, is linked by Kant to the unity of reason. In stronger terms, there is a system, a whole, because of the unity of reason.

The second methodological directive restrains us from venturing definitions prematurely: "A precaution against making judgments by venturing definitions before a complete analysis of concepts has been made (usually only far along in a system) is to be recommended throughout philosophy, but it is often neglected" (*CPr*, pp. 9–10, footnote). The point is that one cannot at the outset give rigorous and thorough definitions of basic concepts, since that would involve already deciding questions which can be settled only in the course of the analysis. For instance, in the investigation of reason, one cannot begin with a definition that would precisely delimit what reason is, for the task of the investigation itself, if it is fundamental, includes determining what reason is. Instead, one must begin with preliminary conceptions, those of common sense or of tradition, and let them be developed and transformed in the course of the inquiry. This is very typical of Kant. In many instances of his being charged with blind dependence on traditional concepts, it is rather a matter of his adherence to this methodological principle.

Thirdly, Kant notes that the *Critique of Practical Reason* presupposes the *Foundations of the Metaphysics of Morals*, "insofar as that work gives a preliminary acquaintance with the principle of duty and justifies a definite formula of it" (*CPr*, p. 8). We can see this relation also in terms of the other two methodological issues. To some extent, we may say that the *Foundations* presents the parts, and the *Critique* the synthetic return to them in light of the whole. Also, the *Foundations* begins with ordinary concepts of common rational knowledge about morality and develops them into more precise and adequate philosophical concepts.

In accord with these various indications, we turn now the *Foundations of the Metaphysics of Morals* in order to prepare for our reading of the *Critique of Practical Reason*.

III. *Foundations of the Metaphysics of Morals*

In the Preface, Kant introduces the concept of ethics, that is, pure moral philosophy, the metaphysics of morals. He refers first to the ancient division of philosophy into physics, ethics, and logic. According to the skeptic Sextus Empiricus, this distinction goes back to Xenocrates, successor of Speusippos, himself the successor of Plato as head of the Academy. Xenocrates claimed to find the basis for this division in Plato's writings. The Stoics took over the division, and from them it was transmitted to the Middle Ages and to modern philosophy. Kant accepts the division. His only addition is to work out the system of divisions wherein this particular division belongs:

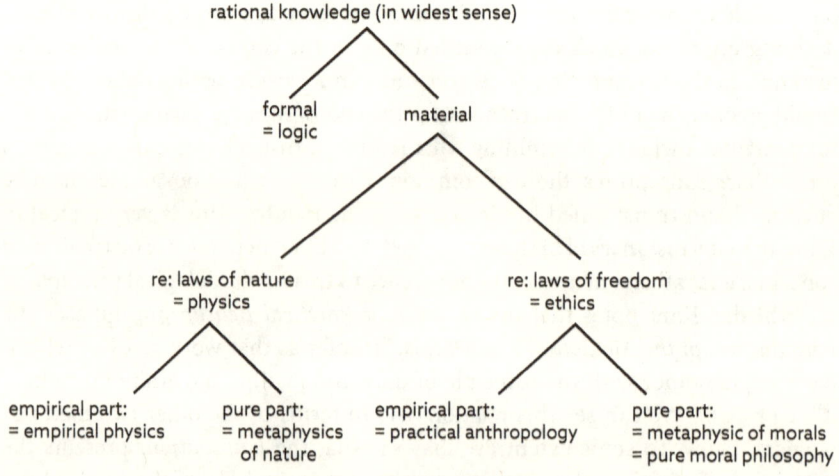

As a preliminary indication that there must be a *pure* moral philosophy, freed from everything empirical, Kant refers to the common conception of duty and of moral law. His point is that according to this common notion, a moral law "must imply absolute necessity," not a necessity based merely on the specific empirical constitution of human nature. For example, the command "Thou shalt not lie," does not apply "to man only, as if other rational beings had no need to observe it" (*FM*, p. 5). Kant concludes: "One must concede that the ground of obligation here must not be sought in the nature of man or in the circumstances in which he is placed, but sought apriori solely in the concepts of pure reason" (FM, p. 5).

But this is no more than a preliminary indication. In fact, the transition it sketches from the common notion to the level of philosophical principles is the transition the entire *Foundations* attempts to carry out. Kant says: "The present foundations ... are nothing more than the search for and establishment of the supreme principle of morality" (FM, p. 8). In other words, it is the transition from the common conception of morality to the level of the fundamental establishment of the principle of morality, the level of a critique of practical reason.

This transition involves three distinct stages, undertaken in the three sections of the *Foundations*:

(1) from the common rational knowledge of morals to the philosophical
(2) from popular moral philosophy to the metaphysics of morals
(3) from the metaphysics of morals to the critical examination of pure practical reason.

As leading up to the level of such a critical examination, the *Foundations* can be taken as an extended introduction to the *Critique of Practical Reason*. In another respect, it is an introduction to the metaphysics of morals: it supplies the principle which is then *applied* in the metaphysics of morals. Thus we should not expect from the *Foundations* any detailed account of the application of moral principles. The examples given in the *Foundations* are merely illustrations, meant to clarify the sense of the principle, and are not detailed applications of it.

(1) First Section. Transition from the common rational knowledge of morals to the philosophical.

This section contains three main parts:

(a) discussion of a good will—provides the starting point
(b) formulation of three principles of morality—leads up to the formulation of the fundamental principle (moral law)
(c) discussion of the relation of practical philosophy to common reason.

(a) A good will.

Here Kant finds within "common rational knowledge of morals" the starting point from which the transition to the philosophical level can proceed. That starting point lies in the concept of a good will. It can serve as an appropriate starting point because there is general accord with regard to it.

Kant begins: "Nothing in the world—indeed nothing even beyond the world—can possibly be conceived which could be called good without qualification except a good will" (FM, p. 9). This means, first, that a good will is the only thing good in all circumstances. Kant does not mean a good will is the only good. In fact, he goes on to enumerate many other things that are good: the gifts of nature and the gifts of fortune. The former include talents of the mind, such as intelligence, wit, and judgment, and qualities of temperament, such as courage, resolution, and perseverance, while the gifts of fortune include power, riches, honor, health, and even happiness. Yet none of these are good in all circumstances, that is, independently of the circumstances. They can be bad at times, for instance if they contribute to enslaving others. They are only conditioned goods. The good will is unconditioned.

Second, a good will is the only thing that is good in itself. That is, a good will is not good because of the effects it produces but only because it is the kind of willing it is. In fact, its goodness is not diminished if it should prove entirely incapable of achieving its proposed end.

Despite the agreement of common reason or ordinary moral consciousness regarding the absolute worth of a good will, there is still ground for suspicion. So Kant introduces some further reflections intended to allay these misgivings. His reflections also serve to bring *reason* explicitly under consideration.

Kant begins with the notion that reason is by nature appointed as ruler of the will. Again, this is not a philosophical thesis but a notion of ordinary moral consciousness and simply expresses the view that human action is not a mere predetermined response. Instead, our action involves both detachment from the situation and self-determination. In other words, our engagement in action is determined, not just by feelings and sense impressions, but by rational considerations. We do things—at least sometimes—because we have reasons for doing them. If we think of will as that by which we engage ourselves in action, this amounts to saying that reason can determine the will. That is what, for common sense, primarily distinguishes a rational being: it is one that can "act rationally."

Kant now asks: what is the function of reason? What is the purpose for which reason was appointed ruler of our will? For what end does reason determine the will?

We might suppose this end to be the satisfaction of our needs, thus our welfare, our happiness. But, Kant argues, reason is *not* suited for realizing such ends, for directing the will to obtain objects by which our needs would be satisfied. Such objects would be much more readily obtained if, as in animals, instinct were the guide.

So if reason is not suited to guide the will in the attainment of such external ends, if it is not suited to guide the will with respect to the will's character as a means to some end beyond itself, then it must be suited to guide the will in some other respect. Which one? It must be with respect to the will's character in itself, regardless of the ends to which it is a means. That is, it must be suited to making the will a good will: "reason's proper function must be to produce a will good in itself and not one that is good merely as a means" (*FM*, p. 12).

Let us look more closely at Kant's argument. Reason's function is to determine the will; it is by nature appointed as ruler of the will. But reason is not suited to determining the will as a means, hence it is suited only to determining it in itself. Therefore, reason's function is to determine the will in itself.

Note the missing premises: reason's function coincides with that for which it is most suited, and reason is especially suited for some end. Thus the argument presupposes a certain purposiveness. Kant expresses that as a conditional clause preceding his conclusion just cited: "As nature has elsewhere distributed capacities suitable to the functions they are to perform, reason's proper function must be to produce a will good in itself and not one that is good merely as a means" (*FM*, p. 12). Presumably Kant presupposes that common human reason would grant such purposiveness, although of course he would also admit that there is ground for suspicion. Let us note that if one rigorously pursued such suspicion and raised it to the level of a philosophical problematic, the result would be a critique of teleological judgment.

(b) Basic propositions of morality.

Here Kant actually carries out the transition to the philosophical level. The starting point has been established: the concept of a good will. The task is to develop this concept. Through the development, "the common rational knowledge of morals" will be raised to the level of philosophical thematization.

Kant proposes to develop the concept, not directly, but by taking up the concept of duty. The point behind this proposal is that under conditions belonging to a *finite* rational being, who must struggle with desires and inclinations, a good will is manifested in action done for the sake of duty. Thus Kant proceeds to formulate three basic propositions concerning duty.

Proposition 1: an action is morally good only if it is done from duty. Here we must distinguish between something done *from* duty and something done merely *in accord with* duty. For example, suppose a person is kind to others. Since it is a duty to be kind to others, his action is in accord with duty. But this does not suffice to give the action moral worth. He may be kind to others for various reasons: for example, because it serves his own interests. Then clearly his action has no moral worth. Or it may be because he is by nature inclined to be sympathetic toward others. Although such action may deserve praise and encouragement, still it has no moral worth. It has moral worth only if he does it *because* it is his duty. So it is all a matter of the motive that determines the action. Only if the action is determined by the motive of duty does it have moral worth.

Proposition 2: "An action performed from duty does not have its moral worth in the purpose to be achieved through it, but in the maxim by which it is determined. Its moral value, therefore, does not depend on the realization of the object of the action but merely on the principle of volition by which the action is done, without any regard to the objects of the faculty of desire" (*FM*, p. 16).

This proposition applies to action the consequences of the earlier account of a good will. A good will is good in itself, not because of its effects but because it is the kind of willing it is. This carries over to the action in which we engage ourselves by our willing. The goodness of the action does not derive from the achievement of some purpose, some effect. Rather, its moral worth is determined by the kind of willing from which it arises. That is, its moral worth is determined by the maxim according to which the action is done or, in other words, by the subjective principle according to which the will is determined to the action. What, then, is the maxim that must rule an action in order that it be done from duty and be morally worthy?

Proposition 3 identifies this maxim. "Duty is the necessity of an action executed from respect for the law" (*FM*, p. 16). This says that the maxim is respect for the law. So to act from duty is to act from respect for the law. This involves letting one's will be determined by the law, submitting one's will to complete determination by the law. Kant explains: "Since an act from duty wholly excludes the influence of inclination and therewith every object of the will, nothing remains which can determine the will objectively except the law, and nothing subjectively except pure respect for this practical law. This subjective element is the maxim that I ought to follow such a law even if it thwarts all my inclinations" (*FM*, p. 17).

Two questions arise. To begin with, what is respect? Kant does not yet actually develop this issue. It is one of the richest in his practical philosophy, and we will return to it when we take up the *Critique*. Here in the *Foundations*, all he says about respect is contained in another footnote (*FM*, pp. 17–18). I will mention only three points:

First, respect is a feeling. It is utterly distinct, however, from all other feelings. The distinctiveness is that respect is not received through any influence, but rather is *self-effected* by a rational concept. So, unlike all other feelings, respect cannot be referred to inclination or fear. It does not arise through affection. It is a "pure" feeling.

Second, the only object of respect is the law. Indeed, we may also have respect for a person, but "all respect for a person is only respect for the law." We still have to see what this really involves. How can respect for a person be respect for the law?

Third, respect harbors a peculiar tension in its basic constitution. We are subject to the law and submit ourselves to it, whereby it thwarts our self-love. Yet it is a law we impose on ourselves. That is, we are subject *to* and subject *of* the law. Action arising out of this tension is action from respect for law, that is, action from duty. Kant expresses this tension in a footnote by saying that respect involves moments analogous to both fear and inclination: "As a law, we are subject to it without consulting self-love; as imposed on us by ourselves, it is a consequence of our will. In the former regard, it is analogous to fear and in the latter to inclination" (*FM*, p. 18). Clearly, we are not yet in a position to understand this tension; we have not yet even thematized the law, much less considered its character as self-imposed. Such a consideration can be carried out only at the level of the *Critique of Practical Reason*.

The second question concerning respect has to do with the law which is the object of respect and which is to determine the will. What sort of law is this? It cannot be a *material* law, one pertaining to some effect expected by an action. That is because the determination of a good will is not a determining of it as a means, that is, with regard to some effect beyond the will. So the law must be purely formal. According to Kant: "Nothing remains to serve as a principle of the will except universal conformity of its action to law as such. That is, I ought never act in such a way that I could not also will that my maxim should be a universal law. Mere conformity to law as such (without assuming any particular law applicable to certain actions) serves as the principle of the will" (*FM*, p. 18). This is the first formulation of the moral law. It is a negative formulation, and it is preliminary.

As regards the moral law, note how this principle serves in practical judgments. It is not a matter of deducing particular moral laws from it but rather of examining the material maxim of a prospective action and accepting or rejecting that maxim depending on whether it can be willed as universal law.

Kant gives the example of a false promise made in distress. Here the material maxim is: to extricate myself from difficulty, I can make a false promise. But I must ask myself: could I will that this maxim should hold as a universal law? No, I could not. For then there would be no promises at all. That is, if everyone did this by law, then it would become impossible to extricate myself from difficulty by a false promise, since no one would believe the promise. In Kant's words: "Thus my maxim would necessarily destroy itself as soon as it was made a universal law" (*FM*, p. 19).

Also note the peculiar "status" of this principle. All that the law prescribes is conformity to law as such. This may seem highly abstract and remote from the "common rational knowledge of morals," despite Kant's intention of merely elevating such knowledge to the level of philosophy. Yet we should notice that immediately after he states the moral law, Kant repeats this methodological intention: "The common reason of mankind in its practical judgments is in perfect agreement with this and has this principle constantly in view" (*FM*, p. 18).

How can Kant make such a claim? I suggest that what the principle expresses is simply what common reason would regard as the *minimal*, most general, requirement for morality. Specifically, a person is good not by merely furthering *his own* interests and satisfying *his own* desires but rather by obeying a law valid *for all*, by following an objective standard that is not merely determined by his own desires and inclinations.

(c) Relation of philosophical thematization to common reason.

What has Kant accomplished by this philosophical thematization? He has not *proved* the moral law, in the sense of deriving it from its ground. He has not yet, as he admits, even discerned its ground. Rather, he has simply thematized, drawn attention to, the *principle* of the moral knowledge of common human reason. As he notes, his procedure here has been Socratic.

In this connection, Kant observes that neither science nor philosophy is required for morality, that is, in order to know how to be honest, good, virtuous: "We might have conjectured beforehand that the knowledge of what everyone is obliged to do, and thus also to know, would be within the reach of everyone, even the most ordinary man" (*FM*, p. 20). Yet such ordinary moral knowledge, such "innocence," is easily led astray. That explains why philosophy is needed in this sphere—not to learn from it but rather to secure the precepts we already have, that is, to secure us against that "natural dialectic" which is provoked by inclinations and leads us to argue against the laws of duty and to make them more in accord with our inclinations: "In this way, common human reason is impelled to go outside its sphere and to take a step into the field of practical philosophy.... It is so impelled on practical grounds ... in order to escape from the perplexity of opposing claims and to avoid the danger of losing all genuine moral principles through the equivocation in which it is easily involved" (*FM*, p. 22).

The step into practical philosophy is precisely what this section has accomplished. It is of utmost importance to see that its ground, the ground of the entire philosophical reflection on morality, ultimately the ground of practical philosophy itself, is a practical rather than a theoretical ground.

(2) Second Section. Transition from the Popular Moral Philosophy to the Metaphysics of Morals.

This section is composed of three main parts preceded by an introduction:

(a) Introduction: sketch of the character of the transition
(b) Imperatives: development of the basis for the transition
(c) Categorical imperative: actual carrying through of the transition
(d) Autonomy and heteronomy: critical application of the results.

(a) Introduction.

Here Kant sketches the character of the transition. The opening sentence provides a negative sketch: "If we have derived our earlier concept of duty from the common use of our practical reason, it is by no means to be inferred that we have treated it as an empirical concept" (*FM*, p. 22). The transition now to be made will enforce that statement. It will carry the concept of duty from the level of the thematization already achieved to the level at which it is totally dissociated from all empirical concepts.

In order to develop this sketch, Kant considers various issues involved in the contention that duty is not an empirical concept. If it were empirical, that would mean it is derived from experience; in other words, we would form the concept of duty by observing in experience various instances and abstracting from them. Kant argues that it is not empirical because action from duty is never discernible in experience. We cannot, on the basis of experience, distinguish between actions done from duty and actions merely in conformity with duty: "It is in fact absolutely impossible by experience to discern with complete certainty a single case in which the maxim of an action, however much it may conform to duty, rested solely on moral grounds and on the conception of one's duty... for, when moral worth is in question, it is not a matter of actions which one sees but of their inner principles, which one does not see" (*FM*, p. 23).

Conversely, Kant argues that if the concept of duty were conceded to be empirical, then we would play into the hands of those who reduce morality to a mere phantom of imagination. Since we do not apprehend with certainty any instances of duty, which seems then to be an empty concept, and, more decisively, when we look closer or with more maturity of observation at instances that might be taken as action from duty, we are repeatedly disappointed and "we everywhere come upon the dear self" (*FM*, p. 23). So to make of duty an empirical concept is ultimately to fall into moral skepticism. The transition Kant is now outlining is intended to preserve the concept of duty (lifted from common rational knowledge of morals) from dissolution in such skepticism.

Kant adds a corollary regarding the role of examples or models in morality: "Nor could one give poorer counsel to morality than by attempting to derive it from examples" (*FM*, p. 25). The point is that no man could serve as a model on which morality could be based, for moral worth would then consist in imitation of this model. On the contrary, any such model would have to be judged in advance according to the principle of morality in order to determine its fitness to serve as an example. This holds not just for any man but even of Christ; even he must be judged by the ideal of rational perfection. So Kant concludes: "Imitation has no place in moral matters, and examples serve only for encouragement" (*FM*, p. 25).

If moral concepts are not empirical, then they must be apriori, originating from reason. So Kant says: "According to what has been said, it is clear that all moral concepts have their seat and origin entirely in reason" (*FM*, p. 28).

Thus we see the character of the transition: from the level of the first thematization of the concept of duty as achieved in the First Section to the level at which duty is thematized in its purely rational, apriori character in distinction from everything empirical. Yet there is still a question we need to pose in order to bring out the full structure of the transition. Does this transition break with common reason? In a certain regard, we must say no. This transition does not involve posing some new concept of duty over against the one lifted from common reason. Rather, it is simply a matter of developing to a higher philosophical level the concept of duty belonging to common reason. But why this development? Is it just a matter of theoretical curiosity? If so, then it would fall completely outside the domain of practical philosophy. For (cf. the end of the First Section) practical philosophy is based on practical rather than theoretical grounds. It is provoked and guided by needs arising in the practical dimension. What is the relevant practical need here? It is the need to preserve the concept of duty from dissolution in moral skepticism. But what threatens to dissolve it that way? Certainly not common reason. Rather, it is a particular theoretical *corruption* of our common knowledge. Kant identifies this as "popular practical philosophy" and says that it "goes no further than it can grope by means of examples." Such popular philosophy is corruptive because it remains tied to experience and to the notion that duty is something empirical, to be discerned in an example.

So this transition is indeed a break—not with "common reason" but rather with "popular moral philosophy" (as stated in the title). And yet, in another sense, it is also a break with common reason: practical philosophy has now to secure the principles of "common reason" against corruption, and for this it cannot simply appeal to common reason. In other words, the transition is now beyond the level of merely making explicit what is already implicit in our common rational knowledge in regard to morality.

(b) Imperatives.
This part proceeds in three stages:

(i) imperatives in general
(ii) classification of imperatives
(iii) possibility of imperatives.

This part develops the basis for the transition. We can see more specifically how it does so if we look at Kant's statement of just how the transition is to be made: "In order to make this advance, we must follow and clearly present the practical faculty of reason from its universal rules of determination to the point at which the concept of duty arises from it" (*FM*, p. 29).

The discussion of imperatives proceeds along the first stretch of this way. It moves from the concept of practical reason up to the point at which the concept of duty can subsequently be formulated in its purely rational character.

(i) Imperatives in general.
Kant begins with the concept of a rational being: "Only a rational being has the capacity of acting according to a conception of laws, that is, according to

principles" (*FM*, p. 29). This again expresses the element of detachment, but now in relation to a determination by law, whereas previously it was treated in relation to sensibility. Something in nature is immediately, directly, determined by laws of physics. But a rational being is determined by law only indirectly; it is detached from the law. Yet how is that possible? It can be determined by the law indirectly only insofar as the rational being itself mediates the determination, that is, applies the law to itself. This amounts to acting according to principles.

Kant continues: "This capacity is will." So will is the capacity for acting according to principles. Will is that character of agents by which they mediate between law and action, that is, mediate the application of the law to their action.

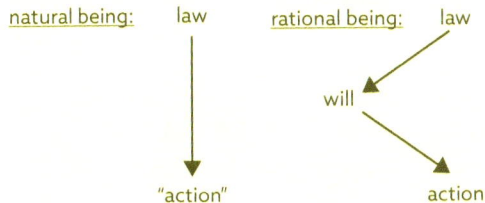

Therefore, only a rational being may be said to have a will. But Kant goes still further: "Since reason is required for the derivation of actions from law, will is nothing else than practical reason" (*FM*, p. 29). So Kant is saying that practical reason and will are the same capacity. We must be careful, however, not to overstrain this identification, such that the distinction between will and reason completely disappears. We cannot take them as simply identical, for Kant's very next sentence begins: "If reason infallibly determines the will. . . ." Reason could not be said to determine the will if the two were identical. So how is the relation to be understood? I suggest that when Kant says the "will is nothing else than practical reason," he means they constitute one and the same capacity or agent. They are not "parts" of the soul. But the agent, the practical subject, does involve various structural moments or dimensions, and that is how we are to understand the distinction. Practical reason is the agent with respect to its being determined by law. Will is the agent with respect to its being determined to action.

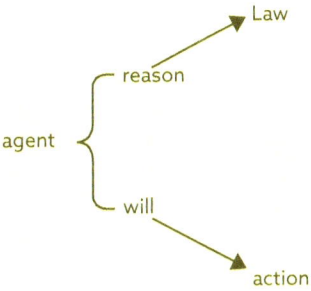

Thus Kant can speak of reason determining the will. That means the agent mediates the application of law to action, lets its action be determined by law.

On the basis of this conception of reason and will, Kant proceeds to define an imperative. First he draws a contrast: "If reason infallibly determines the will, the actions such a being recognizes as objectively necessary are also subjectively necessary" (*FM*, p. 29). This is the condition defining the divine will or holy will. There is total accord between reason and will; only that action is willed which is recognized by reason as good. What is objectively necessary (actions prescribed by law, recognized by reason) are also subjectively necessary (must be willed). By contrast: "If the will is not of itself in complete accord with reason (the actual case with man), then the actions recognized as objectively necessary are subjectively contingent, and the determination of such a will according to objective laws is constraint" (*FM*, p. 29).

That is the condition defining a finite will, where there is no pre-established accord between reason and will. So, in this case, there is no necessity that what is objectively necessary (recognized by reason as good) is actually willed. There exists a possibility of discord between reason and will, between law and the action willed. Then the determination of the will according to objective laws is a matter of *constraining* it into accord. Furthermore, whatever constrains the will has the character of a command. An imperative is the expression of such a command: "The conception of an objective principle, so far as it constrains the will, is a command (of reason), and the formula of this command is called an imperative" (*FM*, p. 30). Kant adds that an imperative is expressed by an "ought." Also, there can be no imperatives for a divine will or holy will: "The 'ought' is here out of place, for the volition of itself is necessarily in unison with the law" (*FM*, p, 31).

(ii) Classification of imperatives.

The main division is between hypothetical and categorical imperatives. The former presents the necessity of some action as a means to achieving something else. If you are to gain a certain end, you must perform a certain action which is the means to that end. (For example: if you are to be elected, you must campaign.) The latter presents an action as practically necessary in itself, without regard to any further end. (For example: love your neighbor.)

Kant also expresses the distinction in terms of the goodness of the action, that is, with regard to whether it is good for some end (hypothetical) or good in itself (categorical). For example, campaigning is good only for some end, getting elected. So the imperative "you ought to campaign" is hypothetical. But loving your neighbor is good in itself. Accordingly, the imperative "you ought to love your neighbor" is categorical. The point is that all moral imperatives are categorical.

There is a secondary division of hypothetical imperatives—in terms of whether the end is merely possible (an end I *can* will) or actual (an end all men do by nature will). A possible end corresponds to a problematical imperative, technical imperative, or an imperative (rule) of skill. An example is campaigning to get elected. As to an actual end, there is one which is actual in all rational beings: happiness. A hypothetical imperative presenting the necessity of an action as a means to the promotion of happiness is an assertorical imperative or pragmatic imperative. Since skill in choice of such means is called "prudence," such imperatives may also be called "counsels of prudence." For example: you ought to care for your health.

(iii) The possibility of imperatives.

Kant poses a question: "How are all these imperatives possible?" In other words, what is their basis? What gives them their validity as imperatives? What makes them binding for all rational beings, such that a fully rational being would have to will as they command?

In the case of hypothetical imperatives, the basis consists in the fact that these imperatives are analytic propositions. In general, an analytic proposition is a proposition in which the predicate is contained in the subject ("a square is four-sided"). In such a case, if one grants the subject, then one must also grant what is asserted in the predicate, must grant that the predicate belongs to the subject—provided one is a purely rational being. So such a being would be bound by an analytic proposition, would have to assert or grant theoretically the assertion expressed in that proposition. In the translation of this situation from the theoretical to the practical sphere, the difference is that a practical proposition expresses a willing rather than an assertion. And so, in an analytic *practical* proposition, the willing expressed in the predicate is contained in the willing expressed in the subject. In such a case, one who willed the subject would also have to will the predicate—provided he was fully rational. The connection between the two acts of willing would be binding for a fully rational being.

So in saying that hypothetical imperatives are analytic, Kant is saying that the willing of the means (the predicate) is already contained in the willing of the end (the subject). Therefore, this connection, what the imperative asserts, is binding on any fully rational being. Kant expresses this very succinctly: "Whoever wills the end, insofar as reason has decisive influence on his action, wills also the indispensably necessary means to it that lie in his power" (*FM*, p. 34). It is essential to see that the purely analytic and hence binding connection is between two acts of will, not between means and end. The connection between means and end can only be determined empirically and thus would be expressed in a theoretical *synthetic* proposition.

This entire development has the purpose of merely bringing out by contrast the state of the same question with respect to categorical imperatives. A categorical imperative cannot be analytic, because it does not connect a willing with another, already presupposed willing. Rather, it connects a willing "directly with the will of a rational being as something which is not contained in it" (*FM*, p. 38, footnote). It merely poses a certain willing as binding on any rational being, although that willing is not simply contained in the *concept* of a rational being. So the connection it establishes is synthetic.

Furthermore, since, as already agued, such a moral imperative cannot be derived from experience, the connection it expresses must be apriori rather than empirical. Thus a categorical imperative is an apriori synthetic practical proposition. Kant does not here answer the question of how a categorical imperative is possible; he only defines the problem more precisely. It is a problem of showing how apriori synthetic *practical* propositions are possible, just as the *Critique of Pure Reason* showed how apriori synthetic *theoretical* propositions are possible. The difficulty of the task in the first *Critique* justifies supposing that the present task will also be difficult, the task of grounding morality. For now, Kant defers this task in order to make the preparation by which he can eventually take it up.

(c) Categorical imperative.

In the initial part of the Second Section, Kant developed the basis for the transition to which the section is devoted. Specifically, he proceeded from the general character of practical reason to the concept of an imperative and then to the concept of a categorical imperative as the kind of imperative proper to morality. In the second part, he will carry through the actual transition. More precisely, from the concept of a categorical imperative, he will derive the basic formula of the moral law. Thus, coming from this different direction, Kant will now take up again the issue broached at the end of the First Section.

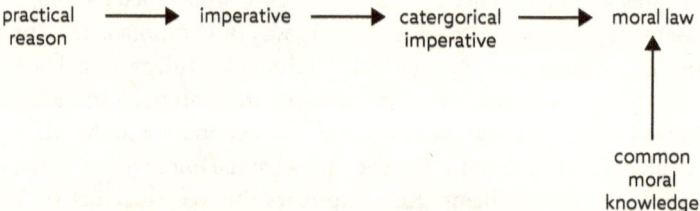

Then Kant will proceed to develop, besides the basic formula of universal law, a series of four additional formulas of the moral law:

(i) formula of universal law
(ii) formula of the law of nature
(iii) formula of the end in itself
(iv) formula of autonomy
(v) formula of the realm of ends.

Through this development, the entire issue will be raised to the pure rational level, the level of a metaphysics of morals. Yet it will still fall short of showing how the moral law is possible, how morality is grounded. Kant will take up that task in the Third Section.

(i) Formula of universal law.

The task here is to derive from the concept of a categorical imperative the specific formula of such an imperative, that is, to discover, from the mere concept, the formula of that imperative which is categorical. Kant expresses this derivation in two very brief paragraphs on pages 38-39. It is one of his most condensed statements.

An imperative expresses an objective principle, a command, as constraining the will. More precisely, the full structure of an imperative involves two moments: the principle or command and the demand, the practical necessity, that the will accord with this command, that its willing be in accord with it, that the maxim (subjective principle) be in accord with the command (objective principle).

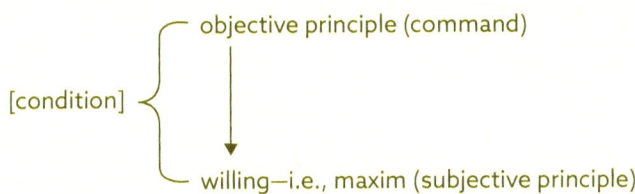

In the case of hypothetical imperatives, there is a third structural moment: the condition, the presupposed willing of some particular end. It is only under this condition that the other two moments are actually constituted. Only under this condition does the command become binding, coercive, a demand. If I do *not* will the end, there is no demand that I will the means. Second, the objective principle (command) is also specified by that condition. What is commanded (the particular means I ought to will) is completely determined by the end that is willed. So the objective principle derives all its content from the condition. Thus Kant writes: "If I think of a hypothetical imperative as such, I do not know what it will contain until the condition is stated" (*FM*, p. 38).

Let us now consider a categorical imperative. It also involves the first two moments:

As categorical, however, it does not involve the third moment, the condition. There is no condition which would then constitute the other moments. Accordingly, the law is commanded *unconditionally*; it is *intrinsically* binding, coercive, a demand on the will. Also, the law does not undergo any specification; there is no condition to give it specific content, and so it receives no special, material determination. That is, it does not become a command that some specific action be willed. Instead, it remains completely unspecified, completely formal.

Yet how can such a totally unspecified law be an imperative at all? What does it contain and hence demand accord with? It contains merely the form of law, the universality of law as such. And so, what it demands is that the maxim conform to this universality, to lawfulness as such. Thus Kant states: "But if I think of a categorical imperative, I know immediately what it contains. For since the imperative contains besides the law only the necessity that the maxim should accord with this law, while the law contains no condition to which it is restricted, there is nothing remaining in it except the universality of law as such to which the maxim of the action should conform; and in effect this conformity alone is represented as necessary by the imperative" (*FM*, pp. 38–39).

Thus Kant arrives at the formula: "Act only according to that maxim which you can at the same time will to become a universal law" (*FM*, p. 38). This is simply a positive version of the statement of the moral law in the First Section.

(ii) Formula of the law of nature.

Kant proceeds immediately to formula #2: "Act as though the maxim of your action were by your will to become a universal law of nature" (*FM*, p. 39). According to formula #1, a maxim must be capable of being willed as a universal law and in this sense be capable of universalization. Formula #2 presents an indirect way of testing this capacity to be universalized, namely, by testing the capacity for an analogous kind of universalization in which the universality is that of natural law. Kant does not indicate here why this indirect way is needed nor what its exact relation is to the basic formula (#1). Such clarification will be given in the *Critique of Practical Reason*.

Kant proceeds in the *Foundations* to discuss four types of duty in terms of formula #2. He shows how certain maxims are not capable of universalization and thus are opposed to duty. Thereby our actual duties in the relevant spheres are illuminated.

The division into four types is based on two distinctions: duty to oneself versus duty to others and perfect versus imperfect duties. Imperfect duties involve a certain latitude that could be decided by inclination. For example, it is my duty to help others, but just *which* others I help can, within certain limits, be decided by inclination. Hence, this is an imperfect duty.

The two distinctions, put together, yield four types:

1. Perfect duty toward oneself.
   Counter-example: suicide.
2. Perfect duty toward others.
   Counter-example: false promise regarding the repayment of a debt.
3. Imperfect duty toward oneself.
   Example: development of one's talents.
4. Imperfect duty toward others.
   Example: helping others.

Kant's discussion of these examples brings out another distinction, one coinciding with that between perfect and imperfect duties. It is the distinction between narrower (imprescribable) duties and broader (meritorious) duties.

1. Narrower duties. A maxim in conflict with such duties will generate a contradiction if universalized. That is, it will prove to be such that it cannot be thought as a universal law of nature without contradiction. That is the case with the first two examples and is clearest in the second: if making false promises to relieve one's difficulties became a universal law of nature, no one would believe such promises, and so the very possibility of relieving difficulties by false promises would be destroyed. At the level of universality, the maxim contradicts itself.

2. Broader duties. Here there is no internal contradiction in the universalized maxim. But it is still impossible to *will* that the maxim be raised to the universality of a law of nature. Such a will would contradict itself. So here the contradiction that decides the issue lies not in the universalized maxim but in the will itself. That is the case with the last two examples. Consider an imperfect duty to oneself. There is no contradiction in the universalized maxim of not developing one's talents. But this cannot be willed, for it would throw the will into contradiction with itself, because, as a rational being, one necessarily wills the development of one's faculties.

(iii) Formula of the end in itself.

Thus far, Kant has dealt with only one aspect of action, namely, the subjective principle or maxim by which the action is accomplished. Now he introduces a second aspect: "Rational nature is distinguished from others in that it proposes an end to itself" (*FM*, p. 56). This says that human action is not mere purposeless activity, but is activity for, activity directed toward, some end. The task is then to formulate a categorical imperative from the perspective of this aspect of action.

What kind of ends could give rise to a categorical imperative? It could not possibly be "subjective ends," by which Kant means specific material ends one poses for oneself on the basis of desire (inclination, incentive). Such ends are relative to a specifically constituted faculty of desire. They have worth only through that relation; they do not possess an absolute worth that would be binding for all rational beings. Such ends can give rise only to hypothetical imperatives, namely, of the form: if you have such-and-such a desire, you should pursue such-and-such an end which is a means to satisfying that desire. There can be no categorical command to pursue such ends.

Kant says there can be a categorical command only in the case of objective ends. These are ends which are not relative to certain desires; they are not merely posited as a means to satisfy certain desires. Accordingly, they must be ends in themselves, not ends which are, in turn, merely the means to something else, the satisfaction of certain desires. Also, these ends cannot be merely relative to our actions, produced by our actions, because any such end would have only relative worth and would not be an end in itself. They must instead be ends existing independently of our actions and desires.

Are there any such ends? Kant answers: "Man and, in general, every rational being exists as an end in himself and not merely as a means to be arbitrarily used by this or that will" (*FM*, p. 46). On this basis, Kant distinguishes between persons and things. All independently existing beings other than rational ones have only relative worth and are called "things," in contrast to rational beings, which are ends in themselves and are designated as "persons." So the formula for the categorical imperative is: "Act so that you treat humanity, whether in your own person or in that of another, always as an end and never as a means only" (*FM*, p. 47).

Such comportment toward persons as persons, as ends in themselves, coincides with letting one's actions be determined by the moral law. Therefore, Kant can extend to our relation with others the term "respect," previously used only with regard to the moral law. Here we see how respect for persons and respect for law are brought together.

(iv) Formula of autonomy.

Kant does not provide a full statement of this formula. But the essential is expressed as follows: "By this principle all maxims are rejected which are not consistent with the universal lawgiving of will" (*FM*, p. 49). The formula could be stated in this way: So act that your will can regard itself at the same time as *making* universal law through its maxim (cf. H. J. Paton, *The Categorical Imperative*, London: Hutchinson, 1947, pp. 129–135).

The relation to formulas #1 and #2 is evident. As in those, this imperative commands that the maxim be capable of universalization, that it have the form of law. The difference is that this formula demands that the universalizable maxim also have the character of being self-given, legislated by the will to itself: "The will is thus not only subject to the law but subject in such a way that it must be regarded also as self-legislative and only for this reason as being subject to the law (of which it can regard itself as the author)" (*FM*, p. 49).

So in this formula we can distinguish two moments: the capacity of the maxim for universalization and the character of the maxim as self-legislative. The first moment corresponds to what was expressed by formulas #1 and #2. Kant relates the second moment to the character of the practical subject as a person or end in himself. In contrast to things, which are merely subject *to* laws, a person is also a subject *of* laws, is self-legislative. So the second moment corresponds to what formula #3 expressed.

These two moments can also be considered in another way, one that indicates more clearly the justification for this formula. They can be considered as corresponding to and specifications of the two general moments we found to belong to the structure of imperatives. The first general moment, the objective principle or law, is expressed in the first moment of the formula of autonomy: what is commanded for the maxim is universality, the form of law. The second general moment, the demand that the will (its maxim) accord with this law or principle, is expressed in the second moment of the formula, namely, the character of the maxim as self-legislated.

Our structural analysis of imperatives showed that in a hypothetical imperative there is always a third moment, a condition, and that only under this condition are the other two moments actually constituted. Specifically, only under the condition does the command become binding, coercive, a demand. Only if I will the end, the condition, is there a demand that I will the means. Or, in the terms Kant now uses, the command is binding only because of some *interest* I have.

The real problem arises when we consider the categorical imperative, where no condition or interest can render the command binding. So how is it possible for a categorical imperative to be an actual imperative, to be binding? Kant argues that as long as we are merely *subject to* laws, there must be some interest that serves as a stimulus to obey these laws; that is, there must be an interest (for example, the reward promised or the punishment threatened) on account of which we submit to the laws. The only case in which one can be bound to law without any interest intervening, hence the only case in which there can be a categorical imperative, is that in which one directly binds oneself, that is, gives oneself the law. So the self-legislative side (the second moment) of this formula expresses the way a categorical imperative can be binding.

(v) Formula of the realm of ends.

This formula may be stated (cf. Paton) as follows: So act as if you were, through your maxims, a member of a realm of ends. This formula follows from the formula of autonomy. The first moment of the formula of autonomy is the capacity of the maxim for universalization, for taking on the form of universal law. Insofar as all rational agents are bound by this formula, all their maxims have this universal form and thus constitute a system, a "systematic union," in contrast to the disunity and conflict among maxims not capable of universalization. So we arrive at the concept of a realm: "By 'realm' I understand the systematic union of different rational beings through common laws" (*FM*, p. 51). This concept is the ideal which, in effect, is posed by the first moment of the formula of autonomy.

The second moment of the formula of autonomy is the character of the maxim as given by the subject to itself. This self-legislative character of the practical subject expresses, as we saw, the character of the subject as a person, as an end in himself. So the realm posed as ideal in this new formula is a realm of ends. Specifically, it is a realm of ends in themselves (rational beings) and of particular ends which these beings posit and which form a systematic union because they are governed by universal law. Kant explains: "Because laws determine ends with regard to their universal validity, if we abstract from personal differences of rational beings and thus from all content of their private ends, we can think of a whole of ends in systematic connection, a whole of rational beings as ends in themselves as well as of the particular ends each may set for himself" (*FM*, p. 51). So the formula poses this realm of ends as ideal: one should act as though he were a member of such a realm.

Kant adds a brief consideration of dignity. He says that everything in the realm of ends has either a price or a dignity. By "dignity" he means absolute worth, in contrast to the merely relative worth of price. What is it that has absolute worth? "Morality and humanity, insofar as humanity is capable of morality, alone have dignity" (*FM*, p. 53). More precisely, what has dignity is that self-legislating explicitly expressed in the formula of autonomy, that giving of the moral law to oneself. It has dignity because it is what determines all other worth. "Autonomy is thus the basis of the dignity of both human nature and of every rational nature" (*FM*, p. 54).

Having dealt with all the formulas, Kant now indicates how they are related. We distinguished five formulas:

Formula of:	(1) universal law	(2) law of nature	(3) end in itself	(4) autonomy	(5) realm of ends
[form] in terms of principle:	universality	universality of nature	--	universality	realm
[matter] in terms of end:	--	--	humanity as end in itself	self-legislation	of ends

Kant regards these as three basically different ways of presenting the principle of morality. Formulas #1 and #2 present the principle in terms of form. "All maxims have a form which consists in universality; and in this respect the formula of the moral imperative requires that the maxims be chosen as though they should hold as universal laws of nature" (*FM*, p. 54). As we noted, the first formulas differ by the fact that #2 specifies the relevant universality to be that of nature. Kant now adds that there is an analogy between these kinds of universality (but this issue actually belongs in the *Critique of Practical Reason*).

Formula #3 presents the principle in terms of matter (content). Kant says that all maxims have "a material, that is, an end; in this respect the formula says that the rational being, as by its nature an end and thus as an end in itself, must serve in every maxim as the condition restricting all merely relative and arbitrary ends" (*FM*, pp. 54–55).

Formulas #4 and #5 present a complete determination, one with respect to both form and content. Kant says that there is "a complete determination of all maxims by the formula that all maxims stemming from autonomous legislation ought to harmonize with a possible realm of ends as with a realm of nature" (*FM*, p. 55). Note the reference to a "realm of nature," which suggests that in formula #5 there is also a specification relating to nature, such as we found in formula #2.

Kant next calls attention to a progression here, with the stages corresponding to the categories of quantity (unity, plurality, totality). "There is a progression here like that through the categories of the unity of the form of the will (its universality), the plurality of material (the objects, the ends), and the all-comprehensiveness or totality of the system of ends" (*FM*, p. 55). But Kant does not indicate what significance this correspondence might have.

Kant concludes the discussion of the formulas by briefly reviewing the entire course of their derivation. Let us note two points regarding this review.

(1) Kant says: "We can now finish where we started, with the concept of an unconditionally good will" (*FM*, p. 55). Kant is referring back to a statement with which the First Section began and which we already cited: "Nothing in the world—indeed nothing even beyond the world—can possibly be conceived which could be called good without qualification except a good will." The entire effort has been to raise this concept to its proper level: first, to raise it out of that common rational knowledge about morals in which it is implicit and then to raise it to a level at which it is freed from all connection with examples and with everything empirical. At the level to which it is now raised, it is thematized as the self-legislative will which in its maxims gives universal law to itself, that is, the autonomous will, a member of a realm of ends.

(2) On the basis of this development, Kant comes finally to define the other basic concepts of morality, including morality itself. "Morality is thus the relation of actions to the autonomy of the will, that is, to possible universal lawgiving by maxims of the will" (*FM*, pp. 57–58). Thus morality consists in the subordination of action to the autonomy of the will. In other words, morality consists in letting action be determined by the self-legislation of the will. Kant adds: "The action

which can be compatible with the autonomy of the will is permitted; that which does not agree with it is prohibited" (*FM*, p. 58).

Lastly, Kant recasts the basic moral concepts in terms of the development now completed; he defines holy will, obligation, and duty: "The will whose maxims necessarily are in harmony with the laws of autonomy is a holy will or an absolutely good will. The dependence of a will not absolutely good on the principle of autonomy (moral constraint) is obligation. Hence obligation cannot be applied to a holy will. The objective necessity of an action from obligation is duty" (*FM*, p. 58).

(d) Autonomy and heteronomy.
Let us consider three issues in this final part of the Second Section.

(1) In the first of the three headings Kant introduces, he repeats and makes more explicit what the transition in the Second Section has established: the autonomy of the will as the supreme principle of morality. He defines this autonomy precisely: "Autonomy of the will is that property of it by which it is a law to itself independently of any property of objects of volition" (*FM*, p. 59). So autonomy means the will gives law directly to itself without the mediation of any objects.

(2) Kant contrasts autonomy with heteronomy. First he defines heteronomy. If the will "goes outside itself and seeks the determining law in the property of any of its objects, heteronomy always results. For then the will does not give itself the law, but the object through its relation to the will gives the law to it" (*FM*, p. 59). So in the case of heteronomy, the will is given its law by something, some object, beyond it.

This contrast is a development of the contrast with which the Second Section began, between the understanding of moral concepts as apriori, that is, as rational, and understanding them as empirical. The understanding of moral concepts as apriori corresponds to the principle of autonomy. Thus the transition has accomplished its goal of raising moral concepts to the level at which they are thematized in their apriori character, their practical-rational character. On the other hand, heteronomy is broader than an empirical understanding of moral concepts, which is only one of two forms of heteronomy. Specifically, the object from which the law is taken may be either empirically presented in feeling or rationally presented in an ideal stemming from thought and so presented in theoretical rather than practical reason. So in his classification of heteronomous principles, Kant deals with four forms, corresponding to two kinds of feeling (physical and moral) and to two types of perfection (the mere rational concept of perfection and the concept of an independent perfection).

The first form of heteronomy (physical feeling) makes happiness its principle. Of the four, it is the most objectionable. The primary reason is that "this principle supports morality with incentives which undermine it and destroy all its sublimity, for such a principle puts the motives to virtue and those to vice in the same class, teaching us only to make a better calculation while obliterating the specific difference between them" (*FM*, pp. 60–61).

The second form (moral feeling) makes feeling its principle. It elevates moral feeling to the level of a principle (Hutcheson). Kant responds: "The appeal to it is superficial, since those who cannot think expect help from feeling, even with regard to that which concerns universal laws" (*FM*, p. 61). Yet Kant places this form above the first one: "Nevertheless, moral feeling is nearer to morality and its dignity, inasmuch as moral feeling pays virtue the honor of ascribing the satisfaction and esteem for her directly to morality and does not, as it were, say to her face that it is not her beauty but only our advantage which attracts us to her" (*FM*, p. 61).

The third form (mere rational concept of perfection) takes as its principle the ontological concept of perfection. But this concept is empty and inadequate. Still, it is better than the fourth form (concept of an independent perfection), which takes as its principle a most perfect divine will. If we suppose that God is good, we do so only on the basis of our knowledge of what moral goodness is. Thus to posit goodness of God as determining moral goodness is to proceed in a vicious circle. On the other hand, if we subtract from the concept of the divine will what we have added to it from our understanding of moral goodness, then "the only remaining concept of the divine will is made up of the attributes of desire for glory and dominion combined with the formidable conceptions of might and vengeance, and any system of ethics based on them would be directly opposed to morality" (*FM*, p. 62).

Of the four forms of heteronomy, clearly the second and third are the least objectionable. And of these, the third (based on the ontological concept of perfection) is less objectionable than the second, "because it preserves the indefinite idea (of a will good in itself) free from corruption until it can be more narrowly defined" (*FM*, p. 60).

(3) Finally, Kant indicates quite precisely what the Second Section has and has not shown. It has shown that the autonomy of the will is the foundation of morality, *if* there is morality. But it has not shown how the moral principle, the categorical imperative, is possible. It has not shown how it is that morality exists. The task of establishing the ground and of grounding morality on it can be taken up only at a still higher level, that of a critique of practical reason.

According to Kant, as we already cited, the *Critique of Practical Reason* presupposes the *Foundations of the Metaphysics of Morals* only insofar as the latter "gives a preliminary acquaintance with the principle of duty and justifies a definite formula of it." We have now satisfied this presupposition by following Kant's derivation of the various formulas for the moral principle. And so we are ready to return to the *Critique*. In fact, the *Foundations* itself returns us to it, for its final section is a transition from the metaphysics of morals to the level of a critique of practical reason.

Within the structure of the *Foundations*, this transition is the last of three fundamental transitions. The *Foundations* began with the concept of an unconditionally good will and proceeded to draw it out of that common rational knowledge about morals in which it is implicit and then to raise it to the level at which it is freed of all connection with examples and everything empirical. Thus the concept was raised to the purely rational level. At that level, the concept was thematized as the self-legislative will, as the will which gives universal law to itself, the autonomous will. Autonomy of will was thus presented as the supreme principle of morality.

(3) Third Section.

(a) The grounding.

A major problem is left unsolved: that of genuinely *grounding* morality. The Third Section is devoted to this problem of grounding. The first four subsections carry through the grounding. The last subsection fixes the limits of that grounding.

The grounding involves five main steps. These steps correspond roughly to Kant's division into subsections, except that the first two steps fall in the first subsection.

First step. Kant traces out certain connections essential to the grounding. He begins with the concept of freedom. Kant first takes freedom simply as detachment, as independence from foreign determining causes. More precisely, freedom is that property of the will "by which the will can be effective independently of foreign causes determining it" (*FM*, p. 64).

Such a concept of freedom is merely negative. Yet a positive concept flows from it. Kant proceeds to trace out the derivation. Will is a kind of causality, one belonging to living beings insofar as they are rational. The concept of causality entails that of law. That is, causality is the lawful coming to be of something through something. And so freedom cannot be lawless but must instead involve its own peculiar lawfulness.

What kind of lawfulness does freedom involve? What kind of causality is freedom? Its lawfulness is one in contrast with that of natural causality. Whereas natural causality is such that every cause is determined to its causality (made to cause some further effect) by something else (something other than itself), freedom is that causality which is *self*-determined. It is "the property of the will to be a law to itself." In other words, the lawfulness of natural causality is heteronomy; that of freedom is autonomy.

So up to this point, Kant has shown that freedom cannot be mere arbitrariness, mere indeterminateness, but rather must be self-determination. A free will must be an autonomous will. Freedom entails autonomy. Kant continues: "The proposition that the will is a law to itself in all its actions, however, only expresses the principle that we should act according to no other maxim than that which can also have itself as a universal law for its object" (*FM*, p. 65). This says that autonomy is merely an expression of the categorical imperative, the moral principle. The same was shown in the Second Section in the establishment of the fourth formula, the one of autonomy.

So Kant has demonstrated that free will must be an autonomous will, which is a will under moral law. That is, from freedom one can derive, by mere analysis of the concepts, autonomy and morality. "Thus if freedom of the will is presupposed, morality with its principle follows from it by the mere analysis of its concept" (*FM*, p. 65). So this is the essential connection: freedom—autonomy—morality. The connection indicates how Kant will approach the problem of grounding morality: if the actuality of freedom could be established, then that of morality would follow.

Second step. Kant now explicitly poses the problem of grounding morality. "But the principle is nevertheless a synthetic proposition: an absolutely good will is one whose maxim can always include itself as a universal law" (*FM*, p. 65). Kant is simply saying what he said earlier with regard to the categorical imperative: it is an apriori synthetic practical proposition and so, in contrast to a hypothetical imperative, is in need of grounding. Thus the problem of grounding morality amounts to establishing this synthetic proposition. What does that require?

Kant continues: "It is synthetic because by analysis of the concept of an absolutely good will that property of the maxim cannot be found" (*FM*, p. 65). So the proposition connects the concept of a good will with that of a maxim capable of universalization, and it is synthetic because the predicate-concept is not contained in the subject-concept. To establish this proposition therefore amounts to exhibiting the ground of the synthesis of the two concepts, that is, exhibiting a third term through which these two are connected. Kant identifies this third term as the positive concept of freedom, that is, freedom expanded into autonomy.

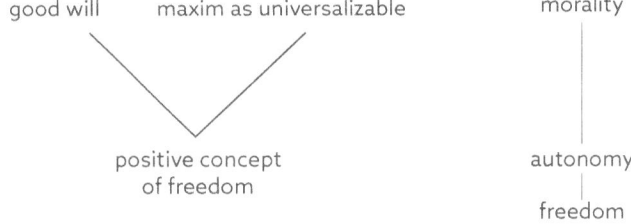

Thus Kant is here posing the same connection as in the first step. But now he does so in explicit reference to the problem of grounding morality. Again, the problem of grounding morality is focused on that of establishing freedom.

Note how Kant's way of posing the problem relates to the preceding sections. The two terms of the synthetic proposition are, in effect, the beginning and end of the First Section. The third term, which Kant poses as the grounding term (positive concept of freedom, autonomy) is the endpoint of the Second Section. So we could say that the First Section supplies the moral principle, the Second supplies the ground, and the Third carries out the grounding.

Third step. It is very brief, comprising only two sentences, and thus is difficult to interpret. Kant begins: "Now I say that every being which cannot act otherwise than under the idea of freedom is thereby really free in a practical respect" (*FM*, p. 66). To be really free in a practical respect (that is, free with respect to praxis, action) means to act freely. But freedom is not mere indetermination; it is a kind of causality involving a peculiar sort of lawfulness. So to act freely is to act on the basis of the laws of freedom. Now, a being which cannot act otherwise than under the idea of freedom is a being which takes the idea of freedom as basic to its action and does act on the basis of (the laws of) freedom. Thus the two (namely, being able to act only under the idea of freedom and being really free in a practical respect) coincide.

Kant continues: "That is to say, all laws which are inseparably bound up with freedom hold for it just as if its will were proved free in itself by theoretical philosophy" (*FM*, p. 66). A being which cannot act otherwise than under the idea of freedom is a being which, in order to be able to act, must postulate its freedom. It is a being which must posit itself as free in order to provide the necessary basis for its acting. Kant's point is that in both cases—whether the subject is really free or only posits itself as free—the laws of freedom provide the basis for action. In other words, the basis of action is the same, regardless of whether that basis actually exists or is merely posited. And so both cases are *practically* the same.

What does all this have to do with grounding? The first two steps showed that the grounding of morality requires a proof of freedom. The third step showed that from a practical point of view, it suffices to prove less, namely, that a rational being cannot act otherwise than under the idea of freedom or, in other words, a rational being must *posit itself* as free.

Fourth step. Why must a rational being posit itself as free? It is on account of the character of reason as one finds it in oneself. Kant explains: "Man does find in himself a faculty by which he distinguishes himself from all other things, even from himself insofar as he is affected by objects. This faculty is reason" (*FM*, p. 70). So we find our reason to be pure spontaneous activity by which we are placed over against all other things, over against everything pertaining to receptivity and sensibility. Kant continues: "On account of this, a rational being must regard itself as intelligence" (*FM*, p. 71). This expresses the issue in terms of the distinction between the phenomenal world (sensible world) and the noumenal world (intelligible world). The point is that we find our reason to be such that we must posit ourselves, qua rational, as belonging to the intelligible realm. But that amounts to positing oneself as free: "As a rational being and thus as belonging to the intelligible world, man cannot think of the causality of his own will except under the idea of freedom, for independence from the determining causes of the world of sense (an independence which reason must always ascribe to itself) is freedom" (*FM*, p. 71).

So by virtue of its character as rational, a rational being posits itself qua reason as free. Reason, in view of its very character qua reason, posits itself as free.

Let me note in passing that this self-positing is related to a basic issue in the *Critique of Pure Reason* which, however, Kant does not bring up in the present context, namely, that self-positing called "transcendental apperception."

Final step. Kant draws the conclusion to which these steps lead. We saw that a rational being posits itself as free (fourth step). Practically regarded, this is equivalent to establishing freedom (third step). But freedom entails autonomy, which in turn entails morality (first step). Therefore, morality is grounded practically.

If we ask in what is morality grounded, we must say: in reason's positing of itself as free. Thereby (that is, because of this self-positing) the categorical imperative is possible and the apriori synthetic practical proposition (as expressed in the second step) is established. "Thus categorical imperatives are possible because the idea of freedom makes me a member of an intelligible world" (*FM*, p. 73).

There is one further refinement. Not only do I posit myself as free but I also intuit myself as sensible, that is, I am given to myself as appearance in inner sense. This duality is required for morality in full, that is, for moral imperatives or commands: "Consequently, if I were a member only of the intelligible word, all my actions would always be in accordance with the autonomy of the will. But since I intuit myself at the same time as a member of the world of sense, my actions *ought* to conform to it, and this categorical 'ought' presents a synthetic apriori proposition" (*FM*, p. 73). Because I belong, in different ways, to both the sensible world and the intelligible world, autonomy is not something to which I conform by necessity but something to which I *ought* to conform.

(b) Limits of the grounding.

The last main subsection ("On the extreme limit of all practical philosophy") is devoted to indicating the limits of the grounding just carried through. These limits are, at the same time, the limits of practical philosophy as such. I will highlight three points.

(i) Kant clarifies the sense in which reason posits itself as intelligible: "When practical reason thinks itself into an intelligible world, it does in no way transcend its limits. It would do so, however, if it tried to intuit or feel itself into it" (*FM*, p. 77). This says that reason merely thinks, posits, itself as belonging to the intelligible; it does not *know* itself as so belonging, nor does it know anything about this world. Such knowledge would require intellectual intuition, which is impossible for a finite subject. The concept of such a world "is therefore only a standpoint which reason sees itself forced to take outside of appearances, in order to think of itself as practical" (*FM*, p. 78).

How does this serve to indicate the limit of the grounding? It makes explicit that morality is not grounded in some intelligible, supersensible content transcending the subject. For example, it is not grounded in pseudo-Platonic ideas or in a divine *logos*. To see in Kant's practical philosophy just a disguised or skeptical Platonism is simply wrong. Furthermore, morality is not grounded in any knowing (intuiting) at all, neither sensible nor intellectual. We could perhaps say it is grounded in a primordial act, in a transcendental praxis, in reason's positing of itself as free.

(ii) Kant indicates another, related limit: "But reason would overstep all its limits if it undertook to explain how pure reason can be practical, which is the same problem as explaining how freedom is possible" (*FM*, p. 78). The limit is that freedom remains an idea whose actuality in itself is doubtful. We cannot prove freedom or explain it in a theoretical sense.

Kant elaborates by saying that we can prove only what falls under natural laws in the broadest sense, including both empirical and apriori laws: "But where determination according to natural laws comes to an end, there too all explanation ceases and nothing remains but defense, that is, refutation of the objections of those who pretend to have seen more deeply into the essence of things and therefore boldly declare freedom to be impossible" (*FM*, p. 79).

So *the* issue of practical philosophy, namely, freedom, falls outside the sphere of nature, to which the *Critique of Pure Reason* has limited positive theoretical knowledge. Freedom is not something to be explained or known in a theoretical sense. The role of theoretical reason with respect to practical philosophy is limited to refuting theoretical claims that would undermine morality. A paradigm case of such practically relevant use of theoretical reason occurs in the critical resolution of the third antinomy in the *Critique of Pure Reason*.

(iii) Finally, Kant states the outcome of the grounding together with the limit of the grounding: "Thus the question of how a categorical imperative is possible can be answered to this extent: we can cite the only presupposition under which it is alone possible. This is the idea of freedom, and we can discern the necessity of this presupposition which is sufficient to the practical use of reason, that is, to the conviction of the validity of this imperative and hence also of the moral law. But how this presupposition itself is possible can never be discerned by any human reason" (*FM*, p. 80).

* * *

At this point, let us return briefly to the directive questions we posed at the outset. To what extent have they been answered by the *Foundations of the Metaphysics of Morals*? Our questions were formulated in terms of the two characters of practical reason on which we focused at the beginning: the character as positing and the character as detaching the subject from immediate sensible determination.

What specific form does the positing take? What does practical reason posit? The answer is that reason posits *itself as free, as intelligible*. Thus the fundamental positing is a self-positing, and that is what grounds morality.

What specific form does the detaching of the subject take? We already noted that the subject, as detached, is just reason itself, and so it is a matter of self-detachment, reason detaching itself. The *Foundations* shows that this self-detachment coincides with the fundamental self-positing, since the latter is precisely a positing of the self as free in the negative sense, which means: as detached.

Thus our third question is answered: we see how the two characters of reason belong together, how they form a unity, coincide.

Finally, we asked: how does practical reason belong together with theoretical reason? How is their unity to be understood? The *Foundations* has provided only some preliminary indications. The book has brought out the role of theoretical reason with respect to practical reason, namely, the protection of practical reason from theoretical undermining, from claims to knowledge which would destroy the foundations of morality.

Kant has noted that in both its theoretical and practical employment, reason has a distinctive independence and distance from sensibility. What reason posits—either transcendental ideas or itself as intelligence—is posited as beyond sensibility, beyond the world of phenomena, beyond nature. We could then say that reason's positing is meta-physical.

Clearly, a more adequate answer to the fourth question is needed. But the same may be said of that question into which the first three have now contracted: what is the character of reason's self-positing as free, as detached? Kant's presentation here remains tied to the context of the *Foundations* and does not fully attain the critical level. He presents the matter as though reason somehow came across itself as having a certain character, namely, spontaneity, and as a result then posits itself as free. It is as though reason first *intuits* itself and then posits itself. But there can be no such intuition, for it would be an intellectual intuition, and I can intuit myself only as appearance. So the question remains: just what is the character of that self-positing which is the ground of morality?

IV. *Critique of Practical Reason*

How in general does the *Critique of Practical Reason* differ from the *Foundations of the Metaphysics of Morals*? In both, the overall project is the same: to work out the foundations of an ethics, that is, to work out a metaphysics of morals. In the *Critique*, this project is posed at a level which the *Foundations* attains only in the Third Section. In the *Critique*, Kant does not raise the moral law out of common moral knowledge, nor does he work out the various formulations of the moral law. Rather, from the outset, the issues are taken up at the level of an analysis of reason, at the purely rational level if not yet at the level of the grounding which Kant attained only in the course of the Third Section of the *Foundations*.

A. The Introduction of the *Critique of Practical Reason*

The Introduction lays out the general character of the project. I will highlight four points.

(1) Kant draws a contrast between the theoretical use of reason and the practical use. In the former, reason passes beyond itself to objects, is directed toward the determination of objects. From the *Critique of Pure Reason*, we know that this determination may take two forms. It may be a determination of the objects of experience, in which case reason is called "understanding." Or it may be an attempt at a determination of objects (soul, world, God) that transcend experience, in which case it is called "dialectical reason."

In its practical use, "reason deals with the grounds of determining the will," that is, reason is directed toward determining the will. But we have seen already that practical reason and will are the same, and so the issue in the practical use of reason is *self*-determination. The contrast can therefore be stated as follows: in theoretical reason, the subject determines the object; in practical reason, the subject determines itself. The contrast could also be drawn by saying that in theoretical reason, the object determines the subject (in sense experience) and in practical reason, the subject determines the object (in action).

(2) Kant poses "the first question: is pure reason sufficient of itself to determine the will, or is it only as empirically conditioned that it can do so?" (*CPr*, p. 15). This amounts to asking: can pure reason be practical? The first chapter of the *Critique of Practical Reason* will be devoted to this question. Kant will attempt to show *how* pure reason can determine the will.

(3) Negatively expressed, this amounts to refuting the claim that only empirically conditioned reason can determine the will. And so the *Critique of Practical*

Reason must "prevent the empirically conditioned reason from presuming to be the only ground of determination of the will" (*CPr*, p. 16). Kant notes that the situation is precisely the opposite of that in the first *Critique*, which showed that theoretical reason (aimed at knowledge of objects) must be empirically conditioned (linked to experience) and that otherwise, as *pure* reason, it leads to illusion. So the *Critique of Pure Reason* insists on the empirical conditioning of reason. Only empirically conditioned reason is theoretically legitimate. The *Critique of Practical Reason* shows that practical reason, aimed at determining the will, must *not* be empirically conditioned. So the second *Critique* insists on the purity of reason and separates reason from empirical conditioning. Only *pure* reason is practically legitimate.

(4) Kant indicates the structure of the *Critique of Practical Reason*. Since here, as in the first *Critique*, pure reason is what is being investigated, the general structure must be the same in the two books. Thus there is a division into a Doctrine of Elements and a Methodology. And the former is divided into an Analytic (which exhibits truth) and a Dialectic (which exhibits and resolves the relevant illusion). But in the second *Critique*, the order of the Analytic is reversed. It proceeds from principles to concepts to senses. This difference is based on the fundamental difference between the two *Critiques*: the *Critique of Practical Reason* has as its central task to establish the empirically unconditioned employment of reason, that is, to establish the non-empirical *principle* in which this employment is expressed. Only then can Kant take up the application of the relevant concepts to objects and the relation of these principles and concepts to the sensuous faculty of the subject. That is to say, Kant must establish the *purity* of practical reason and only then relate it to objects and the senses. In contrast, the *Critique of Pure Reason* begins with sense and with concepts of objects in order to carry these over into principles of theoretical reason.

This same basic difference is also reflected in another structural dissimilarity, which Kant does not mention. In the first *Critique*, the treatment of the empirical, sensible element (Aesthetic) is so important that it is a distinct division. The basic division of the Doctrine of Elements is Aesthetic versus Logic (sensibility versus rationality). The positive part of the Logic is the Analytic, which falls outside the Aesthetic. In the second *Critique*, there is no separate Aesthetic; the treatment of sensibility falls *within* the Analytic. And, appropriately, what is primarily treated there is a form of sensibility or feeling which is rational rather than empirical, namely, respect.

B. Chapter I of the Analytic of the *Critique of Practical Reason*:
Principles of Pure Practical Reason

The task here is to show that and how pure reason can determine the will, that is, to indicate the character of the determining. This task amounts to discovering and formulating the principle by which that determination is expressed. So this first chapter is entitled "Principles of Pure Practical Reason." It corresponds to what Kant undertook in the First and Second Sections of the *Foundations*. In the *Critique*, he is covering much of the same ground, but in a different way. It is worked out more formally and in terms of concepts of reason and freedom, rather than being raised out of common moral knowledge.

I will move quickly through the main steps, omitting those details already developed in the *Foundations*. Kant divides Chapter I into eight numbered sections, followed by two lengthy supplementary discussions.

§1. Definition.

What Kant defines here is what is named in the title of the chapter: practical principles. As principles, they are propositions expressing something general under which several particulars fall. As practical, they pertain to the determination of the will. So: "Practical principles are propositions containing a general determination of the will, having under it several practical rules" (*CPr*, p. 17).

Here we should bear in mind the implied contrast with theoretical principles. The latter are propositions containing a general determination of objects, for example, the principle of cause and effect. By contrast, practical propositions pertain to the determination of the subject (the will) rather than objects. This directedness of practical principles away from objects and toward the subject is strengthened by Kant's insistence that the determination of the will is to be regarded in complete independence of what the will actually can or does accomplish.

Kant proceeds to distinguish between two kinds of practical principles: subjective principles or maxims (pertaining to an individual will) versus objective principles or practical laws (valid for the will of every rational being). We have already seen this distinction.

The long subsequent "Remark" begins: "Assuming that pure reason can contain a practical ground sufficient to determine the will, then there are practical laws. Otherwise, all practical principles are mere maxims" (*CPr*, p. 17). This says that there can be practical laws and not merely maxims only if pure reason can determine the will. The point is that such a law must by definition be valid for all rational beings, independently of their particular sensuous and pathological makeup, and so could be given only by reason. Therefore, Kant's task of showing how reason can determine the will amounts to showing how there can be practical laws; that is, it amounts to discovering the fundamental practical law (cf. §7).

The remainder of the "Remark" develops concepts already familiar: the possibility of a conflict between maxim and law, and hence the character of law as an imperative, specifically as a categorical imperative.

§2. Theorem I: "All practical principles which presuppose an object (material) of the faculty of desire as the determining ground of the will are without exception empirical and can furnish no practical law" (*CPr*, p. 19). The question behind this "theorem" is: what kind of principle can be a practical law? In other words, what must be the character of a practical law? In the *Foundations*, this question was first treated in relation to the concept of a good will: a good will is good in itself, not merely as a means. And so the rational law determining this will must not involve any reference to an end beyond the will, any material or object to which the will would be a means. That is to say, the law must not be a hypothetical imperative in which the will is merely determined to actualize some desired end or object.

Here in the *Critique*, Kant's approach is similar but is adapted to the context. Already he had indicated that a practical law must be given by reason; it must be a law through which pure reason determines the will. So Kant takes up the question of the character of practical laws by asking: what kind of principle would express a determining of the will solely through pure reason? He answers: it would need to be a principle involving no empirical elements but only rational, apriori ones. Now, the kind of proposition described in Theorem I does *not* meet this requirement.

Consider the principle: "Be thrifty." This is a principle which "presupposes an object of the faculty of desire as the determining ground of the will" (*CPr*, p. 19). Specifically, it presupposes that financial security is the object of one's desire. This desire is the condition, and what the principle commands is merely the means of satisfying the desire. In other words, this principle presupposes a certain empirical condition, the presence of the desire. Thus it is not a purely rational principle. We could perhaps go even further: in such a case, what really determines the will is the desire rather than reason. Reason enters in and prescribes a principle only as empirically conditioned and in service to the desire.

§3. Theorem II: "All material practical principles are, as such, of one and the same kind and belong under the general principle of self-love or one's own happiness" (*CPr*, p. 20). By "material practical principles," Kant means those sorts of principles described in Theorem I, those presupposing an object of the faculty of desire. The point is that all such principles are directed toward bringing about satisfaction of the presupposed desire, toward providing that agreeableness or pleasure which is expected from the object and which makes us desire it. Kant concludes: "A rational being's consciousness of the agreeableness of a life which without interruption accompanies that being's whole existence is happiness, and to make this the supreme ground for the determination of choice constitutes the principle of self-love" (*CPr*, p. 20). So all material principles are in service to happiness or self-love.

Kant expresses a corollary: "All material practical rules place the ground of the determination of the will in the lower faculty of desire, and if there were no purely formal laws of the will adequate to determine it, we could not admit the existence of any higher faculty of desire" (*CPr*, p. 21). "Remark I" explains this corollary. Already we have seen that material principles are such that what determines the will is desire for an object. More precisely, it is an *affective* desire, a desire correlative to an expected feeling of pleasure to be obtained through actualizing the object. Kant's point now is that regardless of whether the object of desire is one that is represented in the senses or in the understanding, the expected feeling of pleasure, by virtue of which the object is desired and the will thus determined to actualize it, is always the same.

In other words, one affective desire can differ from another only in degree, even when the object of one desire is sensible and that of the other intellectual: "If the determination of the will rests on the feelings of agreeableness or disagreeableness which a person expects from any cause, it is all the same to him through what kind of notion he is affected. All he considers in making a choice is how great, how long-lasting, how easily obtained, and how often repeated this agreeableness is" (*CPr*, p. 22).

Thus we cannot maintain a distinction between lower and higher faculties of desire on the basis of a distinction between sense and understanding. In both cases, it is just a matter of pleasure. Of course, we may say that intellectual pleasures are more refined, compared to those of sense. But that is "because they are more in our power than others and do not wear out but instead increase our capacity for even more of this kind of enjoyment; they delight and at the same time cultivate" (*CPr*, p. 22). Yet the way of determining the will remains the same: it is still determined by affective desires, correlative to an expected feeling of pleasure.

So there is only the lower faculty of desire, and all material practical principles make this the ground of the determination of the will. More precisely, all *affective* desire is a matter of the lower faculty of desire. If there is a higher faculty of desire, it must be a matter of rationally determined, non-affective desire: "Either no higher faculty of desire exists, or else pure reason alone must of itself be practical, that is, must be able to determine the will by the mere form of the practical rule without presupposing any feeling or consequently any idea of the pleasant or the unpleasant as the matter of the faculty of desire and as the empirical condition of its principles" (*CPr*, p. 23). This higher faculty of desire = pure reason = self-determining will.

§4. Theorem III: "If a rational being can think of its maxims as practical universal laws, such a being can do so only by considering them as principles which contain the determining grounds of the will on account of their form and not their matter" (*CPr*, p. 26). This merely draws the conclusion which follows from

Theorem I: material practical principles cannot be laws. That is, maxims cannot be practical laws by virtue of their matter; they can be laws only by virtue of their form, namely, the form of universal law.

§5. Problem I: "Granted that the mere legislative form of maxims is the sole sufficient determining ground of a will, find the character of will which is determinable by it alone" (*CPr*, p. 28). That is, what must be the character of the will in order for it to be determined by the form of the maxim?

Kant's solution is that the form of a law is an object of reason, not an object of the senses, not an appearance. Thus the determining relation between form and will must be entirely different from that which holds among appearances, namely, natural causality. Thus the will, as determinable by form, must be independent of natural causality. It must be a free will. Therefore, practical law implies freedom.

§6. Problem II: "Granted a free will, find the law which alone is competent to determine it necessarily" (*CPr*, p. 28). Kant's solution is that since a free will is independent of empirical conditions, it must not be determined by the material of the maxim, that is, by affective desire and its object. But then there is nothing else to determine it but the form.

The subsequent "Remark" brings together the solution of the two "problems": freedom and practical law reciprocally imply each other. Then Kant asks: which of these is prior in our knowledge? It cannot be freedom, for we have no immediate knowledge of freedom, nor can we infer it from experience. We have no direct knowledge of freedom. But we do have direct knowledge of the moral law, and it is only from it that we "infer" freedom. "It is therefore the moral law, of which we become immediately conscious as soon as we construct maxims for the will, that first presents itself to us" (*CPr*, p. 29).

§7. Fundamental Law of Pure Practical Reason: "So act that the maxim of your will could always hold at the same time as a principle establishing universal law" (*CPr*, p. 30). This follows from Theorem III.

What is most important is contained in the subsequent "Remark." Kant says consciousness of this fundamental law may be called "a fact of reason" (*CPr*, p. 31). It is a fact because it cannot be derived from any antecedent data of reason, for example from a consciousness of freedom, since such consciousness is not given. And yet it forces itself on us—as mankind's common moral understanding testifies (cf. the *Foundations*). Kant notes that this law would follow analytically if freedom were presupposed. But that presupposition could be established (freedom could be ascertained) only by an intellectual intuition. So the fundamental practical law forces itself on us as a synthetic apriori proposition—based on *no* intuition, pure or empirical.

Kant stresses that calling this consciousness of law a "fact" does not mean it is an *empirical* fact. Instead, it is a fact, the sole fact, *of pure reason*; it is something "given" with reason itself. Here Kant arrives again at that dimension of grounding problems which was attained in the Third Section of the *Foundations*. How is this fact, consciousness of the moral law, related to that fundamental act explicated in the *Foundations*, the act in which reason posits itself as free, intelligible?

The "Corollary" merely draws out the consequences: "Pure reason is practical of itself alone, and it gives (to man) a universal law, which we call the moral law" (*CPr*, p. 32). So it has been shown how pure reason is practical.

The "Remark" incorporates several familiar concepts. Note especially how Kant introduces the concept of a holy will, a will incapable of any maxims in conflict with the moral law. He presents this as a practical ideal toward which finite rational beings must *strive* even though they cannot reach it. Then he defines virtue as continuous progress toward this model.

§8. Theorem IV. It incorporates the other basic concept from the Third Section of the *Foundations*, autonomy in contrast to heteronomy: "The autonomy of the will is the sole principle of all moral laws and of the duties conforming to them" (*CPr*, p. 33). Kant establishes connections (already worked out in the *Foundations*) among autonomy, freedom, and moral law. Autonomy is the positive concept of freedom. Moral law is the expression of autonomy.

The subsequent "Remarks" cover familiar ground and culminate in a classification of material principles of morality, corresponding to the treatment of heteronomy at the end of the Second Section of the *Foundations*.

* * *

The main part of Chapter I is followed by two supplementary discussions. The first is entitled "On the Deduction of the Principles of Pure Practical Reason." The title simply expresses what the main part of the chapter has accomplished, and so this supplement is a *reflection* on that and draws out some further consequences.

At the same time, it is Kant's elaborated answer to a criticism made against the *Foundations* by J. F. Flatt. Kant refers to it in the Preface of the *Critique*. As we already noted, Flatt charged that Kant's argument is circular, using the moral law as a basis for proving freedom and then using freedom to prove the moral law. Kant's general answer was already clear in the Preface: freedom is the *ratio essendi* of the moral law, whereas this law is the *ratio cognoscendi* of freedom. This says exactly the same thing Kant has shown in the main part of Chapter I: we have direct consciousness of the moral law but not of freedom, whereas beings subject to the moral law must be free.

Kant begins this first supplementary discussion by restating certain results. Consciousness of the moral law has been exhibited as a fact of reason. Once this consciousness is granted, freedom may be "inferred," since the moral law and freedom are mutually implicative. So consciousness of the moral law (fact of reason) is "inextricably bound up with the consciousness of the freedom of the will" (*CPr*, p. 43).

Next, Kant appeals to a decisive result of the *Critique of Pure Reason*: "It has been sufficiently proved in another place that if freedom is attributed to us, it transfers us into an intelligible order of things" (*CPr*, p. 43). This expresses the resolution of the third antinomy: freedom can belong to an agent only if that agent belongs to an intelligible (noumenal) order distinct from the domain of appearances (phenomena). Therefore:

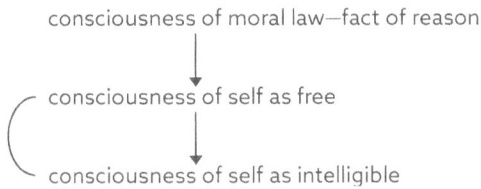

But we can have no intuition of the intelligible. We can only *think* (posit) ourselves as free, intelligible. This marks a significant development. Kant is connecting two basic issues: the fundamental act in which reason posits itself as free and the fact of reason (consciousness of the moral law). Previously, it seemed that this act involved two moments: a self-intuition and then a positing of oneself in the way prescribed by that intuition. The problem was that no such intuition is possible, since it would have to be intellectual. Now we see that the first moment is *not* a self-intuition but rather is the fact of reason, the consciousness of the moral law. In other words, the fundamental act (transcendental praxis) involves as moments: the fact of reason (consciousness of the moral law given with reason itself) and reason's positing of itself as free.

The second supplementary discussion bears the title "On the right of pure reason to an extension in its practical use which is not possible to it in its speculative use." This issue was raised, as a criticism, by H. A. Pistoris in his review of the *Foundations*. As we saw, Pistoris charged that Kant was inconsistent by denying an extension of the categories to the supersensible in the field of speculative reason while affirming such extension for practical reason. The specific issue is: how can the concept of causality be applied to pure reason? How can there be a concept of noumenal causality? It is a problem because the *Critique of Pure Reason* showed that concepts such as causality have objective validity only within the phenomenal domain of experience and do not extend to noumena.

Kant's answer involves two steps. First, he maintains that the category functions here as a pure rather than a schematized concept. It is a pure concept of an object in general, without that link to pure intuition by which it would be referred to objects of experience so as to yield knowledge of them. Here reason (will) is merely *thought* as noumenal cause, merely posited as noumenal cause. More precisely, reason *posits* itself as free and intelligible. But it does not *know* itself as a noumenal cause, for there is no underlying intuition (neither intellectual and pure nor empirical), and intuition is always required for knowledge.

Second, there is nevertheless an actual basis for this use of the category, and so the practical extension is not merely a matter of pure thought, mere positing, sheer logical possibility. The basis is the fact of reason. Specifically, in the consciousness of the moral law, the objective reality of pure will (pure practical reason) is given. And, in turn, the concept of pure will contains that of freedom and so of noumenal causality. Thus the fact of reason testifies to the actuality of a noumenal causality. Therefore, noumenal causality can be affirmed, but only granted the fact of reason, not on the basis of any intuition. In other words, it can be affirmed only practically, not theoretically: "Even though I have no intuition which would determine the objective theoretical reality of a noumenal causality, such causality nevertheless has a real application exhibited *in concreto* in intentions or maxims; that is, its practical reality can be pointed out. All this is sufficient to justify the concept of causality even with reference to noumena" (*CPr*, p. 58).

C. Chapter II of the Analytic of the *Critique of Practical Reason*: The Concept of an Object of Pure Practical Reason

Having dealt with principles in Chapter I, Kant proceeds to deal with concepts of objects, moving, as we noted, in an order opposite to that of the *Critique of Pure Reason*. Chapter II corresponds roughly to the metaphysical and transcendental deductions of the first *Critique*. The main part of this chapter deals with three issues:

(1) the general concept of an object of practical reason
(2) the concept of the good
(3) practical categories.

(1) What is the concept of an object of practical reason? That is to say, what does it mean to call something an object of practical reason? Kant explains: "To decide whether or not something is an object of pure practical reason is only to discern the possibility or impossibility of willing the action by which a certain object would be made actual, provided we had the ability to bring it about (the latter being a matter which experience must decide)" (*CPr*, p. 59). This says that

for something to be an object of practical reason, the action by which it would be produced can be willed; the determination of the will to such action would be in accord with the moral law.

Note how this concept of "practical objectivity" differs from "theoretical objectivity." Whether something is an object of theoretical reason, that is, an object of knowledge, depends on whether it is intuitively given and then determined (formed) by thought. But whether something is an object of practical reason has nothing to do with whether the object is given. Instead, this practical objectivity is determined solely on the side of the subject, determined by whether or not the subject could, in accord with the moral law, determine itself to the action by which the object would be produced.

Here we see again the basic contrast between theoretical and practical reason. In the former, the subject determines the intuitively pre-given object; in the latter, the subject determines itself. We could say that the determination by which objectivity is constituted differs fundamentally in the two cases. In theoretical reason, objectivity is constituted by the subject's determination of the object, that is, by an application of categories to the intuitive manifold. In practical reason, objectivity is constituted by the subject's determination of itself, that is, by an application of categories to itself.

(2) The concept of the good.

Kant defines "the good" as "a necessary object of the faculty of desire" (*CPr*, p. 58). Then he proceeds to contrast the two possible ways of developing the concept of the good. These correspond to the two possible ways the faculty of desire can be determined to desire a particular object: by reason or by feeling.

One way of developing the concept of the good was already sketched in the discussion of objectivity. Whatever is an *object* of practical reason is good. We have seen that such objectivity is determined by whether the subject could, in accord with the moral law, determine itself to the action capable of producing that object. But self-determination in accordance with the moral law amounts to determination by pure practical reason. So in this case what determines the faculty of desire (will) is practical reason. Clearly, this is the way of developing the concept of the good required by what Kant has established in Chapter I.

Note especially that in this case the concept of the good would be based on the moral law, rather than conversely. Kant refers to this as a paradox. It is *para-doxa*, contrary to the usual opinion: "The paradox is that the concept of good and evil is not defined prior to the moral law, to which, it would seem, the former would have to serve as foundation; rather, the concepts of good and evil must be defined after and by means of the law" (*CPr*, p. 65).

Kant says that both the ancients and the moderns made the mistake of beginning with the concept of the good and trying to base the moral the law on it. Also, one of the criticisms by Pistoris, which Kant referred to in the Preface, was that "the concept of the good was not established before the moral principle."

This development can be taken one step further. What is good in the fundamental sense is not the object, but instead is the action and the willing, since the goodness of the object derives entirely from its relation to the action and willing that are in accord with the moral law. "If something is to be, or is held to be, absolutely good or evil in all respects and without qualification, it could not be a thing but only the manner of acting. That is, it could only be the maxim of the will and consequently the acting person himself as a good or evil human being" (*CPr*, p. 62).

Here, at the critical level, Kant has come back to the starting point of the *Foundations*: all that is absolutely good is a good will. Kant says now that the only other alternative for developing the concept of the good is to equate the good with whatever object promises pleasure. In that case, the faculty of desire would be determined by the pleasure expected from the object. The good would become a matter of experience, since we cannot know apriori which objects give pleasure. And the decisive element would be not reason, but "the feeling of pleasure or displeasure as a receptivity belonging to inner sense" (*CPr*, p. 60). In other words, it would be that which is most remote from reason. Kant insists again: such a position leads inevitably to heteronomy and moral empiricism.

(3) Practical categories.

We need to see exactly what the problem is here. In its positive theoretical employment, reason takes the form of understanding. As understanding, it determines (forms) the manifold given in intuition and does so at an apriori level. The apriori determinations applied by the understanding to the intuitive manifold are called "pure concepts of the understanding," "categories." Kant's problem now is this: what are the categories of *practical* reason? That is, what are the apriori concepts by which practical reason determines its object?

A general answer is readily available. Practical reason determines the will. *As what* does it do so, by what concept? It determines it as a good will. In other words, the concept of the good is the category of practical reason, and when Kant goes on to discuss various practical categories (listed on pp. 68–69), they are articulations of this general category. But the actual character of the practical categories has to be worked out in terms of that specific determining to which they pertain. It is a determining of the will, a determining of the subject to action. On the one hand, this action belongs to the conduct of an intelligible being, and the determining of the subject to such action is a matter of freedom, that is, noumenal causality. Therefore, Kant says that these categories "are without exception modes of a single category, that of causality" (*CPr*, p. 67). On the other hand, such action belongs to the domain of appearances, and so the rules of practical reason, practical categories, "are possible only with respect to appearances and consequently in accordance with the categories of the understanding" (*CPr*, p. 67).

Therefore, practical categories are categories of freedom (since the determining they express is *free* causality) and are also in accord with the categories of the understanding (since the action determined belongs to appearances). We might say that practical categories arise by articulation of the concept of *free* causality in accordance with *theoretical* categories.

Kant contrasts theoretical and practical categories. As categories, they are all rules for bringing a many under a one, thus they are rules for a gathering. What are the relevant one and many in each case? With theoretical reason (understanding), the one is the unity of consciousness, that is, transcendental apperception, and the many is the manifold of sensuous intuitions. In the case of practical reason, it is a matter of "the apriori subjection of the manifold of desires to the unity of consciousness of a practical reason commanding in the moral law, that is, of a pure will" (*CPr*, p. 67). So here the one is the practical unity of consciousness (unity of pure will) and the many is the manifold of desires. The questions provoked are: what exactly is this *practical* unity of consciousness? And how is it related to transcendental apperception?

Kant contrasts the two kinds of categories also from another perspective. He appeals to another result from the *Critique of Pure Reason*: theoretical reason determines the intuitive manifold, and such determining is possible only because understanding determines pure intuition (its forms, space and time) in which the intuitive manifold must be given.

$$\text{category} \longrightarrow \text{pure intuition} \longrightarrow \text{sensible intuition}$$
$$\text{(space and time)}$$

So the determining of objects by theoretical reason is mediated by something residing not in reason but rather in receptivity, in pure intuition. By contrast, practical reason's determining of itself as will remains entirely within the compass of reason; no external mediation is required. In other words, it is a *pure* determining, neither conditioned empirically nor in any other way by receptivity.

Kant therefore says that these practical categories "themselves produce the actuality of that to which they refer (the intention of the will)—an achievement which is in no way the business of theoretical concepts" (*CPr*, p. 68). This says that practical categories (or, more precisely, the determining they express) bring forth, create, their object rather than apply determinations to a previously intuited object. (Independent of—and in a sense contrary to—Kant's position, this description can be regarded also as applying to certain forms of imagination. In the mode of phantasy, for instance, imagination brings forth its object.)

In practical determining, reason accomplishes what in the theoretical sphere could be accomplished only by the divine (infinite) subject: instead of needing to receive its object through intuition, it brings it forth. Yet the object practical reason brings forth is just a modality of itself. Here we have a first indication of the character of the *practical* unity of consciousness: it is a bringing oneself forth—a ποίησις of self.

* * *

Following the main part of Chapter II, there is a supplementary discussion entitled "On the Typic of Pure Practical Judgment." The main issue is Kant's justification of the second of the five formulas for the moral law given in the *Foundations*, the "formula of the law of nature," which specified the universality as that of a law of nature: "Act as though the maxim of your action were by your will to become a universal law of nature."

Kant justifies this formula by drawing a parallel, on the side of practical reason, to the problem of the schematism in theoretical reason. The problem of the schematism concerns how the rational (the intellectual, the category) is connected to the sensible (intuition). In the *Critique of Pure Reason*, the problem is solved by the theory of transcendental imagination; categories and intuitions are connected by transcendental schemata provided by the imagination. An analogous problem can be posed for practical reason: how can the moral law, as law of freedom, be applied to events in the sensible world so as to decide whether some action in the sensible world is morally justified? According to Kant, in the case of practical reason, it is understanding rather than imagination that provides the connection, and what it provides is not a schema but a formal natural law or, more precisely, the "type of the moral law." This "type," as distinguished from moral law itself, is what formula #2 in the *Foundations* expresses, the formula referring explicitly to the connection between the maxim of action and sensible nature.

What about imagination here? John Silber suggests that the typic is "a thought experiment for the moral agent." In other words, it is an experiment in which we undertake "to determine the willed consequences of our action . . . by projecting in imagination the sort of world that would come into existence were the maxim of our act to become a universal law of nature" (John R. Silber, "Procedural formalism in Kant's ethics," *Review of Metaphysics*, xxviii, 1974). Indeed, in connection with the account of the typic, Kant writes: "The rule of judgment under laws of pure practical reason is: ask yourself whether, if the action you propose should take place by a law of nature of which you yourself were a part, you could regard it as possible through your will" (*CPr*, p. 72). The question to which Silber, in contrast to Kant, gives an affirmative answer is: Does this "asking yourself," the looking ahead that this "asking" would necessarily prompt, require the power of imagination?

D. Chapter III of the Analytic of the *Critique of Pure Reason*:
The Incentives of Pure Practical Reason

The main content of this chapter lies in the analysis of respect. We need to begin by sketching the context, first in terms of the structure of the Analytic of the second *Critique* in relation to the *Critique of Pure Reason* and then in terms of Kant's concept of incentive, with which he introduces the analysis of respect. Then we will work through the analysis itself and finally consider the significance of respect for the fundamental issues of practical reason. So, we will take up four topics:

(1) the problem of practical sensibility
(2) the problem of incentive
(3) the analysis of respect
(4) the significance of respect.

(1) The problem of practical sensibility.
In Chapters I-II, Kant has dealt first with principles and second with concepts of objects, following an order opposite to that of the *Critique of Pure Reason*. Accordingly, Chapter III, inasmuch as it corresponds structurally to the Transcendental Aesthetic of the first *Critique*, will deal with sensibility. It will analyze *practical* sensibility. That means it will deal with a different element in sensibility, different from the one taken up by the first *Critique*.

What kinds of elements are there in sensibility? According to the *Metaphysics of Morals*, sensibility involves two different kinds of elements: those which can be referred to an object as a means for knowing it (sensations) and those which relate only to the subject and cannot become factors in the knowledge of objects (feelings). Let me again mention in passing that this same distinction occurs in the *Critique of Judgment* as prescribing moments in the structure of judgments of taste.

Sensation, since it pertains to knowledge, falls on the side of theoretical sensibility, whereas feeling is what makes up practical sensibility. Accordingly, Chapter III will analyze feeling. Yet the analysis will treat not feeling as such, not all feeling, but a unique, moral feeling, namely, respect. Just as the Transcendental Aesthetic did not actually deal with all intuition, but only with pure intuition, so likewise the analysis of practical sensibility will deal only with respect, considered as a *pure* feeling.

(2) The problem of incentive.
Kant introduces the analysis of respect in terms of the concept of incentive, hence the title of the chapter. Kant begins with a contrast familiar from the

Foundations, the distinction between action *from* duty and action *according to* duty. He also expresses this distinction as that between morality and legality, between the spirit of the law and the letter of the law. As the *Foundations* stressed, only action *from* duty has moral worth.

The distinction can also be formulated in terms of a second distinction, between two senses in which the moral law may be said to determine the will. It may do so objectively, which means the maxim of the willing is in accord with the law. And it may determine the will subjectively, which means the will is brought into this accord with the moral law *because of* or *by* the moral law. In other words, moral law itself, rather than some feeling, may impel us to act in a certain way. In action merely according to duty, the moral law is only an objective determining ground of the will. In action *from* duty, the moral law is both an objective and subjective determining ground.

Kant defines "incentive" as a subjective determining ground of a finite will (*CPr*, p. 74). So the contrast between action according to duty and action from duty may also be expressed as a contrast between two different kinds of incentives. In action from duty, the moral law is the incentive; in action merely according to duty, feeling functions as the incentive.

The problem is then "to determine carefully in what way the moral law becomes an incentive" (*CPr*, p. 75), to exhibit its character and effect as an incentive. Yet an important qualification must be made here. Kant is not proposing to show how the moral law and hence reason can determine the will. He notes that that would amount to showing how morality and free will are possible, which cannot be shown and is "an insoluble problem for human reason." According to Kant: "Therefore, we shall not have to show apriori why the moral law supplies an incentive but rather what it effects (or better, must effect) in the mind, insofar as this law is an incentive" (*CPr*, p. 75).

In different terms, Kant will exhibit the way we can be bound to the moral law, impelled to act in accord with it, *by* the moral law itself. He will exhibit the way our bond to the moral law can, in the case of genuine morality, proceed from the moral law itself, that is, how we can be drawn by the moral law itself and not merely be impelled to it by some inclination or feeling. He will exhibit the concrete form this drawing or binding takes. More specifically, he will show that it takes the form of an engendering of feeling in the subject *by* the moral law. The feeling thus engendered is respect.

(3) Analysis of respect.

Kant analyzes the structure of respect as a feeling engendered by the moral law, that is, engendered in such a way as to bind the subject to the law. So considered, respect involves two interconnected moments, one negative, one positive.

Kant begins with the *fact* that the will can be determined by the moral law. Again, this fact is not to be proved but rather exhibited. For the will to be determined by the moral law means negatively that it is not determined by sensuous impulses or inclinations. Thus insofar as the moral law determines the will, it thwarts our inclinations. Or as Kant elaborates the matter: the moral law checks selfishness by restricting self-love to agreement with the law and strikes down self-conceit.

But inclinations are matters of feeling, and the negative effect on feeling by the thwarting of inclinations is itself a feeling. So in determining the will, the moral law engenders a feeling in the subject.

There is also a positive moment. As thwarting our inclinations, as humiliating our self-conceit and striking it down, the moral law is an object of positive respect. That is, it engenders in the subject a positive feeling for the law: "If anything checks our self-conceit in our own judgment, it humiliates. Therefore, the moral law inevitably humbles every man when he compares the sensuous propensity of his nature with the law. Now if the idea of something as the determining ground of the will humiliates us in our self-consciousness, it awakens respect for itself insofar as it is positive and the ground of determination. The moral law, therefore, is even subjectively a cause of respect" (*CPr*, p. 77).

Or again, Kant says: "The lowering of the pretensions of moral self-esteem (humiliation) on the sensuous side is an elevation of the moral (that is, practical) esteem for the law on the intellectual side" (*CPr*, p. 81).

Kant concludes that the moral law is a subjective ground of determination, an incentive, "since it has an influence on the sensibility of the subject and effects a feeling which promotes the influence of the law on the will" (*CPr*, p. 78). This feeling is a *pure* feeling. It is not pathological, not caused by the influence of things on our sensibility. Instead, it is practical: it originates from, is engendered by, the moral law and so by pure practical reason. It must be stressed that respect is not some kind of antecedent feeling which impels us to let our will be determined by the moral law. According to Kant, "In the subject, there is no antecedent feeling tending to morality" (*CPr*, p. 78). Respect is rather the feeling engendered in that very determining. Accordingly, Kant says: "Thus respect for the law is not the incentive to morality; it is morality itself, regarded subjectively as an incentive" (*CPr*, p. 78).

Thus far we have dealt with respect as the feeling engendered in the subject's being bound to the law by the law; that is, we have dealt with it only as respect for law. As such, respect proved to involve two interconnected moments: the negative moment corresponding to the thwarting of inclinations and the positive moment of respect proper. In its full structure, this feeling for law, however, is still only one side of respect. There is another side, and to see it we will begin by considering the general structure of feeling.

This structure involves a "double intentionality": a feeling for something is not merely directed at some "object" but also has a reflexive side. In other words, a feeling for something involves also a feeling of oneself, of one's own condition. In having a feeling for something, one also becomes manifest to oneself in and through the feeling.

In both intentionalities, what is felt is manifest in a way that is not intuitive. What is felt is *immediately* manifest, without the distance and objectification involved in intuition. Thus far we have dealt with only one of these intentionalities, only with respect as a feeling *for something*. But it also involves a self-feeling, an affective manifestation *of oneself*. Kant expresses this other side in several ways. For example, he speaks of the negative element in respect for law, that feeling correlative to the constraining, humiliating function of law. Then he adds: "On the other hand, since this constraint is exercised only through the legislation of one's own reason, it also contains something elevating" (*CPr*, p. 83).

To what is someone elevated in respect? He is elevated "above himself as a part of the world of sense" (*CPr*, p. 89). That is, he is elevated to "personality." He is shown the sublimity of his own nature. The moral law, by engendering respect, "lets us perceive the sublimity of our own supersensuous existence and subjectively effects respect for our higher vocation" (*CPr*, p. 91).

More specifically, in respect for law, I subordinate myself to the law. But this means that I subordinate myself to myself *as* pure reason. And that is precisely an elevating of myself: I elevate myself to myself as a free, self-determining, rational being, and so I am disclosed to myself in my higher vocation, in my dignity, namely, as a (moral) person.

Thus in respect there is self-disclosure, a moral self-consciousness. This self-consciousness is radically different from the forms of self-consciousness treated in the *Critique of Pure Reason*. It is not a pure thought of the I (transcendental apperception) nor an empirical experience of oneself (as appearance in inner sense). Instead, it a consciousness of oneself as a person; it is a practical self-consciousness. So in summary:

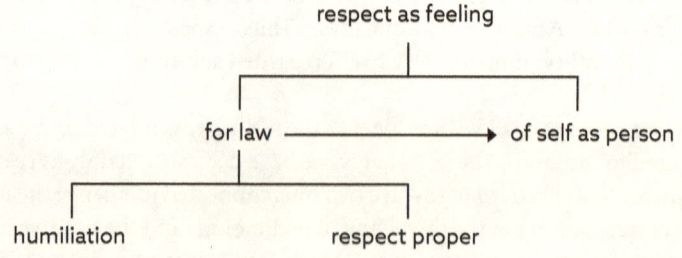

(4) Significance of respect.

In order to grasp the significance of the analysis of respect for the fundamental issues, let us recall briefly how those issues have taken form. The dimension of fundamental issues first appeared in the *Foundations*, Third Section. There Kant exhibited the fundamental act (transcendental praxis) constituting the ground of morality. That act was seen to involve two moments: a self-intuition and then a positing of oneself in the way prescribed by that intuition. But this first account harbored an unresolved difficulty: no such intuition is possible, since it would need to be intellectual.

When we proceeded to Chapter I of the *Critique of Practical Reason*, we saw this issue clarified to some extent: the first moment in the fundamental act is not a self-intuition but rather is that consciousness of the moral law which Kant designates as a fact of reason. So transcendental praxis involves both a consciousness of the moral law and a positing of oneself as free and intelligible.

The most important point is that what Kant describes as respect is identical with that consciousness of moral law (fact of reason) constituting the first moment of transcendental praxis. This identification allows several issues to be clarified:

First, we can see how there can be a consciousness of the moral law without this consciousness being an intuition or a mere thought. It is consciousness in the mode of feeling. In this regard, we note that Kant explicitly refers to the feeling of respect as consciousness: "The *consciousness* of free submission of the will to the law, combined with an inevitable constraint imposed only by our own reason on all inclinations, is respect for the law" (*CPr*, p. 83, emphasis added).

Second, it becomes clear how this primordial consciousness of the moral law is a fact of reason, that is, how it is given with reason itself. The point is that it is a feeling engendered in the subject *by* the moral law, *by* pure reason.

Also, it becomes clear how this consciousness of the moral law belongs together with the other moment of transcendental praxis, namely, the positing of the self as free and intelligible. The point is that this consciousness of the moral law, as a feeling, has a double intentionality: it is also a consciousness of oneself as a person, as free and intelligible. It is to this moral *self*-consciousness that the positing is attached.

E. The Dialectic of Pure Practical Reason

We will first deal with the initial, most difficult, parts of the Dialectic (Chapter I; Chapter II, Sections 1–2). Here we will have to confront the most thorny interpretative problem in all of Kant's practical philosophy. Then, once we have laid out the initial stages of the Dialectic, we will interrupt our textual interpretation in order to bring the problem of practical reason to a deeper level.

(1) The general concept of the dialectic of practical reason.

Kant introduces the general concept of this dialectic by analogy with and then differentiation from the dialectic of theoretical reason. In both its practical and theoretical employment, reason generates a dialectic. It does so as a result of a demand intrinsic to reason: reason "demands the absolute totality of conditions for a given conditioned thing" (*CPr*, p. 111). Let us consider an example: for a particular effect, reason demands the totality of the causal series. Why does this demand generate a dialectic, that is, conflict and illusion? It is because the absolute totality of conditions "can be reached only in things in themselves" (*CPr*, p. 111). Thus by attempting to satisfy this demand, we are led to trespass beyond the limits of experience and knowledge.

According to Kant, what differentiates the dialectic of practical reason is the character of the totality demanded. The one demanded by practical reason is not a putative object of knowledge (such as soul, world, God) but instead is an object of pure will, an object of practical reason. It is an object in which all other objects of will would be gathered into a totality. This object-totality Kant calls "the highest good." Clearly, the first task is to determine with some precision this concept of the highest good.

(2) Concept of the highest good.

The concept of "highest" is ambiguous. It can mean supreme or perfect. As supreme, the highest is the unconditioned condition, the condition subordinate to no other. In this sense, the supreme good would be that which conditions all other good, that by which all other good is good. The Analytic has shown that the supreme good consists in the accord of the will with the moral law. If such accord is regarded not just as a particular occurrence but as something constant, that is, as a totality, then it can be identified with virtue. So the supreme good is virtue.

As perfect, the highest is that whole which is not part of a yet larger whole. The crucial point is that virtue is not the whole or perfect good to which the desire of a finite rational being is directed. Rather, such a being necessarily desires happiness also. Accordingly, the concept of the perfect good includes both virtue and happiness. It is this sense of perfect, whole good that Kant assigns to the concept of the highest good: "The highest good means the whole, perfect good, wherein virtue is always the supreme good, being the condition having no condition superior to it, while happiness, although something always pleasant to him who possesses it, is not of itself absolutely good in every respect but always presupposes conduct in accordance with the moral law as its condition" (*CPr*, p. 115).

So the supreme good equals virtue. The highest (perfect) good equals virtue plus happiness. The question then is: *how* do these two, virtue and happiness, belong together in the concept of the highest good? What kind of connection is there between virtue and happiness?

Two alternatives present themselves. First, the connection may be merely logical or analytic. In that case, the pursuit of virtue and the pursuit of happiness would be absolutely identical. But the Analytic has shown that this is not so. Therefore, the other alternative must hold: the connection must be a real or synthetic connection according to the law of causality.

(3) The antinomy of practical reason.

There are two conceivable synthetic connections that could hold between virtue and happiness: either could be conceived as the cause of the other. An antinomy arises from the fact that both these kinds of connections are impossible. Happiness cannot cause virtue (morality). The Analytic has shown that maxims based on the desire for happiness are not moral. Nor can virtue (morality) cause happiness. Since the connection of causes and effects in the sensible world does not depend only on moral intentions of the will, therefore the effects of the will do not necessarily correspond to the intentions. That is, even if a morally determined will necessarily willed effects that would produce happiness, that could still not suffice to establish a causal relation between morality and happiness, for the effect willed and the effect produced do not necessarily coincide.

Therefore, all forms of connection by which the highest good could be constituted have proved to be impossible. In other words, the highest good has proved to be impossible. Here we arrive at the actual antinomy: "Since the furthering of the highest good, which contains this connection in its concept, is an apriori necessary object of our will and is inseparably related to the moral law, the impossibility of the highest good must prove the falsity of the moral law also. If, therefore, the highest good is impossible according to practical rules, then the moral law which commands that it be furthered must be sheer phantasy, directed to empty, imaginary ends, and as a consequence inherently false" (*CPr*, p. 118).

So the conflict (antinomy) is this: the moral law commands that we further the highest good, but the highest good is impossible. Unless this conflict is resolved, one must conclude that the moral law and hence practical reason as such are empty, false. Thus the antinomy threatens to undermine practical reason completely.

At this point we encounter the most difficult problem of interpretation: why does Kant say the moral law commands that we further the highest good? In other words, what is this connection between moral law and the highest good, a connection presupposed by the antinomy and without which there would simply be no antinomy?

Kant himself warns us near the beginning that this is a delicate matter. After reiterating certain basic connections, he says: "This reminder is of importance in a case as delicate as that of the definition of moral principles, where even the slightest mistake perverts their character" (*CPr*, p. 113). A few lines later, he adds: "This order of concepts of the determination of the will should not be lost from sight, for otherwise we misunderstand ourselves and believe we are contradicting ourselves when everything really stands in the most perfect harmony" (*CPr*, p. 114).

Despite these warnings, nearly all interpreters, including Beck, have ended up condemning Kant's position here as self-contradictory. They have simply given up looking for that "most perfect harmony." This is especially remarkable not only in view of Kant's explicit warnings but also in view of the fundamental status of the antinomy and hence of this crucial connection in Kant's practical thought. The postulates of the immortality of the soul and of the existence of God, that is, answers to questions of ultimate importance to human beings, originate through the resolution of this antinomy.

Considering the care and precision Kant gives to matters of immeasurably less import, it is almost inconceivable that he would here have fallen into the kind of gross confusion and thoughtless self-contradiction with which he is charged. So rather than trying to excuse our own failure to understand by bringing accusations against Kant, let us attempt to think the matter through as far as we can.

The problem is: how are the moral law and the highest good connected so as to allow Kant to say that the moral law commands us to further the highest good? Let us begin with Kant's reminder that the issue is "delicate": "Consequently, although the highest good may be the entire *object* of a pure practical reason, that is, of a pure will, it is still not to be taken as the *determining ground* of the pure will. The moral law alone must be seen as the ground for making the highest good and its realization or promotion the object of the pure will" (*CPr*, p. 113).

The last sentence is of utmost importance, and we need to ask: how does the moral law serve as such a ground? In other words, how does the moral law make the highest good the object of pure will, that to which the will is directed, that which the will is to further?

It is quite clear how it does so in regard to the first component of the highest good, namely, virtue. Virtue is simply the continuing of that accord with the law (more precisely: that determination by law) which the law as imperative commands. So the question comes down to this: how is it that in being directed toward virtue, the will is also directed toward a proportionate happiness?

To be directed toward virtue means to be directed toward being continually determined subjectively by the moral law. But, as the Analytic (Chapter III) showed, when the moral law subjectively determines the will, there is also an engendering of feeling, a determining of practical sensibility by the moral law, by reason. So, to aim at a continual subjective determination of the will by the moral law (that is, to aim at virtue) is also to aim at a consequent determination of practical sensibility by the law (that is, an engendering of respect).

The crucial point is that happiness and unhappiness are matters of practical sensibility, feeling. And so happiness depends on the way practical sensibility gets determined. In the case we are considering (pure will—moral will), the will aims at a situation in which sensibility (feeling) would be determined completely by the moral law. The state of sensibility engendered would be respect or what may equally be called "intellectual contentment." But this is just a kind of utter ideal happiness in which all suffering caused by pathological determination of sensibility would be suppressed.

So, to conclude, in aiming at virtue (complete subjective determination of the will by the moral law), we tacitly and consequently aim at a complete determination of practical sensibility by the moral law, that is, happiness. We are commanded by the moral law to aim at virtue and so also to aim at a consequent happiness. Therefore, the moral law commands us to promote the highest good.

* * *

Interruption of the commentary: the gathering of practical reason.

I want now to pause our commentary on Kant's texts and bring the problem of practical reason to a deeper level. In order to do so, let us return to our point of departure, namely, that brief reflection on the meaning of "reason" with which we began and which provided the basis for our initial directive questions. We took our clues from the Greek roots of the concept of reason, namely, the Platonic concept of λόγος, and from the concept of reason operative in the *Critique of Pure Reason*.

As regards the Platonic concept of λόγος, we considered Socrates' account of how, in his development, he came to have recourse to λόγοι. We asked what is accomplished by that recourse. We answered that, among other things, it makes possible the universality of theoretical knowledge, in contrast to a mere gazing at particulars. That is, it makes possible a knowing in which the particulars are *gathered* under universal concepts and principles. Now, it is this connection between λόγος and gathering that we need now to take in a more radical way.

Specifically, I propose, and have undertaken to show in my book *Being and Logos*, that λόγος means fundamentally: gathering of many into one. For Kant, reason is fundamentally the power of gathering many into one. We can make the connection between λόγος and gathering more definite if we briefly consider the *Critique of Pure Reason* in terms of gathering.

The basic movement traced out by that *Critique* is a complex gathering involving various levels or modes. At the level of intuition, the forms (space and time) serve to gather into extensive unity the utterly dispersed manifold of sensations. At the level of understanding, the categories serve as the ones into which the manifold of intuitions is gathered. And these categories are themselves gathered into the oneness of transcendental apperception. Finally, at the level of dialectical reason, there is an attempted gathering at a still higher (that is, metaphysical) level: for example, a gathering of all appearances into the idea of the world as a whole, an unconditioned totality. But this final gathering in theoretical reason proves impossible to attain, and its failure is attested by the emergence of conflicts and antinomies. The task of the Transcendental Dialectic of the *Critique of Pure Reason* is to exhibit this failure and thus to restrain theoretical reason to its proper sphere.

In all of these modes, reason has its specifically *theoretical* character, namely: a determining of *objects*. That is, in all of these modes, the subject gathers objects into unity. That is the case even at those points where theoretical reason deals with the self: it deals with the self as something empirically intuited, as an object. The only exception occurs at that point where the I posits itself, that is, transcendental apperception. It is an important exception and can perhaps even be seen as something like a point of transition from the theoretical to the practical.

The question then is: what form does the gathering of reason take in the case of practical reason? Practical reason is a determining of the subject and not of objects. Thus in practical reason, the subject gathers the subject into unity, gathers itself into unity. In other words, practical reason is essentially a self-gathering. Kant already referred to this openly at one important juncture. In discussing the practical categories, he described them as rules for "the apriori subjection of the manifold of desires to the unity of consciousness of a practical reason commanding in the moral law, that is, of a pure will" (*CPr*, p. 67). So there is at this level a gathering of the manifold of desires into the unity of a pure will, that is, under the unity of the moral law.

We have seen a higher level of the practical gathering come into question at the beginning of the Dialectic of the second *Critique*. The question of the possibility of the highest good, as a question of the peculiar connection between virtue and happiness, is essentially a question of the gathering of man's manifold sensuous aspect, his sensibility, into his rational aspect. Or, if we think of man as the rational animal, it is a matter of gathering his animality into his rationality. But remember that this gathering is posed by reason itself; so it is reason's gathering of sensibility into reason itself.

(3) Resolution of the antinomy.

Let us return to the antinomy. Its resolution follows the same course as that of the third antinomy in the *Critique of Pure Reason* and so hinges on the distinction between phenomena and noumena.

Kant focuses on the conclusion in the antinomy: the highest good is impossible. This conclusion followed from the fact that both ways the highest good might be constituted, that is, both ways its components might be connected, proved impossible. The proposition that "happiness causes virtue" does not hold. Kant has shown this repeatedly. In discussing the resolution, Kant reaffirms his position: this proposition is "absolutely false" (*CPr*, p. 119). What is decisive for the resolution is that the other proposition ("virtue causes happiness") is not *absolutely* false. Instead, it is "false only insofar as this disposition [virtue] is regarded as the form of causality in the world of sense. Consequently, it is false only if I assume existence in that world to be the only mode of existence of a rational being, and therefore it is only *conditionally* false" (*CPr*, p. 119).

Thus it is necessarily false only if we do not open up the distinction between phenomena and noumena. Specifically, as long we consider only phenomenal causality, virtue (or moral intention) cannot be regarded as the cause of happiness. That is because happiness does not depend only on virtue but also on other causal factors, for example, on the physical ability to bring about what is willed. That is to say, our sensible condition (and whether or not it is one of happiness) is determined by various causes, not just by moral intention.

This difficulty is removed, however, if we avoid regarding virtue as just another cause in the sensible order. It is removed if we distinguish phenomena and noumena and set virtue as noumenal cause over against all natural causes, in a different order from them.

Indeed, this move is justified. Not only can I *think* of myself as noumenal (intelligible), but this character is also attested practically in the moral law. So there is a positive practical ground for opening up the distinction. And if this distinction is granted, then it must also be granted that it is not impossible for virtue to be the noumenal cause of happiness.

To grant this distinction amounts to positing the moral subject as free. In other words, what is granted is the postulate of freedom. So we may formulate the result as follows: there is a positive practical ground, namely, the attestation of the moral law, for the postulate of freedom, and this postulate grounds the general theoretical possibility (non-impossibility) of the connection between virtue and happiness. That is to say, it grounds the possibility of what reason absolutely requires on practical grounds, namely, the possibility of the highest good.

Yet more is still required. This general theoretical possibility (non-impossibility) must be exhibited more positively and more specifically. Before Kant proceeds to this task, however, he offers a short account of the general relation of theoretical and practical reason, namely, the primacy of the practical over the theoretical.

Kant defines primacy: "By primacy between two or more things connected by reason, I understand the prerogative of one on account of which it is the prime ground of determination of the combination with the others" (*CPr*, p. 124). Thus if two things are combined (related), the prime thing is the one that determines the combination (relation). Kant goes on to define "primacy" in a more specific sense: it is "the prerogative of the interest of one insofar as the interest of the others is subordinated to it and is not itself inferior to any other" (*CPr*, p. 124). That is, something has primacy if other interests are subordinated to its interest.

What does Kant mean by "interest"? He says: "To every faculty of the mind an interest can be ascribed, that is, a principle which contains the condition under which alone its exercise is advanced" (*CPr*, p. 124). Consider, for instance, theoretical reason. Under what condition is the exercise of theoretical reason advanced? In the first place, what constitutes an advancement of theoretical reason? That is simply its coming to know objects. So its interest is the knowledge of objects. Thus Kant says: "The interest of the speculative use of reason consists in the knowledge of objects up to the highest apriori principles" (*CPr*, p. 124). He adds that the interest "of the practical employment of reason lies in the determination of the will with respect to the final and perfect end" (*CPr*, p. 124). So the interest of practical reason is the determination of the will.

Then to say that practical reason has primacy over theoretical reason means that the interest of theoretical reason (knowledge of objects) is subordinated to the interest of practical reason (determination of the will) and that therefore the relation between theoretical and practical reason is determined by the practical.

Yet why is there a problem of combination and primacy? Are not theoretical and practical reason with their respective interests so distinct that there could be no question of combination? This would be so if practical reason did not involve postulates. In other words, there is a problem of combination and primacy because of the postulates attaching to practical reason. Kant says that practical reason "has of itself original apriori principles [that is, the moral law] with which certain theoretical positions [that is, postulates] are inseparably bound but which are beyond any possible insight of speculative reason (although not contradictory to it)" (*CPr*, p. 125).

The point is that there are certain postulates, such as that of freedom, falling "in between" theoretical and practical reason and hence posing a problem as regards the combination (relation) of the theoretical and the practical. More specifically, such postulates are bound to practical principles, required by practical reason; for example, the postulate of freedom is required in order to grant what practical reason demands, namely, the possibility of the highest good. In themselves, however, these postulates are theoretical rather than practical; that is, they express a cognitive determination rather than a moral one.

So the problem is: how are these practically grounded theoretical propositions (postulates) to be combined with the propositions of theoretical reason proper? Specifically, how are the results to be combined in those cases, such as freedom, where practical reason postulates the relevant proposition and theoretical reason proves incapable of establishing it?

Kant stresses that they *must* be combined. Why? Because "it is only one and the same reason which judges apriori by principles, whether for theoretical or practical purposes" (*CPr*, p. 125). That is, the unity of reason itself requires that these propositions be combined, subordinated to one another. As Kant says: "Without this subordination, a conflict of reason with itself would arise" (*CPr*, p. 126).

Which is to be subordinated to which? Answer: the theoretical to the practical. That is to say, the positive theoretical postulates of practical reason (for example, the affirmation of freedom) take priority over the corresponding results of theoretical reason (demonstration of nothing more than the logical possibility of freedom).

What is the ground of this priority? What actually constitutes the primacy of practical reason? At the very end of this section, Kant says: "Nor could we reverse the order and expect practical reason to submit to speculative reason, because every interest is ultimately practical, even that of speculative reason being only conditional and reaching perfection solely in practical use" (*CPr*, p. 126). That is, the primacy of practical reason lies in the fact that every interest, even that of theoretical reason, is ultimately practical. Kant does not elaborate. We will return to this issue later.

(4) The postulates.

We have seen that practical reason demands the possibility of the highest good, that it commands us to further the highest good, and that if the highest good were not possible, then practical reason would be empty, false. The task thereby raised is to show what this possibility requires theoretically. That is, what theoretical postulates must be granted in order to grant the possibility of the highest good?

Already Kant has shown that the postulate of freedom is required. What further postulates are required in order to exhibit the possibility of the highest good more specifically? Kant proceeds to show that there are two such postulates. In order to grant the first component of the highest good, the postulate of the immorality of the soul is required; and in order to grant the second component, the postulate of the existence of God.

(a) The immortality of the soul.

Kant's demonstration of the postulate of the immortality of the soul is very compact. It proceeds in six steps:

1. The highest good is possible. This possibility is demanded by practical reason.
2. So, the first component of the highest good is possible, namely, virtue, which equals complete fitness of will to the moral law, which equals holiness.

3. But holiness cannot at any time be realized in a finite rational being.

4. Yet, since holiness must be possible, it must be realized in some other way, namely, not at any time but rather in an endless progress to holiness.

5. Endless progress is possible only if the soul is immortal.

6. Therefore, "The highest good is practically possible only on the supposition of the immortality of the soul, and the latter, as inseparably bound to the moral law, is a postulate of pure practical reason" (*CPr*, p. 127).

Steps 3 and 4 and are the most crucial. As regards step 3, the question arises: why can holiness not be realized at any time in a finite rational being? It is because, as the *Critique of Pure Reason* showed, what constitutes the finitude of the finite rational being is its receptivity, the fact that it is affected and determined by something external to it. That is exactly the contrast with the infinite subject. So a finite subject, on account of its finitude, remains susceptible to affection and thus is never fully determined by the moral law and so is never holy.

Step 4 says that since holiness is not possible at any time, it must be realized only through the totality of time, that is, in endless progress. In other words, a finite subject cannot *be* holy without relinquishing its very character as finite but can only *become* holy. Yet there is a problem here: to say that holiness is realized only in endless progress toward it would seem tantamount to saying: holiness cannot be realized, is impossible. So how is it that *becoming* holy, without ever being such, constitutes a realization of holiness and thus in a sense is equivalent to *being* holy?

Becoming, endless progress, could not have this significance were it not possible for it to be regarded from two different perspectives: that of time (which, as we are presently constituted, is linked to the sensible) and that of the eternal or noumenal: "Only endless progress from lower to higher stages of moral perfection is possible to a rational but finite being. The Infinite Being, to whom the temporal condition is nothing, sees in this series, which is for us without end, a whole conformable to the moral law" (*CPr*, p. 127).

The point is that from the perspective of eternity (of the completely noumenal), endless progress appears as the form of holiness appropriate to a finite rational being. It is "a progress which in God's sight is regarded as equivalent to possession" (*CPr*, p. 128, footnote). Notice the consequence: this wholly noumenal perspective, namely, God, is presupposed, and to that extent the postulate of immortality is dependent on that of the existence of God.

(b) The existence of God.

Kant's demonstration of this postulate is more straightforward. It proceeds in three steps.

1. The second component (happiness) of the highest good is possible, proportional to and consequent upon morality (virtue). This is demanded by practical reason itself, which otherwise would be empty, false. The question is: what is required to guarantee this component, this connection of happiness to virtue?

We saw already that the non-impossibility of this connection requires the postulate of freedom, that is, the opening up of the distinction between phenomena and noumena, the lifting of moral intention out of the context of natural causal conditions. But this move did not yet show positively how such a connection is possible. Instead: "There is not the slightest ground in the moral law for a necessary connection between the morality and the proportionate happiness of a being who belongs to the world as one of its parts and as thus dependent on it. Not being nature's cause, his will cannot by its own strength bring nature, as it touches on his happiness, into complete harmony with his practical principles" (*CPr*, p. 129).

2. In other words, there is a gap, a bifurcation, between the moral determination of the will and the natural determination on which happiness depends, a gap a finite being cannot bridge because, as finite, such a being does not simply determine nature, cause it, but rather is determined by it.

3. So if the highest good is to be possible, a cause must be postulated capable of bridging this gap and connecting the dissociated terms. "Therefore, also the existence is postulated of a cause of the whole of nature, itself distinct from nature, which contains the ground of the exact coincidence of happiness with morality" (*CPr*, p. 129). More specifically, "Therefore, the highest good is possible in the world only on the supposition of a supreme cause of nature which has a causality corresponding to the moral intention" (*CPr*, p. 129). This being is God. And so, Kant says: "Therefore, it is morally necessary to assume the existence of God" (*CPr*, p. 129).

* * *

Outlines of the demonstration of the practical postulates of immortality and God.

Immortality.

1. The highest good is possible.
2. Holiness is possible.
3. Holiness cannot at any time be realized in a finite rational being.
4. Holiness must be realized in endless progress.
5. The soul must be immortal.
6. Therefore, the possibility of the highest good requires the postulate of the immortality of the soul.

God.

1. The second component of the highest good is possible, namely, happiness proportional to morality.
2. But there is a gap between these.
3. Therefore, a cause capable of bridging this gap, God, must be postulated.

V. Conclusion to the Course

At the outset, we developed a preliminary determination of practical reason, and then in terms of that determination, we posed four directive questions. We kept these questions in view in our study of the *Foundations*, and at the end of that study, midway in the course, we returned to those questions. We found that the first three had coalesced into a single one: what is the character of reason's positing of itself as free, as detached? In other terms, what is the character of reason's fundamental self-positing? The fourth question remained at that point largely unanswered, the question of the relation between theoretical and practical reason. We need now, in conclusion, to take up these questions again and consider what further light has been cast on them by the *Critique of Practical Reason*.

(1) We already noted several stages of the further development with respect to the question of the character of the practical self-positing. In the characterization at the end of the *Foundations*, it appeared that the two components in the full structure of such self-positing are an intuition of self and a positing of the self as intuited. We noted at that point, however, that such an intuition would be impossible. When we came to the *Critique of Practical Reason*, we found a more adequate characterization of this first component: initially, it was characterized simply as consciousness of the moral law (fact of reason, but not an intuition). Subsequently, this consciousness was characterized as respect.

We also found that within the structure of respect there is a practical self-disclosure, a practical disclosure of the self as free, intelligible. This consciousness of the moral law, that is, respect, self-disclosure in respect, is then the first moment, the condition, of the self-positing. So what this entire development does is to exhibit the condition of the self-positing. The Dialectic carries the development still further and shows that this same condition is also the condition for positing the immortality of the soul and the existence of God. In other words, it is the condition for the practical postulates.

(2) The *Critique of Practical Reason* has thrown considerable light on the question of the relation between theoretical and practical reason. We have seen that in both employments, reason is a determining, a positing of determinations, or, at the deeper level we tried to open up, a gathering. The difference, then, is this: theoretical reason is a determining of objects; practical reason is a determining of the subject, the self. The Dialectic has developed this question in terms of the issue of the primacy of practical reason.

Now we can take this development one step further. Recall how Kant characterized the ground of the primacy: it lies in the fact that every interest, even that of theoretical reason, is ultimately practical. Specifically, as we quoted: "... every interest is ultimately practical, even that of speculative reason being only conditional and reaching perfection solely in practical use." The question is: in what sense can it be said that theoretical reason remains conditional, that it reaches perfection only in practical use?

We can interpret it as follows. The ultimate condition on which theoretical reason rests, that on which its categorial determining of objects is grounded, is transcendental apperception, theoretical self-consciousness. But transcendental apperception itself remains, in a sense, ungrounded, conditional, less than perfect. Why? —Because it is a mere *thought* of self, a mere empty positing of oneself as subject of knowing. What happens when we come to the sphere of practical reason? There too we find a fundamental self-positing, but one that is not merely a matter of thought. It is self-positing for which a supporting condition can be exhibited. So the theoretical self-positing of transcendental apperception reaches perfection and is grounded only in practical self-positing. It is thus that there is a primacy of practical reason.

* * *

With the issue of the primacy of practical reason, we come back to the very beginning of our reflections on Kant's practical philosophy, namely, our description of the *situation* from out of which we attempt to dialogue with Kant. One of the chief features of that situation is the emphasis placed on praxis (for example, in pragmatism or Marxism), the demand that philosophy be brought into relation with praxis, that the theoretical be brought back into relation with the practical. In Kant, especially in the issue of the primacy of practical reason, we have an attempt to think through such a demand, to think back to its ground.

Yet what about that other feature of the situation to which we referred through the words of Levinas and Nietzsche, namely, the suspicion surrounding morality today and, presumably, infesting any reflection on morality, any practical philosophy? I suggest that in the movement of Kant's practical philosophy, there is worked out an appropriate direction of response to this side of our situation. Kant thinks back from morality to its ground. That ground does not itself depend on morality, but rather conversely.

The ground is "transcendental praxis." Its full structure may be regarded as consisting of three basic moments. One moment is the subjective determination of the will by the moral law. Another moment is the correlative respect, the consciousness of the moral law. The third moment is the consequent self-positing. The fundamental moment is the subjective determination by the moral law. Yet such determination simply means, at this level, determination by reason. In turn, determination by reason means genuine *self*-determination, freedom in the full positive sense. At this level, freedom is neither an act of a subject nor a quality of such acts. Instead, as a condition of self-positing, it is that event by which a subject is first constituted. So Kant's practical philosophy is no mere reflection on morality; it is instead a thoughtful regress to the domain of transcendental praxis, the domain of that primordial event of freedom by which there is first constituted both the practical subject and consequently the possibility of anything like morality in the usual sense. The fundamental problem of Kant's practical philosophy is situated—to use Nietzsche's phrase—"beyond good and evil."

Part Three.
Kant, *Critique of Judgment*

Lecture course presented at Boston College
Spring 2011

With supplementary material from lecture course at Boston College
Spring 2019

I. Introduction

KANT'S *CRITIQUE OF Judgment* is a pivotal work, that is, a work in which a decisive turning occurs, a fundamental redirection, reorientation, of philosophical thought. This pivotal character is what makes the book so significant. It is also what makes it so difficult and so resistant to definitive interpretation. What is the turning carried out in the third *Critique*?

Kant says repeatedly that the *Critique of Judgment* brings the critical project to completion. Yet it is not at all a mere filling out of a project already securely sketched. It is anything but a mere extension of what the first two *Critiques* had accomplished. The *Critique of Judgment* contains a wealth of new insights, ones falling outside the range of the *Critique of Pure Reason* and the *Critique of Practical Reason*. Most importantly, the third *Critique* involves the discovery of an entirely new, unforeseen direction or area of critical thought. In this book, we witness the elaboration of this discovery, whose successive stages are layered into the work—hence the complexity of the text.

We first hear of this discovery in a letter Kant wrote to Karl Reinhold in December 1787, shortly after the completion of the *Critique of Practical Reason*. Reinhold went on to become an important philosopher in his own right. He was the first who sought to go beyond the critical philosophy, and to that extent, he set the stage for German Idealism. He exercised great influence on Fichte and the young Schelling.

At the time of Kant's letter, however, Reinhold was known for his popularizing of Kant's ideas. Reinhold's book, *Letters on the Kantian Philosophy*, published in serial form beginning in 1786, was primarily responsible for drawing widespread attention to Kant's writings. In his letter, Kant compliments Reinhold. Then, turning to his own work, Kant speaks of having discovered certain ways of investigation that were unexpected: "I am now at work on the critique of taste, and I have discovered a kind of apriori principle different from those heretofore observed" (*Philosophical Correspondence 1759–99*, p. 127). Kant explains that previously he thought it impossible to find such principles. That is, he thought that taste, discrimination with regard to beautiful things, was merely empirical, without any apriori principles. But he says he has now discovered such principles, and this discovery "gives me ample material for the rest of my life, material at which to marvel and if possible to explore. . . . I hope to have a manuscript on this completed though not in print by Easter [1788]; it will be entitled 'Critique of Taste'" (p. 127).

In fact, Kant did not complete the work until 1790, and it bore the title "Critique of Judgment." This change in title points to the complex development the project underwent during the two intervening years. Perhaps the most important development was the elaboration of the concept of judgment and especially the introduction of the notion of reflective judgment. In the most general terms, the concept of reflective judgment is a way of thinking the relation between universal and particular that is different from the traditional way, in which the particular is subsumed under the universal. This notion, which does not occur in the first two *Critiques*, moves to the center of Kant's project in the third. Then, since there can be reflective judgments not only of taste but also in regard to teleology, the project, as a critique of (reflective) judgment, comes to have two parts: Critique of Aesthetic Judgment and Critique of Teleological Judgment.

An additional development eventuated at least partially in response to certain contemporary controversies, especially the "pantheism controversy" provoked by the revival of interest in Spinoza. Kant introduced, alongside the analysis of beauty, an analysis of the sublime. At the outset of his "Analytic of the Sublime," he observes that "the beautiful and the sublime are similar in some respects.... Both presuppose that we make a judgment of reflection" (*CJ*, p. 97). In this regard, there are certain anticipations of the *Critique of Judgment* in Kant's early pre-critical work *Observations on the Feeling of the Beautiful and Sublime*, which dates back to 1764, almost two decades before the *Critique of Pure Reason*. As the title indicates, the relation of the subject to the beautiful and the sublime is here regarded as *feeling* rather than as judgment. Yet, it is significant that already in this work, Kant includes the sublime along with the beautiful and gives examples that would accord with the analysis in the *Critique of Judgment*:

> Finer feeling, which we now wish to consider, is chiefly of two kinds: the feeling of the *sublime* and that of the *beautiful*. The stirring of each is pleasant, but in different ways. The sight of a mountain whose snow-covered peak rises above the clouds, the description of a raging storm, or Milton's portrayal of the infernal kingdom, arouse enjoyment but with horror; on the other hand, the sight of flower-strewn meadows, valleys with winding brooks and covered with grazing flocks, the description of Elysium, or Homer's portrayal of the girdle of Venus, also occasion a pleasant sensation but one that is joyous and smiling. In order that the former impression could occur to us in due strength, we must have a *feeling of the sublime*, and, in order to enjoy the latter well, a *feeling of the beautiful*. Tall oaks and lonely shadows in a sacred grove are sublime; flower beds, low hedges and trees trimmed in figures are beautiful. Night is sublime, day is beautiful. (*Observations on the Feeling of the Beautiful and Sublime*. Berkeley: University of California Press, 1965, pp. 46–47)

Furthermore, in the *Critique of Judgment*, Kant came to emphasize the ethical relevance of beauty. This culminates in the famous §59: "On beauty as the symbol of morality."

These developments compounded the work so thoroughly that, just prior to its publication, Kant completely rewrote the Introduction. The striking differences between the two Introductions are an index of the complexity of the development.

So the *Critique of Judgment* arises from the discovery that there are apriori principles in judgments of taste, that is, in judgments regarding beauty. This amounts to a discovery that a transcendental grounding of such judgments and indeed of beauty as such is possible. But in working out this discovery, a host of other issues emerges, and all of these issues enter into the text in the form it finally had when it appeared in print in 1790.

* * *

The *Critique of Judgment* turned out to be pivotal in another sense as well, that is, not only in Kant's own thought but also in the overall development of modern philosophy. In very general terms, the third *Critique*, more than any other work, is the site of the transition from the Enlightenment to the era of Romanticism and German Idealism. The transition can perhaps be seen most clearly with respect to two themes: nature and imagination.

(1) Nature. With the rise of Galilean-Newtonian physics, nature came to be regarded as a totality of masses in motion, operating by efficient causality and governed by the mathematical laws of physical science. Thus nature was stripped of everything eidetic and purposive and was conceived as sheer mechanism.

This concept of nature is taken over by Kant in the *Critique of Pure Reason*: "By nature . . . is meant the sum of appearances insofar as they stand, in virtue of an inner principle of causality, in thoroughgoing interconnection" (B446). Even though Kant regards nature as a sum of *appearances*, that is, of objects as they appear to us, not as they are in themselves, nature nevertheless remains sheer mechanism, devoid of all characteristics other than the causally determined properties treated by natural science.

In the *Critique of Judgment*, however, Kant discovers a way to take seriously certain other features we experience in nature, namely, beauty and sublimity. Kant discovers that these are not merely subjective and empirical but that they have a transcendental ground. In other words, there is some basis for our judging certain things to be beautiful or sublime. And there is a basis for the way the experience of beautiful things is pleasing and enlivening and the experience of sublime things emotional and uplifting.

Thus, with regard to our experiences, nature proves to exceed its purely objective, causally determined character. In such experience of nature, something else comes to be disclosed, something about our relation to nature. In Kant's words, in a famous Reflection, "Beautiful things tell us that human beings belong to nature" (*Reflexionen*, no. 1820a, in vol. 16 of *Gesammelte Schriften*, Akademie Ausgabe. Berlin: De Gruyter, 1924, p. 127).

How thoroughly this development transforms the concept of nature can be seen in Schiller's "On naive and sentimental poetry," written in 1795 under direct influence of the *Critique of Judgment*: "There are moments in our lives when we extend a kind of love and tender respect to nature in plants, minerals, animals, and landscapes, as well as to human nature in children, in the customs of country folk, and in the primitive world, not because it pleases our senses, nor even because it satisfies our understanding or taste . . . , but merely *because it is nature*" (Friedrich Schiller, "On naive . . ." in *Essays*. New York: Continuum, 1993, p. 179).

This concept of nature came to be developed further—still under Kant's influence—in German Idealism. For example, Schelling writes in 1800: "What we call nature is a poem that lies locked in a mysterious, wondrous script. Yet the enigma would unveil itself if we could recognize the odyssey of the spirit within it, which, in seeking itself, wondrously deceived, flees from itself" (F. W. J. Schelling, *System des transzendentalen Idealismus*, in *Schriften von 1799–1801*, Darmstadt: Wissenschaftliche Buchgesellschaft, 1967, p. 628).

(2) Imagination. Kant's analyses in the *Critique of Judgment* show that what is at the core of our experience of beauty and of the sublime is imagination. But, precisely as he shows this, the notion of the imagination, the very sense of what imagination is, undergoes a transformation. We can gain an idea of the extent of the transformation if we turn back to pre-Kantian conceptions of imagination.

Hobbes' *Leviathan* was published in 1651. In that book, Hobbes says: "Imagination therefore is nothing but *decaying sense* and is found in men and many other living Creatures, as well sleeping as waking" (Thomas Hobbes, *Leviathan*, ed. R. Tuck. Cambridge: Cambridge University Press, 1991, p. 15).

Or consider Burke's *Philosophical Enquiry into the Origin of our Ideas of the Sublime and the Beautiful*, written a century later, in 1757. This is a book Kant read in German translation as he was working on the *Critique of Judgment*. Burke grants that imagination is more than mere decaying sense, that it involves wit, fancy, and invention. Yet Burke insists that "this power of the imagination is incapable of producing anything absolutely new; it can only vary the disposition of those ideas it has received from the senses" (Edmund Burke, *Philosophical Enquiry* . . . , ed. J. Boulton. Notre Dame: University of Notre Dame Press, 1968, p. 17).

In a certain respect, the *Critique of Pure Reason* takes over this concept of the imagination: "Imagination is the faculty of representing in intuition an object that is not itself present" (B151). Yet in Kant's formulation, something further is suggested: not only that the imagination can reproduce an image no longer given to the senses but that it might also produce an image *not yet* given to sense. So already in the first *Critique*, Kant distinguishes between a merely reproductive and a productive imagination. This "freeing" of imagination cleared the way for the most decisive development.

The Transcendental Deduction of the *Critique of Pure Reason* showed that the productive imagination is what brings about the synthesis essential to all experience, all knowing of objects, such that without imagination "we would have no knowledge whatever" (A78/B103). Thus imagination is not just derivative, not just "decaying sense." Neither is it merely a supplement to experience, a power of merely varying, altering, reconfiguring what sense has provided, as when I imagine a monster by representing together what does not occur together in nature—the head of a lion, the body of a man, and the tail of a horse. Instead, imagination is presupposed by experience, is a precondition for a knowledge of objects. Hence, imagination is "a fundamental power of the human soul" (A124).

The *Critique of Judgment* goes still further by showing that certain apprehended forms can set the imagination in play and that then there occurs a "free play" between imagination and understanding or between imagination and reason. This free play is at the core of our experiences of beauty and the sublime. Even beyond this, imagination is able to envisage "aesthetic ideas" and discover a way to express these through the creation of works of art.

This more powerful conception of the imagination is taken up and developed in German Idealism. Schelling speaks of imagination as that which mediates between the theoretical and the practical. He says that ideas are "mere products of imagination" (*System*, p. 559) and that even reason is simply imagination considered in a certain respect. Hegel repeats that idea: "And the imagination is nothing but reason itself" (Hegel, *Faith and Knowledge*. Albany: SUNY Press, 1977, p. 73).

This conception of the imagination resounds throughout Romanticism in Germany and England. The most prominent example is Coleridge, who writes in 1817: "The imagination then I consider either as primary or secondary. The primary imagination I hold to be the Living Power and prime Agent of all human perception and as a repetition in the finite mind of the eternal act of creation in the infinite I Am. The secondary I consider as an echo of the former" (Samuel Taylor Coleridge, *Biographia Literaria*. Princeton: Princeton University Press, 1983, p. 304).

So with respect to the themes of nature and imagination, we can see how momentous is the transformation effected by the *Critique of Judgment*. And we begin to get some sense of just how much is at stake in that work.

On the other hand, one might be tempted to say that, however essential the *Critique of Judgment* was in leading over from earlier thought to Romanticism and German Idealism, what is ultimately more significant is not the "bridge" but that to which it leads. The question is whether the *Critique of Judgment* is only a bridge, only the effecting of a transformation that is taken over into the further development, or whether—granting German Idealism its due—there is still an essential intrinsic need to return to Kant's work.

Heidegger suggests the latter in a lecture course from 1935–36. He refers to German Idealism and mentions Fichte, Schelling, and Hegel. Then Heidegger says: "This philosophy leaped over Kant with all due respect but did not overcome him. This could not be done, if for no other reason than the fact that his essential foundation was not attacked but only abandoned. It was not even abandoned, because it was never taken up; it was only skirted. Kant's work remained like an unconquered fortress behind a new front . . ." (Martin Heidegger, *What is a Thing?*, tr. W. B. Barton and V. Deutsch, Chicago: Regnery, 1967, p. 59).

* * *

The *Critique of Judgment* is a notoriously difficult book. One reason, as mentioned, is that it involves the working out of a discovery. In this process, the initial conception of the book is displaced, and several other themes get layered onto the text, interwoven into it. This complexity is reflected especially in the Introduction. It is arguably the most difficult part of the book, the kind of introduction for which one needs already to have read the book. And yet, reading the book without it is also not feasible. Here we gain an indication of the enormous question of beginning, of where to begin.

Kant himself discusses this question in the Preface to the second *Critique* (*CPr*, p. 10). There, he frames it in terms of the relation between parts and whole, that is, between an analysis focused on individual parts and a synthetic or synoptic view of the whole. He says that we must begin with an exact and complete delineation of the parts, so far as is possible. But he adds that it is also necessary to grasp correctly the idea of the whole and then see those parts in their reciprocal interrelations in light of their derivation from the concept of the whole. So we could say that an understanding of the parts requires an understanding of the whole, and vice versa. Thus what is required is a kind of hermeneutical movement, a circling, between whole and parts.

Therefore, we will begin by discussing, very selectively, a few indispensable passages in the Introduction. From these, we will gain a preliminary view of the whole. Then we will proceed to the *Critique* itself and go through it part by part. The intention is to come then to a more adequate synthetic or synoptic view of the whole. Thus part and whole will play off against each other.

Another reason for the difficulty of the *Critique of Judgment* is that it presupposes the first two *Critiques*, especially since Kant conceives the third as bringing the entire critical project to completion. The difficulty of the *Critique of Judgment*, however, does not derive from some willful obfuscation on Kant's part nor from an inability to write with precision and clarity. I suggest it stems rather from the difficulty and intrinsic obscurity of the very matters at issue. Heidegger, in the work just quoted, maintains that Kant has in common with Greek philosophy an "incorruptible clarity of thought and speech," although this does not exclude the questionable, nor does it "feign light where there is darkness" (p. 56).

II. Judgment

RECALL THAT THE *Critique of Judgment* arises from a discovery, namely, that there are apriori principles operative in taste. Once Kant makes this discovery, it becomes imperative for him to investigate these principles, a task he could not have foreseen at the time of the first two *Critiques*. The new investigation would be a critique of taste, and taste refers to discernment with regard to beautiful things. Such discernment is exercised in judgment—when one judges that a thing is beautiful. Thus the apriori principles Kant discovers are principles pertaining to judgment, to the particular kind of judgment Kant will call a "judgment of taste" or "aesthetic judgment."

In order to gain a first look at what these apriori principles of judgment involve and what a critique of judgment must undertake, we need to begin by *situating* judgment and the critique of judgment, that is, by constructing a kind of map showing how judgment is related to the other mental powers and, prior to that, a map detailing how the *Critique of Judgment* is related to the other phases of the critical project.

At the end of the Preface to the *Critique of Judgment*, Kant writes: "With this, I conclude my entire critical enterprise" (*CJ*, p. 7). So the third *Critique* concludes, completes, the critical enterprise. What is the sense of completion here? How does the *Critique of Judgment* bring critique to its conclusion?

It does so in the sense that it connects the other two parts of the critical project, making it a unified whole. These other two parts are the *Critique of Pure Reason* and the *Critique of Practical Reason*. In their positive import, the former deals with the domain of the understanding, the latter with the domain of reason. Thus the *Critique of Judgment* must deal with the connection, the mediation, between these two domains.

What does Kant mean by "domain"? In section II of the Introduction to the *Critique of Judgment*, Kant distinguishes domain (*Gebiet, ditio*, place where one's dicta have authority) from various other spheres of objects, such as field (*Feld*) and territory (*Boden, territorium*). The domain of a specific cognitive power is the sphere of objects within which that cognitive power is legislative, that is, prescriptive of the laws governing whatever occurs in that sphere. So the *Critique of Judgment* must deal with the connection between the sphere in which understanding is legislative and the sphere in which reason is legislative. What are these two domains, and why is their connection problematic?

The domain of the understanding is nature. To see in what sense this is established by the *Critique of Pure Reason*, let us begin with Kant's famous comparison of his own project to Copernican astronomy. Kant draws this comparison in the course of a discussion about metaphysics. Metaphysics aims at a knowledge of objects that is not derivable from an experience of those objects; in other words, metaphysics aims at apriori knowledge of objects. Since such knowledge is independent of our experience, it is available *prior* to our experience of the objects; thus it is *apriori*. Furthermore, metaphysics attempts to gain such knowledge purely through concepts, that is, without any intuition, not even the pure intuition that plays a role in mathematical knowledge, as when I have the insight, the intuition, that the sum of the angles of a triangle = 180°.

Kant asks: how is metaphysics possible? How is such apriori knowledge of objects possible? To show this possibility, the *Critique of Pure Reason* (B xvi–xvii) proposes a revolution, a turning around of a basic assumption, analogous to Copernicus' revolution. Kant notes that "hitherto it has been assumed that all our knowledge must conform to objects." But every metaphysics based on this assumption has ended in failure. Therefore, let us suppose that objects must conform to our knowledge, whereby it would be possible to have knowledge of objects apriori. Kant then compares this proposal to Copernicus' primary insight: "Failing of satisfactory progress in explaining the movements of the heavenly bodies on the supposition that they all revolved around the spectator, he tried for better success by making the spectator revolve while the stars remained at rest."

Kant's proposal might seem diametrically opposed to that of Copernicus, who effected a shift *away from* the human subject: the Earth is no longer the center. Kant carries out a shift *toward* the subject; he makes the understanding legislative. But the point of the analogy is that Copernicus explained the apparent movement of the stars and planets by taking into account the movement of the Earth, the movement of the observer.

The simplest case is that of the stars. They do not move, but the apparent turning of the entire sky, as if it were a sphere in which the stars are set, is a result of the rotation of the Earth. More complex, but for Kant more consequential, is the case of the planets. In Copernican theory, the apparent movement of the planets is treated as a resultant of two movements: the actual moment of the planet, now taken to revolve around the sun, and the movement of the observer, that is, of the Earth rotating and itself also revolving around the sun (see the figure on the next page).

Analogously, the *Critique of Pure Reason* treats the appearance of an object as the "resultant" of the object itself, the object as it is in itself, and that which is contributed by the subject. The subject contributes a certain form, and in order for an object to appear, what is actually given by the object, namely, the content, the sense-material, must be set into that form. Thus the object must conform to our knowledge, to the forms operative in our cognitive activity. If so, then apriori knowledge of objects is possible, specifically with regard to the forms all appearances must exemplify. For instance, if one such form is the cause-effect relation, then we can know apriori that every appearance, every apparent object, is the effect of some cause. If another such form is that of substance with qualities, then we can know apriori that every appearance, every appearing object, will have—will exhibit—this form; in other words, every object that appears will have the form of a substance with qualities.

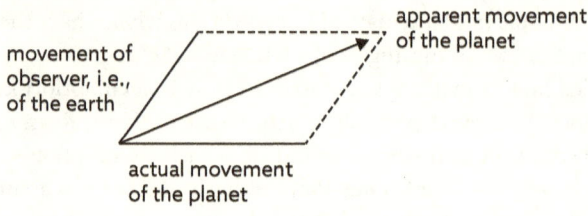

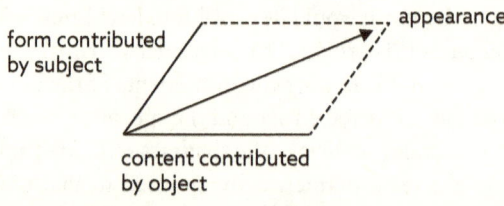

An important consequence of the revolution is that it places a severe limitation on human knowledge. If appearance—the appearing object, the object as it appears to us—results from the melding of sense-content derived from the object as it is in itself and forms supplied by the subject, then the appearance must be distinguished from the object as it is in itself. Since we have no access to objects except as they appear to us, our knowledge is limited to appearances. We have no knowledge of objects as they are in themselves, of what Kant calls "things in themselves."

The cognitive power that supplies the forms of appearances is the understanding. That precisely is the legislation, the law-giving: the understanding gives the law, the general forms, to appearances. These forms are expressed in the categories of the understanding. The totality of appearances is nature. So the understanding is legislative for nature; its domain is nature.

There is a broader issue arising in relation to the discussion of nature as the domain of understanding. It is broached in the Preface to the Second Edition of the *Critique of Pure Reason*: "Thus it does indeed follow that all possible speculative knowledge of reason is limited to mere objects of *experience*. But our further contention must also be duly borne in mind, namely, that though we cannot *know* these objects as things in themselves, we must yet be in a position at least to *think* them as things in themselves; otherwise we should be landed in the absurd conclusion that there can be appearance without anything that appears" (B xxvi). Kant thus insists on the condition that in order for there to be appearance, there must be things that appear, things in themselves. But we can experience—can know—*only* appearances, only things as they appear, not things as they are in themselves. And yet, there must be some relation to things in themselves in order for us even to posit them, to suppose that they are. Hence, Kant says that, though we have no knowledge of things in themselves, we can *think* them. So Kant introduces a distinction between knowing and thinking: thinking is a relation to something—a positing of something—something that is not necessarily given to intuition. This distinction and its far-reaching consequences have remained problematic. The distinction has been taken up again and again; it has been reformulated, recast, criticized, rejected, from the time of Kant's immediate successors such as Jacobi, Reinhold, and Fichte up to that of Nietzsche and Heidegger.

The other domain, the domain of reason, is freedom. Here too it is a matter of legislation, law-giving. It is a matter of a cognitive power that gives a law to something. The cognitive power is reason, and the law it gives is the moral law, the categorical imperative: "So act that the maxim of your will could always hold at the same time as a principle establishing universal law" (*CPr*, p. 30). Reason gives this law to the will, to the power of desire, as the law by which the will ought to be determined rather than being determined by sensuous inclination.

Why does Kant speak here of freedom? It is because the moral law presupposes freedom: we can be bound by the moral law, obligated to act in accordance with it, only if we are free and not determined by nature. But then to say we are free and self-determining is to say we are essentially detached from nature, outside nature. So as practical subject, as free, self-legislating, self-determining subject, we are outside nature, while as theoretical subject engaged in knowing objects, we are within nature—experiencing it and giving it form.

Here we begin to see why mediation is necessary: one and the same subject is both in nature and outside nature. It is this mediation that will be traced by the *Critique of Judgment*.

Let us consider still more precisely what the problem is and why mediation is needed. Understanding and reason have their respective domains: nature and freedom. Each cognitive power is legislative within its domain. And yet, according to Kant: "the territory on which the domain of our cognitive power is set up and on which it exercises its legislation is still always confined to the sum total of the objects of all possible experience, insofar as they are considered nothing more than mere appearances" (*CJ*, p. 13). This says that the territory, the sphere of objects, in which the legislation of these two cognitive powers would be exercised—that is, would have its effect—is in both cases nature. Then Kant goes on: "Hence understanding and reason have two different legislations on one and the same territory of experience. Yet neither of these legislations is to interfere with the other" (*CJ*, p. 13).

Kant then mentions that the *Critique of Pure Reason* has shown it is possible, without contradiction, to think of these two legislating powers as coexisting in the same subject. He is referring to the Transcendental Dialectic, specifically to the antinomies. There Kant showed that if the distinction is drawn between appearances and things in themselves, it is then possible to think that appearances operate solely by natural causality while, with respect to things in themselves, there is freedom. Yet it was *not* shown that this is actually the case, only that it is logically possible, can be thought without contradiction.

Kant continues: "Although these two different domains do not restrict each other in their legislation, they do restrict each other incessantly in the effects their legislation has in the world of sense" (*CJ*, p. 14). The point is that despite the mutual irreducibility, the separation between the domain of nature and that of freedom, nevertheless freedom or self-determination does issue in action, is aimed at action. Thus freedom is meant to have an influence in nature, to produce an effect in nature. In other words, self-determination through the moral law is intended by its very meaning to actualize in the world of sense, that is, in nature, the purpose proposed by the moral law.

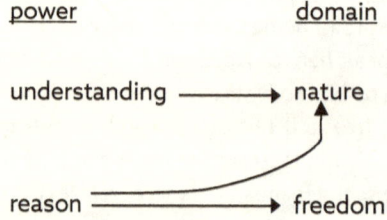

Kant is saying that freedom ought to influence nature: "the concept of freedom is to make actual in the world of sense the purpose enjoined by its [freedom's] laws" (*CJ*, p. 15). Kant then concludes: "Hence it must be possible to think of nature as being such that the lawfulness of its form will harmonize with at least the possibility of achieving the purposes we are to carry out in nature according to laws of freedom" (*CJ*, p. 15).

The question is: exactly *how* must nature be thought in order to be conceived as harmonious with purposes to be effected according to laws of freedom? Kant's answer: nature must be thought as purposive. Thus the mediation, the transition between nature and freedom, will involve a certain thinking of the purposiveness of nature.

Yet the mediation will involve not merely *thinking* this purposiveness but also *experiencing* it. This experience occurs preeminently in the experience of the beauty of nature. Most remarkably, such experience falls completely outside the experience in which we come to *know* objects. In Kant's language, aesthetic judgment, although it involves our cognitive powers, is something quite different from the cognition of objects. In an often cited statement from the Preface, Kant says about aesthetic judgments: "although these judgments do not by themselves contribute anything whatever to our cognition of things, they still belong to the cognitive power alone" (*CJ*, p. 6). So aesthetic judgments contribute nothing to our knowledge of things. That is, to judge things of nature or works of art to be beautiful is not to come to know anything about them. For example, to say the sky is beautiful is quite different from saying the sky is blue.

Here we begin to see that the *Critique of Judgment* is not just the completion of what was undertaken in the first two *Critiques*. For, the experience to which it is primarily addressed, namely, aesthetic judgment, not only mediates between theoretical and practical knowing but falls completely outside the scope of knowing. In coming to address such experience, Kant has made a genuine breakthrough, a discovery extending the bounds of critical thought.

The question that remains—even in our time—is that of truth. Does the fact that aesthetic judgment contributes nothing to knowledge entail that it does not in any way reveal truth? Are knowledge and truth identical? Or can there be truth that is not knowledge?

Kant also thinks of the mediation at issue here in other terms, namely, in terms of the ancient distinction between the sensible and the supersensible. As free subjects apart from nature, we belong to the intelligible or supersensible: "If freedom is attributed to us, it transfers us into an intelligible order of things" (*CPr*, p. 43). Furthermore, natural things, since they are merely appearances, must have a noumenal or supersensible substratum underlying them, namely, things in themselves. So the mediation can be thought as between these two supersensibles, although of course no theoretical knowledge of them is possible: "Thus there must after all be a basis uniting the supersensible that underlies nature and the supersensible contained practically in the concept of freedom" (*CJ*, p. 15).

This conception of the mediation proved decisive for German Idealism. Schelling stressed the unity between these two supersensibles and maintained that they are the same although appearing in different guises. Identifying the supersensible with spirit, Schelling concluded that nature is visible spirit. We might indeed suspect that here Kant was, as Heidegger says, merely skirted rather than overcome.

* * *

Let us turn to the second map we need to construct, one that situates judgment with respect to the other powers of the soul. Kant's expression is *Seelenvermögen oder Fähigkeiten*, powers or capacities by which the soul or the subject does something. That something may be to know, to desire, or to feel pleasure and displeasure. The powers should not be thought as parts of the soul or as faculties. For example, understanding is not that which knows but that by means of which *I* know.

The map is sketched in a single passage in section III of the Introduction:

> Between the cognitive power and the power of desire lies the feeling of pleasure, just as judgment [*Urteilskraft*: power of judging] lies between understanding and reason. Hence we must suppose, at least provisionally, that judgment also contains an apriori principle of its own and also suppose that since the power of desire is necessarily connected with pleasure or displeasure (whether this [pleasure or displeasure] precedes the principle of this power [power of desire], as in the case of the lower power of desire, or, as in the case of the higher one, only follows from the determination of this power by the moral law), judgment will bring about a transition from the pure cognitive power, that is, from the domain of the concepts of nature, to the domain of the concept of freedom, just as in its logical use judgment makes possible the transition from understanding to reason. (*CJ*, pp. 17–18)

Judgment lies between understanding and reason. In dealing with whatever pertains to cognition, Kant usually begins with the logical conceptions, with the way the matters have been conceived in logic. His beginning with logic and logical concepts is not just arbitrary; it is not as though he could have begun with some other discipline. In the Preface to the Second Edition of the *Critique of Pure Reason*, Kant writes as regards logic: "Since Aristotle it has not been required to retrace a single step.... It is remarkable also that to the present day this logic has not been able to advance a single step and is thus to all appearance a closed and completed body of doctrine" (B viii). Thus, Kant regards logic as the one science that is completely developed and that consequently can be considered completely rigorous. For this reason, it can serve as a valid starting point for other disciplines, such as that which describes and differentiates the powers of the soul. As he proceeds, the concepts are transformed from the logical to the transcendental. The prime example is the transformation of the logical functions of the understanding into apriori categories. In the present case, Kant is drawing initially on formal logic, on the traditional order: concepts, propositions, arguments. Concepts are formed by the understanding, for example by abstracting from a multiplicity of instances. Concepts are then joined together to form propositions, accomplished through the power of judgment. Propositions, judgments, are then connected to form syllogisms, by which an inference is made from premises to a conclusion. The power of inference accomplishing this is reason.

```
E.g., red things
         ↓
concept:    red
         ↓
judgment:   the house is red
         ↓
inference:  red things are expensive

(syllogism) ∴ the house is expensive
```

So, logically, judgment lies between understanding and reason, concept and inference. That is how Kant maps judgment amid the other cognitive powers. But the mapping of the powers of the soul continues with Kant placing the feeling of pleasure between the cognitive power and the power of desire. He takes these three powers to be *the* three basic ones, that is, *all* the basic powers of the soul: "For all of the soul's powers or capacities can be reduced to three that cannot be derived further from a common basis: the cognitive power, the feeling of pleasure and displeasure, and the power of desire" (*CJ*, p. 16). Here Kant is maintaining the traditional division of the powers of soul into reason, will, and feeling, although in the course of critique these come to be interrogated anew and redetermined.

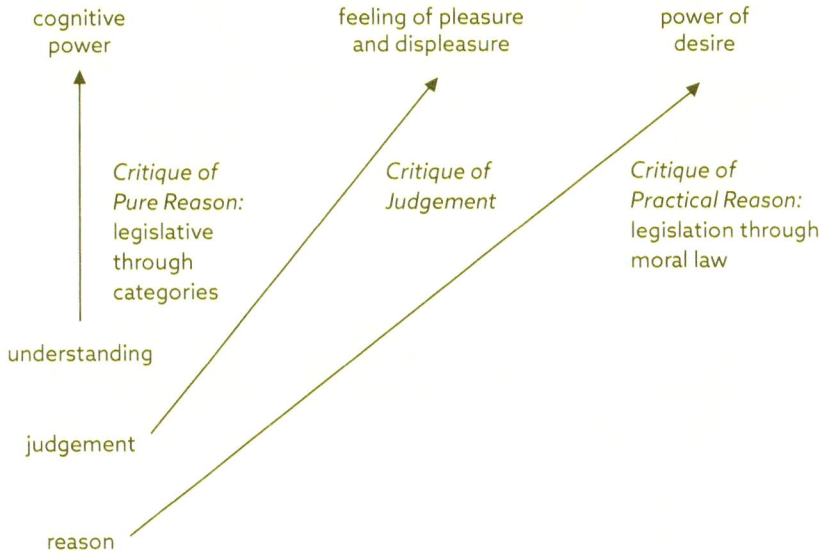

Kant focuses on one side, namely, the connection between the feeling of pleasure and the power of desire. It is this connection that is addressed by the parenthetical remark in the long passage quoted above. For the lower, sensuously determined power of desire, it is pleasure or the prospect of pleasure that determines it; the satisfaction of one's desire is what gives or will give pleasure. For the higher power of desire as determined by the moral law, the determination of the power of desire precedes the feeling or anticipation of pleasure and brings about that feeling or anticipation. In other words, here one desires what is morally right or good, not what promises pleasure. Yet desiring in this way, as self-determination through the moral law, can itself produce a certain feeling of pleasure, namely, that uniquely pure feeling Kant calls "respect."

Kant says we must suppose that "judgment also contains an apriori principle of its own" (*CJ*, p. 18). This again is Kant's great discovery. To say that judgment contains an apriori principle is to say that it is legislative, that it gives the law, determines something apriori. So to what does judgment give the law? What does it determine apriori? Already in the Preface, Kant asks whether judgment "gives the rule apriori to the feeling of pleasure and displeasure" (*CJ*, p. 5). It will indeed turn out that certain types of judgment do determine the feeling of pleasure. But the legislating carried out by judgment is not primarily its determining of feeling; that is little more than a concomitant result. So Kant concludes: "Judgment will bring about a transition from the pure cognitive power, that is, from the domain of the concepts of nature, to the domain of the concept of freedom" (*CJ*, p. 18), corresponding to the logical transition from understanding to reason.

In other words, since judgment mediates between understanding and reason and since, through its apriori principle, it at least in some cases determines the feeling of pleasure, it effects a transition, a mediation, from cognition and nature (as domain of theoretical cognition) to desire and freedom (as domain of practical reason). We could say that judgment serves to bind together the primary powers of the soul, namely, understanding and reason, that is, theoretical reason and practical reason, cognition and desire. Thus judgment serves to gather the soul to itself.

But what is judgment? Kant defines it at the beginning of section IV of the Introduction: "Judgment in general is the ability to think the particular as contained under the universal" (*CJ*, p. 18). The word "particular" here is ambiguous. It can mean either the specific (species) or the singular (individual). Thus judgment can consist in thinking a species as contained under a universal, a genus (for example: humans are mortal) or in thinking something singular (an individual) under a universal (for example: Socrates is human).

Kant distinguishes between the two main types of judgment as follows: "If the universal (the rule, principle, law) is given, then judgment, which subsumes the particular under it, is determinative. . . . But if only the particular is given and judgment has to find the universal for it, then this power is merely reflective" (*CJ*, p. 18). So if the universal is given, then we have a determinative judgment. If the universal is not given but only the particular for which the universal must be found, then the judgment is reflective.

Note that Kant extends the sense of universal beyond that of mere concepts, hence beyond, though not excluding, such judgments as "Humans are mortal" or "Socrates is human." In fact, when Kant indicates what he means by universal, he does not explicitly mention concepts; instead he refers to rules, principles, laws. So he includes—and even emphasizes—judgments in which:

(1) a specific principle is subsumed under a more universal principle. For example, the principle prohibiting certain crimes such as robbery can be subsumed under the more universal principle of respect for all humans.
(2) singular phenomena are brought under a specific law. Then a manifold of specific laws is subsumed under a more universal law. For example, Galilean laws for falling bodies are subsumed under Newton's universal law of gravitation.

These more complex examples make clearer what is at stake in the distinction between determinative and reflective judgments. If it is merely a matter of subsuming the particular (Socrates) under a universal, then it would seem that there are always universals given and known, under which to subsume it. And then reflective judgment would seem to differ from determinate judgment only in that we might hesitate regarding whether to subsume it under this or that universal. But if we think of the example from physics, the distinction is clearer: at first, there were only singular phenomena. Then there was a time when physicists had only the more specific laws of falling bodies, thus when the universal was *not* given. Newton's accomplishment was precisely to *find* the one universal law under which to subsume the previous specific ones.

Kant deals with reflective judgment in its simplest empirical form at first. We have seen that the understanding legislates nature, gives law to nature in such a way as to determine the universal form and connection of nature. These forms and connections are prescribed by the categories, to which nature must conform. Yet understanding determines in this way only the most universal laws of nature: for example, objects are substances having properties, objects are extended in space, objects are causally connected. Everything else is left undetermined by these laws. All further determination of nature is by merely empirical laws.

It is in the search for these empirical laws that reflective judgment comes into play and, with it, the apriori legislative principle that belongs to such judgment. Reflective judgment ascends from the particular in nature to the universal. That is, it seeks laws under which various singular things or events can be subsumed: thus for all falling bodies near the Earth, $s = \frac{1}{2}gt^2$. Then for particular laws, it seeks more universal laws.

The crucial point is that in ascending from the particular in nature to the universal, reflective judgment requires a principle. This principle cannot be borrowed from the experience of nature, since the principle is to provide the very basis for the reflection allowing us to ascend to universal laws. Instead, this principle must originate from the power of judgment itself; yet it must be a principle that the power of reflective judgment gives *only to itself*. For here, in contrast to the legislating of nature by the understanding, there is no basis for supposing this principle is legislative with respect to nature. Instead, it serves only for our *reflection* on nature. What is this principle?

It is one that represents nature as being such that the empirical diversity of nature is comprehended under laws, and in turn the variety or manifold of laws under a higher unity. That is to say, the principle represents nature as having the same kind of synthetic unity at the empirical level that the *Critique of Pure Reason* showed it to have at the apriori level, the level of its general, categorial form. And yet in this principle, nature is merely *thought* as having such unity at the empirical level. It is not supposed that we could ever fully fathom such comprehensive unity. Nor is this unity actually ascribed to nature. Reflective judgment merely gives this principle to itself as the principle for its own reflection on nature.

Two important consequences follow from Kant's identification of this principle of reflective judgment.

(1) In this principle, nature is thought as having at the empirical level the kind of unity it would have if its unity were supplied to it by an understanding.

> This principle can only be the following: since universal natural laws have their basis in our understanding, which prescribes them to nature (although only according to the universal concept of it as a nature), the particular empirical laws, as regards what the universal laws have left undetermined in them, must be viewed in terms of such a unity as they would have if they too had been given by an understanding (even though not ours) so as to assist our cognitive powers by making possible a system of experience in terms of particular natural laws. That does not mean we must actually assume such an understanding, for it is only reflective judgment that uses this idea as a principle, indeed a principle for reflection rather than determination; in using this principle, judgment gives a law only to itself and not to nature. (*CJ*, pp. 19–20)

(2) In reflective judgments, at least of this type, the principle is presupposed and already in play. In other words, prior to reflective judgment, nature has already been thought, that is, intended, as purposive. Now Kant says: "The attainment of an aim [intention] is always connected with the feeling of pleasure" (*CJ*, p. 27). Therefore, if in an actual judging, nature shows itself as purposive in a particular actual regard, then the attainment of such conformity, the fulfillment of an intention, is the source of a feeling of pleasure: "When we discover that two or more heterogeneous empirical laws of nature can be unified under one principle comprising them both, the discovery does in fact give rise to a quite noticeable

pleasure, frequently even admiration, even an admiration that does not cease when we have become fairly familiar with its object" (*CJ*, p. 27).

* * *

At this point, let us review and set the stage for further developments. Beginning in section III of the Introduction, Kant maps out three powers of the soul:

(1) cognitive power
(2) power of desire (= will)
(3) between these: feeling of pleasure.

In turn, there are three cognitive powers:

(1) understanding, which is legislative for cognitive powers, that is, determines the objects of cognition (= nature) through categories
(2) reason, which is legislative for the power of desire, that is, determines the will through the moral law (through freedom)
(3) between these: judgment, which can at least in some cases determine the feeling of pleasure.

It is important to see, however, that the determination of the feeling of pleasure is not the primary legislative role of judgment but is instead only a result. Kant says that judgment brings about the transition from the cognitive power to the power of desire, from nature to freedom.

Continuing our review, we recall that judgment is the power to think the particular as contained under the universal. Kant, as we said, distinguishes between determinative judgment, in cases where the universal is given, and reflective judgment, if the universal is not given but only the particular is given, for which the universal must be found. The *Critique of Judgment* is concerned primarily with reflective judgment. Indeed, it was Kant's discovery that an apriori principle is operative in such judgments which constituted his decisive breakthrough, as mentioned in his letter to Reinhold.

What is this principle? In other words, what kind of legislation (determination) is involved apriori in reflective judgment? In order to show what it is, Kant begins, not with the kind of reflective judgments that are his main concern, aesthetic judgments, but with reflective judgment in its simplest empirical form, namely, as the search for ever more universal laws of nature. Kant shows that in such judgments, there must be an apriori principle that judgment gives itself as directive for its reflection in search of the universal. The principle represents (thinks) nature as having at the empirical level the same kind of synthetic unity it has at the apriori level by virtue of the categories. But such is equivalent to saying that the principle represents nature as having at the empirical level the kind of unity it would have if its unity were supplied in the same way that it is at the apriori level or, in other words, as if its unity were supplied by an understanding.

Here Kant introduces his conceptions of purpose and purposiveness. Kant's definition is very precise but also very abstract: "Insofar as the concept of an object also contains the basis for the actualization of the object, the concept is called the purpose of the thing" (*CJ*, p. 20).

Consider the concept of a bed, which is the concept of something to sleep on. I may simply think (intend) this concept. Then the concept is just a concept, not a purpose. But I may also build a bed and make the object actual in order to have something to sleep on. Then the concept is not just a concept but is also the basis for the actualization of the object. In such a case, it is the purpose of the object, that for the sake of which something exists or is made.

In this concept of purposiveness, Kant is rethinking—deliberately or not—the Aristotelian concepts of formal cause, efficient cause, and final cause. In this regard, Kant's concept of purposiveness represents an advance beyond the reduction, fostered by the science of the time, of causality to efficient causality alone.

Kant continues: "and a thing's harmony [correspondence, accord] with that character of things which is possible only through purposes is called the purposiveness of the form" (*CJ*, p. 20). This says that whatever is of such a character that it serves a purpose is purposive. More precisely, whatever by virtue of its character *could* serve a purpose, regardless of whether it actually does or not, is purposive. Still more precisely, whatever appears as *suited* to serve a purpose (as if it were made for that purpose) can be called purposive, even if in fact no conception of purpose was involved in its fabrication. Hence it is possible to have "purposiveness without purpose." Kant concludes: "Accordingly, the principle of judgment concerning the form that things of nature have in terms of empirical laws in general is the purposiveness of nature in its diversity. In other words, through this concept we represent nature as if an understanding contained the basis of the unity of what is diverse in nature's empirical laws" (*CJ*, p. 20).

Thus for nature to appear or be thought as purposive means that it appears or is thought as having the basis of its actualization in a concept (purpose), that is, in something belonging to an understanding. In turn, this means that nature appears or is thought as having the synthetic unity it would have if its unity were supplied by an understanding. So the principle of judgment (which it gives to itself) represents (thinks) nature as purposive. If, then, in an actual judging, nature shows itself as purposive (as having this kind of unity), then this conformity (fulfillment of intention) produces a feeling of pleasure.

Let us conclude these considerations of judgment in general by noting that here we have the first connection in which judgment determines the feeling of pleasure, that is, determines feeling as pleasurable, that is, determines feeling to feel pleasure. This legislating is very different from that of the understanding. With an apriori principle of judgment, it is not a matter of concepts given to (imposed on) nature. Instead, the legislating is *to itself*: judgment gives itself a principle for its reflection and does so by representing nature as purposive. Here we begin to see more specifically—not merely in terms of a logical schema—how judgment is *between* reason and understanding. Like practical reason, its legislation is self-legislation, although it gives itself not a law for itself but only a principle to guide reflection. On the other hand, like understanding, its legislation (its apriori principle) has to do with nature, although rather than giving law to nature, it merely gives itself a principle by which to reflect on nature.

III. Aesthetic Judgment

Up to this point, we have considered only the simple empirical kind of reflective judgment. In such a judgment, nature proves to have a synthetic unity such as it would have if given this unity by an understanding. That amounts to saying: in such a judgment, nature displays a certain conformity to the understanding (to its forms of unity), or, more generally, nature or a natural object displays a certain conformity with the cognitive powers, that is, proves to be purposive with respect to the cognitive powers.

Let us now turn to the kind of reflective judgment Kant calls "aesthetic judgment." In this case, the judgment is not a matter of cognition. Rather than knowing the object, it is a matter of merely apprehending the form of the object. An aesthetic judgment occurs when this apprehended form proves to have a certain conformity with our cognitive powers and so proves to be purposive.

In somewhat different terms, the conformity to our cognitive powers entails in particular that the form of the object proves to be purposive; that is, the cognitive powers constitute the purpose to which the form conforms, with which it agrees, to which it is oriented, so as to be purposive. In terms of reflective judgment: our cognitive powers constitute the universal, and the form of the object is the particular. When we experience this agreement, when nature appears in conformity with our cognitive powers, then we experience a feeling of pleasure. Since the apriori principle by which nature is thought as purposive will be operative when the apprehended form displays such purposiveness, a feeling of pleasure will be produced.

Here we already have the primary moments of aesthetic judgment, its basic structure. Aesthetic judgment involves:

(1) apprehension of the form of the object
(2) conformity (agreement, harmony) of the form to the cognitive powers
(3) production of a feeling of pleasure.

Over and against aesthetic judgment, Kant distinguishes another kind of reflective judgment: teleological judgment. It will be the topic of Part II of the *Critique of Judgment*. We can think of the purposiveness involved in aesthetic judgment as having a subjective basis, as being a subjective purposiveness. It is a matter of the harmony of the form of the object with the cognitive powers, that is, with something in the subject, something subjective. But there can also be purpose on an objective basis, objective purposiveness. In that case, it is a matter of the harmony of the form of the object with a prior concept of the thing, a concept that prescribes the form the thing is to have, and thus harmony with an objective purpose.

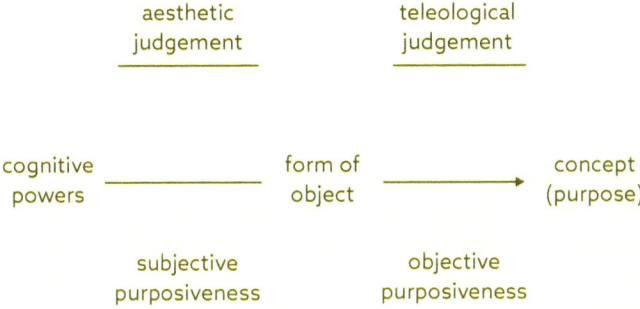

Let us look more closely at aesthetic judgment. Such a judgment has to do only with the form of the object and not at all with what is material in the object as it appears. In other words, it does not have to do with mere sensation, with sensory content. Aesthetic judgment disregards the material for the sake of the pure form. Furthermore, aesthetic judgment has to do with the object only as apprehended, the way something is apprehended in being merely intuited. It has to do only with the apprehended or intuitive form.

Kant contrasts this with the case in which, rather than being merely apprehended, the object is *known*, cognized. Cognition involves both intuition and concept: intuition through which objects are given and concepts through which they are thought. For example, I see an object in intuition and then, in an act of recognition, I refer that seen object to the concept "tree." Then I know (as I say): This thing is a tree. So, in general, cognition involves both intuition and concept and occurs through the referral of the intuition to the concept. In aesthetic judgment, by contrast, there is no cognition of the object—not even of its form. That means the apprehended form of the object is *not* referred to a concept. So the way the form is taken up in aesthetic judgment will be different from referral to (subsumption under) a concept.

Thus there is something almost paradoxical about aesthetic judgment. On the one hand, it involves no cognition of its object; it "contributes nothing to the cognition of its objects" (*CJ*, p. 35). Yet, on the other hand, in aesthetic judgment, what is involved is conformity of the object to the cognitive powers.

Let us turn now to the key paragraph (*CJ*, pp. 29–30, section VII of the Introduction), which begins: "When pleasure is connected with the mere apprehension (*apprehensio*) of the form of an object of intuition and we do not refer the apprehension to a concept so as to give rise to determinate cognition . . ." Here Kant is laying out the moments of aesthetic apprehension:

(1) apprehension of the form of an object
(2) pleasure connected with this apprehension
(3) but without any cognition; the apprehension is not referred to a concept.

The passage continues: "then we refer the representation not to the object but solely to the subject . . ." That means the representation, the apprehended form, is not used for cognition of the object. Instead, it is taken solely in its relation to the subject, as purposive with respect to the subject, as displaying a certain conformity to the subject's cognitive powers.

Kant goes on: "and the pleasure cannot express anything other than the object's being commensurate with the cognitive powers that are, and insofar as they are, brought into play when we judge subjectively, and hence the pleasure expresses merely a subjective formal purposiveness of the object." This says that the pleasure expresses—is produced as a result of—the conformity of the object—its pure form—to the cognitive powers, that is, its subjective purposiveness. Note that in reflective judgment, the cognitive powers are not simply, inactively, dormantly there but rather are *in play*.

Let us consider more precisely the apprehension of the form of the object. What is the character of this apprehension? Up to now, it has seemed to be merely a matter of intuition. Certainly, it is an act taking place at the level of intuition and, in particular, prior to any thought, any concept, indeed without even being oriented toward a concept to which it might subsequently be referred. Yet this apprehension, unlike sheer sense intuition, is not merely receptive, for rather than intuiting the object, it apprehends only the form. That is, in and through this apprehension, the form becomes detached from the object itself, separated from the sensory content.

Such apprehension requires imagination. Thus the passage continues by referring to the "apprehension of forms by the imagination" or, to translate more literally, the apprehension takes the forms up *into* the imagination [*in die Einbildungskraft*]. Note that imagination is preeminently the intermediate power; it mixes receptivity and activity (spontaneity), as, for instance, in a simple phantasy image.

What then happens once the forms are taken up in this way? The passage continues: "For this apprehension of forms by the imagination could never occur if reflective judgment did not compare them, even if unintentionally, at least with its ability in general to refer intuitions to concepts." So once the forms are apprehended, they are compared to the power by which intuitions are referred to concepts. But that power, the power of concepts, is primarily the understanding. Thus once the forms are taken up into imagination, these forms (held in imagination) are compared to the understanding. In other words, imagination (as holding these forms) is referred to the understanding.

Accordingly, the passage continues: "If in this comparison the imagination (as the power of a priori intuitions [here Kant expresses the mixed, receptive-active character of the imagination]) is, through a given representation, unintentionally set into accord [harmony] with the understanding (as the power of concepts), and thereby a feeling of pleasure is aroused, then the object must be regarded as purposive for the reflective judgment." This shows more clearly the character of the accord at the center of aesthetic judgment. In this judgment, the form taken up into imagination proves such that imagination is thereby (that is, by holding this form) set in accord with the understanding. And when there is such accord between imagination and understanding, a feeling of pleasure is aroused. For, the object—by virtue of having such form—will have proved to conform to our cognitive powers.

As the passage continues, Kant makes several further points.

(1) Aesthetic judgment is not based on any concept and does not produce a concept. In different terms, aesthetic judgment is always singular. The singular form of this singular object proves to set imagination in harmony with the understanding. But there is no cognition, no concept under which the singular is subsumed.

(2) Because only the form of the object is involved and not the sensory material, which would vary from one individual subject to another, an aesthetic judgment, despite its singularity, has a certain universality. That is, the judgment holds—presumptively at least—for everyone who judges this object. The issue of the universality of aesthetic judgment is of major concern to Kant, and he will approach it from several different perspectives. Here we have only a first indication.

(3) When the form of the object sets imagination in accord with the understanding and arouses a feeling of pleasure, then the object is said to be beautiful. The ability to judge with regard to beautiful objects is called "taste." So judgments with regard to beauty can be called "judgments of taste."

(4) Yet not all aesthetic judgments are judgments of taste. Kant says that, just as there can be a purposiveness of the object with respect to the subject's powers, that is, the purposiveness involved in judgments of taste, there can also be a purposiveness of the subject with respect to the object. This is the kind of purposiveness that defines the sublime. Thus, along with judgments of taste, there are also judgments of the sublime. These are the two kinds of aesthetic judgments.

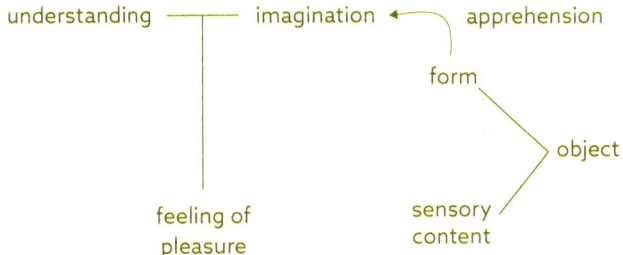

There is an additional passage in section VII of the Introduction we need to consider, since it clarifies the universality and the character of the accord between understanding and imagination occurring in judgments of taste: "In the same way, someone who feels pleasure in the mere reflection on the form of an object, without any concern about a concept, rightly lays claim to everyone's assent, even though this judgment is empirical and singular. For the basis of this pleasure is found in the universal, although subjective, condition of reflective judgments, namely, the purposive agreement [*Übereinstimmung*] of an object (whether a product of nature or of art) with the mutual relation of the cognitive powers (imagination and understanding) that are required for every empirical cognition" (*CJ*, p. 31).

Thus the purposive agreement of the object is its agreement with the mutual relation between imagination and understanding, as they are related in all empirical cognition. (Here is the first of the affinities or proximities between aesthetic judgment and cognition.) More specifically, in the judgment of taste, the imagination takes up the form of the object into itself, and thereby that form is set into a relation of agreement with the understanding. Imagination takes the form up into the very same relation imagination and understanding must have in cognition, although in the judgment of taste there is no cognition. In other words, imagination and understanding are set in this relation in such a way that what occurs is not cognition but merely *play* between them. Indirectly, it is the form (as held by imagination) that brings about the relating of understanding and imagination.

We could say, then, that apprehended form proves harmonious with what is universal in the subject (not just *is* universal—shared by all—but is the very *source* of universality). This is what the passage calls "the universal although subjective condition of reflective judgment." It is on account of this subjectively universal condition that the singular and empirical aesthetic judgment has its proper universality.

IV. Analytic of the Beautiful

This Analytic takes as its point of departure the general analysis of the judgment of taste. Especially in the first part of the Analytic, Kant elaborates that earlier analysis and draws out certain consequences.

To understand the elaboration, we need to formulate some questions, ones remaining unanswered by the analysis as presented in the Introduction.

(1) What is the more specific character of the relation assumed between imagination and understanding in the judgment of taste? And what is the character of the agreement of form with the imagination and understanding in their relation?
(2) How is this relation itself "experienced"? That is, how are we aware of it? To what power is it revealed?
(3) What is the relation between this "experience" that imagination and understanding are so related and the production of pleasure occurring in the judgment of taste?

(1) We have seen that in judgments of taste, imagination and understanding are set into a harmonious relation. It is the same relation as the one required for cognition. It is the same relation imagination and understanding *would* have in cognition, even though in aesthetic judgment there is no cognition. In the judgment of taste, they must be set in this relation in a different way, namely, as play. Kant already followed up this theme: "The cognitive powers, which are set into play by this representation, are thereby in a free play, because no determinate concept restricts them to a particular rule of cognition" (*CJ*, p. 62). So when the form (representation) is taken up into imagination, the cognitive powers (imagination and understanding) are set into a relation of *free* play. Why? —Because there is no concept at work, no cognition to which their relation would be bound, harnessed. We could say that rather than the form (in imagination) being brought under a concept (of understanding), so that the understanding would rule over the imagination, there is free play between the two powers, a freeing, releasing, of the imagination from the yoke of the understanding.

In the first Introduction Kant wrote, he refers to the "harmonious play of the two cognitive powers involved in judgment: imagination and understanding" (*CJ*, p. 413) and says that the distinctive power of each is such that "they further each other," that is, transport, carry, promote each other. Kant also says in the second Introduction that the play of imagination and understanding is "quickened [*beleben*] by their reciprocal harmony [*Zusammenstimmung*: literally, voicing together]" (*CJ*, p. 63), that is, enlivened, animated, by it. We could then say that in the judgment of taste, the relation between imagination and understanding is such that in their free play, they prove to be harmonious, to operate together as they would in cognition, yet they do so freely, unintentionally, without cognition, and in addition their harmonious operation enlivens their free play, whereby each furthers the other.

But in what sense is the form accordant, in agreement, with the play of understanding and imagination? What is the character of this accord, this agreement? The form agrees with the play in that it evokes the play, sets the reciprocal relating going, initiates the motility, precisely as it is taken up into imagination. Because of the active character of understanding, it can be regarded as energizing the play in contrast to the more (but not entirely) passive character of imagination as it holds the form.

(2) How is this harmonious free play "experienced" or presented to us? How are we aware of it? To what mental state or power is it revealed? Kant says: "Hence the mental state in this representation must be a feeling of the free play of the representational powers in connection with the given representation and directed to cognition in general" (*CJ*, p. 62). This says that the harmony, the harmonious free play, is *felt*. The mental state to which it is disclosed is feeling. This is corroborated by another passage: "Indeed, the judgment is called aesthetic precisely because the basis determining it is not a concept but the feeling (of the inner sense) of that accordance in the play of the mental powers insofar as it can only be sensed" (*CJ*, p. 75). Kant's last word in this quotation is *empfunden*, which could also be translated as "felt." It should be understood in terms of what in Greek is called αἴσθησις.

Or again, Kant says about the reference to the feeling of pleasure: "This reference designates nothing whatever in the object, but here the subject feels itself as it is affected by the representation" (*CJ*, p. 44).

(3) What is the relation between this feeling of the harmonious free play and the production of pleasure? Kant in effect identifies this feeling with the one of pleasure produced in the judgment of taste. Kant refers to the pleasure in an aesthetic judgment and then writes: "The very consciousness of a merely formal purposiveness in the play of the subject's cognitive powers, accompanying a representation by which an object is given, is that pleasure" (*CJ*, p. 68). Yet he also says that the aesthetic judging "precedes the pleasure in the object and is the basis of this pleasure, one taken in the harmony of the cognitive powers" (*CJ*, p. 62).

Analytic of the Beautiful | 207

Thus we do not judge or feel that there is harmonious free play *because* we feel pleasure; it is the reverse: we feel pleasure because we feel the harmonious free play. More generally, in this way we experience the actual purposiveness of nature, its purposiveness—in this singular instance—with respect to our cognitive powers. Thus the apriori principle of judgment is fulfilled (that is, the thought of nature as purposive), and in this experience we feel pleasure.

A still more precise formulation is suggested by a phrase Kant uses later. The context is one in which he again refers to a representation, an apprehended form, that engenders a harmonious free play of imagination and understanding. In such a case, we come "to feel [or: sense] the representational state [the mental state of harmonious free play] with pleasure" (*CJ*, p. 159). So, strictly speaking, there is not first a feeling of the harmony and then consequently, as a product, a feeling of pleasure. Rather, when the harmony of the free play is felt, it is felt with pleasure. Thus, the pleasure refers not to the object of the feeling but to its "quality." The object of the feeling is the harmonious free play of imagination and understanding.

Before we look at the broader consequences of Kant's analysis of the judgment of taste, let us note two further points.

(1) Kant says that the harmony between the imagination and the understanding enlivens (quickens) their free play, promotes its continuation. Kant also relates this character (or at least something very similar) to the pleasure with which one feels the harmonious free play. The pleasure has "an inner causality." The pleasure "does have a causality in itself, namely, to keep us in the state of having the representation itself, to keep the cognitive powers engaged in their exercise without any further aim. We linger in our contemplation of the beautiful, because this contemplation reinforces and reproduces itself" (*CJ*, p. 68).

(2) What does the judgment of taste, with this elaborate structure, have to do with reflective judgment as defined in the Introduction? How is the judgment of taste a reflective judgment, one in which the particular is subsumed under a universal without the universal being given in advance?

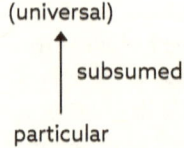

In a judgment of taste, the (singular) form of the object corresponds to the particular. This form (the particular) is referred to the subject's powers; that is, the apprehension of the form elicits a feeling of the harmony of these powers. In other words, the affective apprehension of the form lets it show its purposiveness with respect to the subject's powers.

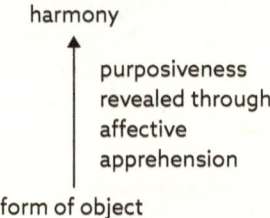

So the referral or subsumption to a universal here becomes felt purposiveness with respect to the subject's powers. Yet how does this amount to a referral to a universal? The crucial point is that for the understanding and imagination to be in harmonious relation means that they are in the same relation they would have in cognition, yet without cognition taking place. But this relation is that from which all universality arises. That is to say, it is a universality in the subject, a subjective universality or, rather, the subjective source, the origin, of universality.

* * *

Let us consider an example. In the Preface to the first edition of the *Critique of Pure Reason*, Kant addresses the question of clarity and of the reader's legitimate demand for clarity. Kant distinguishes between discursive or logical clarity (through concepts) and intuitive or aesthetic clarity (through examples and other concrete illustrations). He says he has sufficiently provided the first kind of clarity. But to have provided the second kind would have enlarged the book too much. So there are indeed almost no examples in the first *Critique*.

In the *Critique of Judgment*, examples are not nearly as lacking. There is even a section (§14) entitled "Elucidation by examples." Yet even here, although Kant mentions a few concrete examples (tone of a violin, colonnades around magnificent buildings), he simply mentions them without any substantial explanation or concrete development. So, taking some distance from Kant's text, let me offer an example.

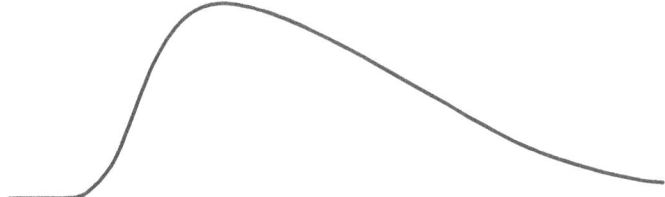

Picture yourself, at dusk, looking at the contour of a mountain. You are looking toward the west. The sun has set behind the mountain. In the dim light, little can be seen distinctly on the slopes, whereas the contour of the mountain, the line it traces against the sky, is all the more conspicuous.

Suppose, then, that you focus on this contour, not just passively perceiving it, but actively engaging your vision with it, looking at it in something like the way you would immerse yourself visually in a painting: one of Monet's Water Lilies or one of the drip paintings of Jackson Pollock. Such a vision is not a mere seeing but rather is an imagining. It is an imagining that is not, like phantasy, set apart from perception but one that animates perceptual vision. It both engages vision with what is seen and simultaneously detaches it so that it can trace and retrace the visible in ever varying ways.

Suppose, then, that you *free* your imagination in this way as you regard the contour of the mountain. Suppose you actively engage your vision with the curving line and let your vision, sensitive to the varying curvature, run back and forth along the contour of the mountain as it is silhouetted against the darkening sky. Perhaps then you will be drawn into the scene, no longer just observing from a distance but in a sense absorbed in it—even as your imagination continues playfully tracing and retracing this figure, the form your imagination has taken up.

This being drawn into the scene might be described by saying that one no longer merely *sees* the contour of the mountain but has a *feeling* for it; the scene has aroused within us a certain affection linked to our imaginative vision. It would not be amiss to describe this feeling as pleasant, although it is a pleasure quite different from that which comes from the satisfying of desires or appetites. Both the feeling and the pleasure it brings are *contemplative.*

Through this affective, imaginative vision, we *understand* something about the scene. We are given something to understand, just as an imaginative engagement with a painting yields something to understand. But such understanding has little to do with knowing, with the production of knowledge. There is perhaps no better indication of this than the experience—when standing before a beautiful natural sight such as the mountain contour or before a painting—that speech is inhibited by such sights. Indeed, the more we engage ourselves imaginatively and understandingly in the sight, the less inclined we are to venture to say what we see. Such a sight entices us into the most active exercise of imagination and understanding and yet demands from us silence.

We linger in the contemplation of something beautiful. We are drawn along in our playful contemplation, and it is as if there were a mutation of time itself, a relief from the incessant rush from one moment to the next. Then also it may seem marvelous that this figure drawn in nature, drawn by nature, offers itself to us this way. It may seem marvelous that it is drawn in such a way that it can engage our imagination, arouse our feelings, and yield something to understand. It is as if it had been drawn in just the right way, with our subjective powers in view, tailored to them—drawn, as we say, on purpose and not simply as a result of the causal mechanism of nature. It is as if—to paraphrase Kant as quoted earlier—this beautiful thing tells us we humans belong to nature.

* * *

Our concern has been with Kant's analysis of judgment regarding the beautiful, that is, judgment of taste. We have distinguished three moments that constitute the whole of such judgment. This whole can be regarded as an *articulated structure* or as an *event* in which beauty comes to light. Let us now consider these moments once again in order to see how they are related so as to constitute this whole.

There is, first, the apprehension of the form of the object. It is the object that is to be judged beautiful. If, in the case of a particular object, the structure proves to be entirely intact, if the event of judging actually, positively occurs, then the object will be judged beautiful. The apprehension detaches the form from the object; thus, it must be carried out, not by mere intuition, but by imagination. As the form is apprehended, it is *taken up into imagination* and is held by, retained within, imagination. From this point on, the judgment of taste has nothing to do with the object but only with the form; the judgment is related to the object only in that it is the object that is to be declared beautiful. But even then beauty is not attributed to the object itself: if one says "The object *is* beautiful," the meaning of the "is" has been displaced from the usual sense. Nothing simply *is* beautiful. Here, then, there emerges a different meaning of being.

The form is referred to our cognitive powers, that is, to understanding; if the object is indeed one that will be judged beautiful, there will be agreement of the imagination with understanding, that is, free play between them, free play evoked by the form that is held by imagination. In playing freely, they will voice together, sing together. Their harmony quickens, enlivens, their play.

But what exactly is this *free* play? What is here the sense of freedom? What happens in the play? Are there constraints? Two points bear on these questions. First, Kant writes: "The judging person feels completely *free* as regards the liking he accords the object" (*CJ*, p. 54). Thus, the freedom is not just within the connection between imagination and understanding; rather, it is a freedom that pertains to the entire event and that is felt by the one judging. Kant continues: "Hence a person will talk about the beautiful as if beauty were a characteristic of the object ... even though in fact the judgment is only aesthetic and refers the object's presentation merely to the subject." Still more directly: "such judgments do not deal with the object at all" (*CJ*, p. 58). Therefore, the freedom is that of the subject as such; it is a freedom from any constraints imposed by the object, for, once the form is detached, the event of judgment goes its way independent of the object.

The second point concerns a difficult but important question: although the play of imagination and understanding is free of the object, is there some other constraint? There is a passage in which, referring to the unity in the relation of the cognitive powers, Kant says that the sensation has the effect of "quickening the two powers (imagination and understanding) to an activity that is indeterminate but, as a result of the prompting of the given presentation, is nonetheless accordant: the activity required for cognition in general" (*CJ*, p. 63). Consequently, in the play, the relation between imagination and understanding must still conform (be "accordant") to the relation they have in cognition in general. In other words, imagination and understanding cannot be related in just any way but only in the activity in which imagination holds the form and understanding unifies its moments. This is accordant with the activity that goes on in cognition; in the judgment of taste, however, it is presumably an activity that can go on and on in ever different configurations, that is, in play.

The third moment in the judgment of taste is feeling. The harmonious play is *felt*, is experienced through feeling, through feeling that is pleasurable. It is through feeling that we are aware of the free play, that it is disclosed to us; it is the free play that is the object of the feeling—that is felt—and not the pleasure. Kant stresses that the pleasure is not the basis of the judgment, but conversely, we feel pleasure because we feel the free play.

There are two further observations regarding feeling that need to be mentioned. First, in describing the feeling that belongs to the judgment of taste, Kant refers to it as a *feeling of oneself*. This connection is almost self-evident: the feeling in the judgment of taste is a feeling of one's own imagination in its play with one's own understanding. It is a feeling that is not shared with others, that is, it is singular; and it is not directed beyond oneself, is not a feeling of anything outside oneself but is subjective. Thus, it is a feeling that is strictly and exclusively a feeling of oneself. One could even say it is a feeling that provides a certain self-awareness.

The second observation concerns Kant's description of this feeling as *feeling of life*. In the *Metaphysical Foundations of Natural Science* (Indianapolis: Bobbs-Merrill, 1970, p. 105), Kant writes: "Life means the capacity of a substance to determine itself to act from an internal principle." In the case of humans, this self-determination consists in determining oneself—one's actions—in accord with the moral law. But life also involves the capacity to act in the sensible world, to carry out in the sensible world, which is governed by efficient causality, what is prescribed by reason in its free self-determination. So, the feeling of life is an awareness of oneself as, on the one hand, a free, self-determining being and, on the other hand, capable of acting, of bringing about effects in the sensible world.

Kant's account of the judgment of taste has a number of very significant consequences. These are woven into the fabric of the Analytic of the Beautiful, woven in the sense that Kant does not present them in a linear fashion but rather shuttles back to each in various different connections. This manner of composition accounts, at least in part, for the complexity of the text but also for its richness. I will discuss five consequences.

(1) Kant distinguishes between logical judgment and aesthetic judgment, specifically, the judgment of taste. A logical judgment proceeds by way of concepts. We might say, for example, that "the tree is green," thereby subsuming the particular tree under the concept "green." In this judgment the quality "green" is actually attributed to the tree; it is judged to be a real property of this object. On the other hand, in an aesthetic judgment, all that counts is whether the form of the object evokes a play of imagination and understanding, which, in turn, is felt with pleasure. But whether it does so, whether an event of such aesthetic judgment takes place, says nothing about the object itself; it does not ascribe to the object any property, does not predicate beauty of it. Thus, a judgment of taste "does not deal with the object at all" (*CJ*, p. 58). Again: "apart from a reference to the subject's feeling, beauty is nothing by itself" (*CJ*, p. 63). Thus, when we judge that an object is beautiful, we do not bring it under a *concept*. As far as judgment of taste is concerned, there is no concept of beauty. Such judgments are completely outside the entire domain of concepts.

Since no concept is involved in the judgment of taste, such judgments are singular. Kant writes: "In their logical quantity all judgments of taste are *singular* judgments. For since I must hold the object directly up to my feeling of pleasure and displeasure, but without using concepts, these judgments cannot have the quantity that judgments with objective general validity have." Kant goes on to say that once we have made a judgment of taste, we can compare it to other such judgments and "convert the singular presentation of the object into a concept . . . and so arrive at a universal judgment" (*CJ*, p. 59). If, for example, we judge a rose to be beautiful, we may then compare this judgment with others and thereby form the universal judgment "Roses in general are beautiful." But then the judgment is not solely aesthetic; it is a logical judgment based on aesthetic judgments.

(2) The judgment of taste involves purposiveness and, specifically, purposiveness without purpose. Kant explains what he means by purpose: "Now insofar as a purpose as such is something the concept of which can be regarded as the basis of the possibility of the object itself, presenting objective purposiveness in a thing presupposes the concept of the thing, i.e., *what sort* of thing it is [meant] to be" (*CJ*, p. 74). So, the purpose of a thing is the same as its concept, the concept of what it is meant to be. A thing is purposive if it is governed by this purpose. For example, a tree is purposive if it is governed by the concept of what a tree is meant to be, if, for instance, its growth aims at realizing this purpose, at becoming a mature tree. Since, on the other hand, the judgment of taste involves no concept, no purpose is operative in it but only purposiveness, which Kant describes as follows: "If the form of the object unintentionally evokes harmony of imagination and understanding (and so a feeling of pleasure), then the object must thereupon be regarded as purposive for the reflective power of judgment" (*CJ*, p. 30). Again: "And since this harmony of the object with the powers of the subject is contingent [*zufällig*], it brings about the presentation of a purposiveness of the object with regard to the subject's cognitive power" (*CJ*, p. 30). Thus, if the referral of the form to the cognitive powers is unintentional, contingent, accidental, then the form is not intrinsically directed to the harmony of the cognitive powers *as* a purpose; *and yet*, since the form brings about this harmony *as if* it were directed at it, the form is purposive—though without purpose. In a broader perspective, it is as though nature proved to correspond to our cognitive powers even though there is no actual connection between nature and those powers.

(3) The judgment of taste is devoid of interest, is disinterested.

In order to see what this consequence means, we need to begin with the general concept of "liking." Kant's term is *Wohlgefallen*. A common German expression runs: *Das gefällt mir*, "I like that," or, more literally, "that pleases me," "that is pleasing to me." So liking is a positive affective comportment to an object. But liking must be kept distinct from pleasure and the feeling of pleasure.

An interest is a certain kind of liking: "Interest is what we call the liking we connect with the representation of the existence of an object" (*CJ*, p. 45). Now, a judgment of taste is precisely *not* this kind of liking. That is, it involves no interest; it is disinterested. The beautiful, as correlate of a judgment of taste, is an object of disinterested liking. Kant's other term for such liking is contemplation (*Betrachtung*).

Kant explains the disinterested character of the judgment of taste as follows. Suppose someone asks me whether I consider something beautiful: "All that person wants to know is whether my mere representation of the object is accompanied by a liking, no matter how indifferent I may be regarding the existence of the object of this representation. We can easily see that, in order for me to say an object is beautiful, and to prove that I have taste, what matters is what I do with this representation within myself and not the way I depend on the existence of the object" (*CJ*, p. 46).

So all that counts with respect to beauty is whether, in merely apprehending the form of the object, I feel with pleasure an ensuing harmonious free play of imagination and understanding. This feeling is what, in turn, provides the basis for my liking the object. In other words, because it engenders such feeling, the object is pleasing to me. But such judgment is indifferent, disinterested, as regards the existence of the object. That is, the judgment of taste involves a certain *epoché* of the existence of the object. This can also be seen in the character of the imaginative apprehension; it detaches the form from the object, takes it up into itself, and from that point on has no further involvement with the object.

Kant contrasts the disinterested liking for the beautiful with two other forms of liking, having to do respectively with the agreeable and the good. Let us begin with the liking for the agreeable (*angenehm*, pleasant, pleasing). The agreeable is "that in sensation which pleases the senses" (*CJ*, p. 47). So this is a liking oriented to gratification of the senses, the pleasures of the senses. Such liking is a matter of interest; it is connected with the *existence* of the object. Kant explains: "That a judgment by which I declare an object to be agreeable expresses an interest in that object is already obvious from the fact that, by means of sensation, the judgment arouses a desire for objects of such a kind, so that the liking presupposes something other than my mere judgment about the object [as in the case of judgments of taste]: it presupposes that I have referred the existence of the object to my state insofar as this state is affected by such an object" (*CJ*, p. 48).

So, whereas in judgments of taste it is the mere form, the mere shining (Hegel), of the object that counts, the liking for the agreeable or pleasurable awakens a desire for the existent object. I want not merely to contemplate its appearance but, for instance, to consume it, which accounts for the interest in its existence. I could contemplate a picture of it, but if I am to eat it, the object itself must be there, must exist.

The second contrast is with the liking for the good. Kant writes: "The good always contains the concept of a purpose, consequently a relation of reason to (at least a possible) volition, and hence contains a liking for the existence of an object or action. In other words, it contains some interest or other" (*CJ*, p. 48–49). This concept of the good can be formulated at two levels. The first is the ordinary, utilitarian level. According to this conception, for something to be judged good, it must have a purpose and must be such that it fulfills or could fulfill this purpose. For example, to judge that something is a good knife means that it is in accord with the concept of knife, that it can realize the purpose of a knife, namely, to cut. Yet there is also the ethical level. Here it is also a matter of purpose, specifically, of *willing* to fulfill this purpose through action. But in order for this willing (and the action that might follow from it) to be good, the purpose must be one that is in accord with the moral law and hence with reason. At both levels a concept or purpose is involved, and there is interest (liking) for the existence of the thing or action in accord with the concept of purpose. Then Kant contrasts such things with those that are said to be beautiful. Here we have one of the few passages in which Kant provides examples: "Flowers, free designs, lines aimlessly intertwined and called foliage, signify nothing, depend on no determinate concept, and yet we like them [better translation: they please]" (*CJ*, p. 49).

(4) The fourth consequence is that the beautiful is the object of a universal liking.

Kant regards this consequence as entailed by the first one, the disinterested character of the judgment of taste. The point is that if in one's liking there is no interest involved, no sense-inclination, no desire for the object, then there is no merely *private* condition underlying the liking. So the beautiful object can be expected to be liked by everyone:

> For if a person likes something and is conscious that he himself does so without any interest, then he cannot help judging that it must contain a basis for being liked which holds for everyone. He must believe he is justified in requiring a similar liking from everyone, because he cannot discover, underlying his liking, any private conditions on which only he might be dependent. Consequently, he must regard it as based on what he can presuppose in everyone else as well. He cannot discover such private conditions, because his liking is not based on any inclination or on any other considered interest whatever; rather, the judging person feels completely *free* as regards the liking he accords the object. (*CJ*, pp. 53–54)

Because our judgment that something is beautiful is not simply based on some private condition such that it could be beautiful for one person and not for another, we tend to speak of beauty as if it were a characteristic of the object, even though there is no cognition and no cognitive attribution of properties to the object. So a judgment of taste is universal, in that one may assume it is valid for everyone. But "this universality cannot arise from concepts" (*CJ*, p. 54). Kant calls it a "subjective" or "aesthetic" universality.

Thus Kant stresses that there is no general rule by which to judge whether things are beautiful. In this sense, there can be no science or metaphysics of the beautiful. Here Kant breaks with German aesthetics (Baumgarten) just as, with his insistence on universality, he breaks with the opposite school, the British position as represented by Edmund Burke.

Rather than admitting a general rule, a judgment of taste requires us to bring the singular thing before our own eyes: "We want to submit the object to our own eyes, just as if our liking of it depended on that sensation. And yet, if we then call the object beautiful, we believe we have a universal voice and lay claim to the agreement of everyone, whereas any private sensation would decide solely for the observer himself and his liking" (*CJ*, pp. 59–60).

What is the basis of this subjective universality? Granted the negative basis, namely, that no merely private condition is involved, what is its positive basis? Kant refers to this basis as "the universal communicability of the mental state" (*CJ*, p. 61) involved in judgments of taste. Yet Kant says that nothing can be communicable universally except cognition or a representation related to cognition: "If we are to think that the judgment about this universal communicability of the representation has a merely subjective determining basis, that is, one which does not involve a concept of the object, then this basis can be nothing other than the mental state we find in the relation between the representational powers [imagination and understanding] insofar as they refer a given representation to cognition in general" (*CJ*, pp. 61–62).

Here again we touch on the peculiar affinity or proximity of the judgment of taste to cognition, even though they remain rigorously distinguished. The basis for the universality is the mental state in which imagination and understanding are, in their free play, related as they would be in cognition. That is what Kant means here by cognition in general: imagination and understanding related not so as to produce any determinate cognition, but the way they would be related in any cognition, although they are now in free play. Kant makes this especially clear:

> But the way of representing in a judgment of taste is to have subjective universal communicability without presupposing a determinate concept; hence this subjective universal communicability can be nothing but that of our mental state when imagination and understanding are in free play (insofar as they harmonize with each other as required by cognition in general). For we are conscious that this subjective relation suitable for cognition in general must hold just as much for everyone and hence be just as universally communicable as any determinate cognition, since cognition always rests on that relation as its subjective condition. (*CJ*, p. 62)

So the condition that makes the judgment of taste universal subjectively is the "cognitive-like" relation between imagination and understanding. This relation, as "cognitive-like," is nothing merely private but rather is universal.

(5) The fifth consequence is that the judgment of taste is independent of charm and emotion.

Kant is emphatic: "Any taste remains barbaric if its liking requires that charms and emotions be mingled in, let alone if it makes these the standard of its approval" (*CJ*, p. 69). This follows from the thesis that the determining basis of the judgment of taste is "solely the purposiveness of the form" (*CJ*, p. 69). Both charm and emotion are bound up with the mere sensuous and material aspect of an object, hence they, and especially charm, pertain to the agreeable, not the beautiful. Nevertheless, it will turn out that emotion, although it has no pertinence for beauty, is significant for the sublime.

In §14, Kant provides a classification of the formal elements that pertain to beauty, and in relation to this classification he introduces, for the first time in the *Critique of Judgment*, a discussion of the arts. In fact, this is a first, preliminary, classificatory schema of the arts; the preliminary character is most evident in that poetry as such is omitted.

form	determination of form	arts
shape	design (*Zeichnung*)	painting
		sculpture
or		architecture
play	composition	
of shapes		mimetic art (drama?) and dance
of sensations (in time)		music

Throughout this discussion, Kant stresses that the form—and the form alone—is the basis of beauty. He insists that even tones and colors cannot as such be beautiful. At best we can say that a pure, simple color is beautiful, but only on account of its uniformity, its form in abstraction from the quality of its sensations. All that such material elements, even abstracted from their materiality, can contribute to beauty is to accent the form. The agreeableness that they add is in no way constitutive of the beautiful. What counts is the form—either as design (drawing) or as composition. Everything outside the form is accessory:

> The charm of colors or of the agreeable tone of an instrument may be added, but it is the design in the first case and the composition in the second that constitute the proper object of a pure judgment of taste; that the purity of the colors and of the tones, or for that matter their variety and contrast, seem to contribute to the beauty does not mean that, because they themselves are agreeable, they furnish us, as it were, with a supplement to, and one of the same kind as, our liking for the form. For all they do is make the form intuitable more precisely, determinately, and completely, while they also enliven the representation by means of their charm by arousing and sustaining the attention we direct toward the object itself. (*CJ*, p. 72)

* * *

Having worked through the five major consequences of Kant's analysis of the judgment of taste (non-conceptuality, purposiveness, disinterestedness, universality, independence of charm and emotion), let us now consider a final issue in the Analytic of the Beautiful.

In distinguishing the judgment of taste from other kinds of liking, Kant gives some examples. In a passage already cited, he writes: "Flowers, free designs, lines aimlessly intertwined and called foliage signify nothing, depend on no determinate concept, and yet we like them." In a judgment of taste, these things would be judged beautiful. And yet—we cannot but ask—are such things the only ones that are beautiful? Is the extent of the beautiful not here so severely restricted that beauty could not be ascribed even, for instance, to works of art? This apparent limitation points ahead to the final development in the Analytic of the Beautiful, which is a kind of shift or reorientation, one that will prove decisive for the later discussions of art and even of nature.

Through much of the Analytic, a primary concern is to distinguish the pure form of the object, which is all that counts for beauty, from other aspects, namely, the sensory content (the merely agreeable) and the concept of the object (what the object ought to be, its "good," its perfection). Judgments determined solely by form Kant calls "pure" judgments of taste. If, on the other hand, a judgment of taste is connected to a judgment about the agreeable or the good, then it would be contaminated. As the Analytic proceeds, Kant continues to insist on the separation between the beautiful and the merely agreeable. Nevertheless, once purely formal beauty has been distinguished, he begins to refer to certain cases in which the purely formal aspect is mixed with a conceptual aspect. That is, he refers to certain non-pure judgments of taste. This transition is clearly marked in the text, at the beginning of §16: "There are two kinds of beauty: free beauty (*pulchritudo vaga*) [*vagus*: wandering, unsettled, vague] and merely accessory [adherent, dependent] beauty (*pulchritudo adhaerens*). Free beauty does not presuppose a concept of what the object is meant to be. Accessory beauty does presuppose such a concept as well as the perfection of the object in terms of that concept" (*CJ*, p. 76).

Kant adds: "When we judge free beauty (according to sheer form), then our judgment of taste is pure" (*CJ*, p. 77). This is to be contrasted with judgments in which we judge the object both with respect to form and also with respect to its perfection, its matching up to its concept.

This terminology (free beauty and pure judgment versus accessory beauty and non-pure judgment) seems to posit a clear priority. It suggests that free beauty and pure judgment have priority over the other, derivative types. But we begin to wonder about this supposed priority if we consider the examples (*CJ*, pp. 76–77) Kant provides of each type of beauty. Free beauties are flowers, birds, crustaceans, designs à la grecque, foliage on borders or wallpaper, music without words. Here no concept of what the object is is involved. We merely contemplate the shape (*Gestalt*), and, in this, "imagination is playing." Accessory beauties are the beauty of a human being, of a horse, of a building (church, palace, etc.).

The point is that the priority of free beauty and pure judgment is merely logical. It is a logically distinct type of representation. In fact, accessory beauty (mixed judgment) will be more prominent and even primary from here on in the *Critique of Judgment*. Indeed, Kant grants that there is a gain in moving from pure to mixed judgments: "It is true that taste gains by such a connection of aesthetic with intellectual liking, for it becomes fixed . . ." (*CJ*, p. 78). He goes on to write of "uniting taste with reason, . . . a union that enables us to use the beautiful as an instrument for our aim regarding the good" (*CJ*, p. 78). He says finally: "It is the complete power of representation that gains when the two states of mind harmonize" (*CJ*, p. 78).

Thus there is a structural shift, a displacement of the center:

previously:

```
mere sensory ──── formal ──── conceptual
                     ✕
                     │
                 judgement
                  of taste
```

now:

```
mere sensory ──── formal ──────────── conceptual
                 = free           accessory
                 beauty            beauty
                   │                  ✕
                   │                  │
            pure judgement    mixed judgement
               of taste           of taste
```

Kant's discussion of the *ideal* of beauty shows that in this case, it is precisely the mixed rather than the pure judgment of taste that has priority. On the one hand, Kant continues to insist on differentiating beauty from the conceptual. So he declares that there can be no rule that would allow us to determine by means of concepts what is beautiful. On the other hand, the ideal of the beautiful (a highest example, exemplary beauty) is *not* independent of concepts. We might expect it would be free beauties corresponding to pure judgments of taste that would admit such an ideal. And yet, it is not so: "We must be careful to note that if we are to seek an ideal of beauty, then beauty must be fixed rather than vague, fixed by a concept of objective purposiveness. Hence this beauty must belong not to the object of an entirely pure judgment of taste but to the object of a partly intellectual one" (*CJ*, p. 80).

So only accessory beauty (fixed rather than vague beauty) can have such an ideal. Thus there is no ideal of beautiful flowers. In the end, there is only one thing that has such an ideal: that being which has its purpose within itself, is an end in itself, namely, the human being.

Kant concludes by asserting that the ideal of beauty is not a matter of a mere, pure judgment of taste. Here he comes to the threshold of a more complex beauty, such as will be found in fine art, and also to the threshold of a form of imagination that will be not merely playful but creative.

V. Analytic of the Sublime

KANT INTRODUCES THE judgment of the sublime by indicating what it has in common with the judgment of taste and then by differentiating the two judgments. That provides a first sketch of the structure of the judgment of the sublime.

What do the two judgments have in common? In what respects are they similar?

(1) Both are reflective judgments in which we like the object freely and for its own sake, not because it is agreeable (such a liking would be based on sensation) and not because it is good (such a liking would be based on a concept). Both judgments involve mere formal, disinterested apprehension of the object.

(2) Both also involve a harmonizing or agreement of the imagination with what Kant now calls simply "the power of concepts" and specifies as either understanding or reason. So as the judgment of taste involves a relation of accord between imagination and understanding, in the judgment of the sublime, there is a relation of accord between imagination and reason, even if the specific character of the relation is different.

(3) Both are singular judgments. And both have subjective universality—not because of any cognition of an object but because they involve a universal and not a private relation between our subjective powers, a relation akin to cognition. This relation between our powers is something *felt*.

So the judgment of the sublime also involves three moments:

(1) formal apprehension
(2) relation of imagination to a cognitive power
(3) a feeling of this relation.

How, then, do the two types of aesthetic judgment differ? This difference can be articulated in terms of the three moments.

(1) Whereas the judgment of taste involves the apprehension of the form of the object, the judgment of the sublime may be oriented to a formless object: "The beautiful in nature concerns the form of the object, which consists in the object being bounded. But the sublime can also be found in a formless object, insofar as we represent unboundedness" (*CJ*, p. 98). So in the case of the sublime, the object can be formless, that is, can lack (yet does not necessarily lack) a form that would delimit and bound it. What, then, is actually apprehended in

the case of the sublime? Certainly not that which Kant opposes to form, namely, the sense-content, the sensations. The judgment of the sublime is just as detached from and disinterested in sense-content as is the judgment of taste. In the case of the sublime as well, what is apprehended must have to do with form, even in cases where the object is formless. What is essential is that, whether the object is formed or formless, "we represent unboundedness," unlimitedness. In other words, the object must be such that what we apprehend is a certain formal unboundedness, a certain exceeding of form. So in the judgment of the sublime, the typical apprehension is of nature: either in its greatness, as absolutely large and beyond all comparison (mathematically sublime) or in its might (dynamically sublime).

In what kind of objects is such unboundedness to be apprehended? In order to ensure the purity of such judgments, their independence from concepts, Kant privileges a certain region. Referring specifically to the mathematically sublime, he writes:

> Here I shall only point out that if the aesthetic judgment in question is to be pure (unmixed with any teleological and hence rational judgment), and if we are to give an example of it that is fully appropriate for the critique of aesthetic judgment, then we must point to the sublime not in products of art (buildings, columns, etc.), where both the form and the magnitude are determined by a human purpose, nor in natural things whose very concept carries with it a determinate purpose (such as animals with a known determination in nature), but rather in crude [raw] nature (and even in it only insofar as it carries with it no charm nor any emotion aroused by actual danger), that is, merely insofar as crude nature contains magnitude. (*CJ*, p. 109)

So the region in which an unboundedness is apprehended is raw or crude nature, nature in its chaos, "in its wildest and most ruthless disarray and devastation, provided nature displays magnitude or might" (*CJ*, pp. 99–100). Kant offers these examples of the mathematically sublime: "shapeless mountain masses piled on one another in wild disarray with their pyramids of ice, or the gloomy raging sea," and of the dynamically sublime: "bold, overhanging, and, as it were, threatening rocks, thunderclouds piling up in the sky and moving about accompanied by lightning and thunderclaps, volcanoes with all their destructive power, hurricanes with all the devastation they leave behind, the boundless ocean heaved up, the high waterfall of a mighty river, and so on" (*CJ*, p. 120).

(2) The second moment involved in the differentiation between the judgment of taste and the judgment of the sublime concerns the cognitive power to which, in each case, imagination is related.

In the case of beauty and the judgment of taste, the imagination, in apprehending the form, is set into accord with the understanding, but with an indeterminate concept of the understanding. The term "indeterminate" indicates that there is no cognition, and so no determinate concept, but only an affinity or proximity to cognition.

In the case of the sublime, the imagination, as it takes up objects in their unboundedness, is set in accord with reason and specifically, as Kant says, with an indeterminate concept of reason. What defines reason—in distinction from the understanding—is its demand for totality. Whereas understanding corresponds to the causal linking of one thing to another, and of this to still another, reason posits the concept of the totality of causally linked things, that is, the idea of the world as a whole.

Thus every concept of reason is a totality, and the indeterminate concept of reason is simply the concept of totality without any specification. Therefore, in judgments of the sublime, the boundlessness of the object (taken up into the imagination) is set in relation to the concept (thought) of totality. That is what Kant says as he continues a passage we already cited: "The beautiful in nature concerns the form of the object, which consists in the object being bounded. But the sublime can also be found in a formless object, insofar as we represent unboundedness, either as in the object or because the object prompts us to represent it, while yet we add to this unboundedness the thought of its totality. So it seems we regard the beautiful as the exhibition of an indeterminate concept of the understanding and the sublime as the exhibition of an indeterminate concept of reason" (*CJ*, p. 98).

If the apprehension is of nature in its greatness, then the relation of accord will be with theoretical reason, yielding the mathematically sublime. If the apprehension is of nature in its might, then the relation of accord will be with practical reason, the power of desire, yielding the dynamically sublime.

Kant notes that the sublime induces a certain mental agitation: "So the imagination will refer this agitation either to the cognitive power [theoretical reason] or to the power of desire [practical reason]. The first kind of agitation is a mathematical, the second a dynamical, attunement of imagination" (*CJ*, p. 101).

(3) The third moment constitutive of the difference between the two kinds of aesthetic judgment concerns the type of feeling involved in each.

Whereas the feeling of the accord between imagination and understanding is a feeling of pleasure in the judgment of taste, the feeling is more complex in the judgment of the sublime, a kind of sequence of displeasure and pleasure. Accordingly, whereas the judgment of taste installs us in restful contemplation, the judgment of the sublime exposes us to a kind of movement of the mind, a mental agitation. In other words, its feeling is an *emotion*, and instead of play, there is seriousness:

> The two likings are very different in kind. The one liking, for the beautiful, carries with it directly a feeling of the furtherance of life and hence is compatible

with charms and with an imagination at play. But the other liking, the feeling of the sublime, is a pleasure that arises only indirectly; it is produced by the feeling of a momentary inhibition of the vital forces followed immediately by an outpouring of them that is all the stronger. Hence it is an emotion, and so it seems to be seriousness, rather than play, in the activity of the imagination. Hence, too, this liking is incompatible with charms, and, since the mind is not just attracted by the object but is alternately always repelled as well, the liking for the sublime contains not so much a positive pleasure as rather admiration and respect, and so should be called a negative pleasure. (*CJ*, p. 98)

Kant proceeds to say that the most important difference between the two types of aesthetic judgment has to do with purposiveness. In the case of beauty, there is purposiveness of the apprehended form with respect to our cognitive powers. It is as though nature were so constituted as to be suited to our cognitive powers: "(Independent) natural beauty carries with it a purposiveness in its form, by which the object seems as it were predetermined for our power of judgment" (*CJ*, pp. 98–99). In the case of the sublime, however, there is no such purposiveness. Indeed, even further, the sublime is contrapurposive: "On the other hand, if something arouses in us, merely in apprehension and without any reasoning on our part, a feeling of the sublime, then it may indeed appear, in its form, contrapurposive for our power of judgment, incommensurate with our power to exhibit, and as it were violent to our imagination, and yet we judge it all the more sublime for that" (*CJ*, p. 99).

So a sublime object does violence to the imagination and is not suited, not purposive, with respect to our powers. Instead, it shows itself as counter to our powers. Now, something rather odd is occurring here. We saw in the Analytic of the Beautiful that the purposiveness of the judgment of taste is what marks it as an aesthetic judgment. Yet the judgment of the sublime is also an aesthetic judgment, and so the sublime object should be purposive with respect to our powers. Thus a contradiction arises: the sublime both must be, and yet is not, purposive with respect to our powers. How does Kant resolve this?

He declares that the object itself is not sublime. Then he continues: "We see from this at once that we express ourselves entirely incorrectly when we call this or that *object of nature* sublime" (*CJ*, p. 99). No object of nature is sublime in the proper sense; such an object is merely "serviceable for exhibiting a sublimity that can be found in the mind" (*CJ*, p. 99). So the sublime proper lies not in the object but in the subject. Therefore, if we can say that no object simply is beautiful, in the sense that an object is beautiful only in correlation with the subject, with the judgment of taste, then we can say that nothing in nature is sublime. The sublime is withdrawn into the subject.

The consequence is a privileging of the beautiful over the sublime, since in the case of the beautiful an actual purposiveness in nature is exhibited:

> This shows that the concept of the sublime in nature is not nearly as important and rich in implications as that of the beautiful in nature. The sublime indicates nothing purposive whatever in nature itself but only in what use we can make of our intuitions of nature so that we can feel a purposiveness within ourselves entirely independent of nature. For the beautiful in nature we must seek a basis outside ourselves, but for the sublime a basis merely within ourselves and in the way of thinking that introduces sublimity into our representation of nature. This is a crucial preliminary remark, which separates our ideas of the sublime completely from the idea of a purposiveness of nature and turns the theory of the sublime into a mere appendix to our aesthetic judging of the purposiveness of nature. For through these ideas we do not represent a particular form in nature but only develop the purposive use the imagination makes of the representation of nature. (*CJ*, p. 100)

Therefore, the theory of the sublime is a mere appendix to the critique of aesthetic judgment.

* * *

Let us now see how Kant fills out this initial sketch of the judgment of the sublime. We will go through the three moments again in turn.

(1) The first moment in this judgment is an apprehension of a certain unboundedness in crude nature—either in the order of magnitude (the mathematically sublime) or of might or power (the dynamically sublime).

Kant contrasts the mathematical estimation of magnitude with the aesthetic estimation. The former is based on a definite measure, an invariable standard valid for all, a universal. Aesthetic estimation is based on a subjective standard derived from common experience, primarily from the average size of the things we see. Now, the apprehension of the mathematically sublime is a matter of an *aesthetic* (not mathematical) estimation of magnitude. In the case of the dynamically sublime, it is not a matter of an estimation of an object but rather of comportment to an object that is so powerful that it arouses fear. Yet we must not actually be afraid; we must be in a safe place—for instance, in a shelter as the storm rages outside. A dynamically sublime object is one that would offer such resistance that it would never yield at all to our exertions against it. Kant writes: "Hence nature can count as a might, and so as dynamically sublime, for aesthetic judgment only insofar as we consider it an object of fear. We can, however, consider an object *fearful* without being afraid *of* it, namely, if we judge it in such a way that we merely *think* of the case where we might possibly want to put up resistance against it, and that any resistance would in that case be utterly futile" (*CJ*, pp. 119–20). The effect of the dynamically sublime is that it can make the mind *feel* its own sublimity, its own elevation above nature.

Let us focus more closely on the mathematical sublime, since Kant develops this analysis in more specific terms.

In the apprehension of the mathematical sublime, there is a dual operation of imagination:

- (a) apprehension proper (*Auffassung*). Since the magnitude is excessive, apprehension proper is in every instance partial and proceeds sequentially. In other words, there is a sequence of discrete, partial apprehensions of the object, one part at a time.
- (b) comprehension (*Zusammenfassung*). This is required precisely because of the partial, sequential character of the apprehension. Comprehension is an operation in which we seek to encompass and bring into view the many parts that have been apprehended sequentially. It is oriented toward gathering the parts into a whole, toward presenting the object in its full magnitude.

Apprehension proper can continue on—sequentially—ad infinitum, proceeding from one part to the next. But comprehension attains a certain maximum. Here is how Kant describes this restriction:

> The imagination must perform two acts: apprehension (*apprehensio*) and comprehension (*comprehensio aesthetica*). Apprehension involves no problem, for it may progress to infinity. But comprehension becomes more and more difficult as the apprehension progresses, and it soon reaches a maximum, namely, the aesthetically largest basic measure for an estimation of magnitude. For when apprehension has reached the point where the partial representations of sensible intuition that were first apprehended are already beginning to be extinguished in the imagination, as it proceeds to apprehend further ones, the imagination then loses as much on the one side as it gains on the other; and so there is a maximum in comprehension that it cannot exceed. (*CJ*, p. 108)

So comprehension—hence the entire phase of apprehension in imagination—encounters a limit, a limit to what can be encompassed and brought into view by the imagination. Kant offers a pair of examples. They are very curious, for two reasons. First, Kant never visited either of the places he refers to in the examples but only read about them in travel accounts. Second, they are not *pure* examples, not things in crude nature without purpose, hence they are not without a concept of perfection. Instead, they are products of art.

The first example is the pyramids in Egypt. They illustrate well how the mathematically sublime exceeds the imaginative capacity to comprehend: if one is situated close enough to apprehend the parts distinctly, then imagination proves incapable of encompassing the whole.

> In order to receive the full emotional effect from the magnitude of the pyramids, one must neither get too close nor stay too far away. For if one stays too far away, then the apprehended parts (the stones on top of one another) are

represented only obscurely, and hence their representation has no effect on the subject's aesthetic judgment; and if one gets too close, then the eye needs some time to complete the apprehension from the base to the peak, but during that time some of the earlier parts are invariably extinguished in the imagination before it has apprehended the later ones, and hence the comprehension is never complete. (*CJ*, p. 108)

The second example is St. Peter's in Rome:

Perhaps the same observation can explain the bewilderment or kind of perplexity that is said to seize the spectator who for the first time enters St. Peter's Basilica in Rome. For there is here a feeling of the inadequacy of his imagination for presenting the idea of a whole wherein imagination reaches its maximum and, in striving to surpass it, sinks back into itself, but thereby is transposed into an emotional satisfaction [liking]. (*CJ*, pp. 108–09)

This latter example is important because it traces the course followed by the imagination in its comprehensive striving to encompass all the apprehended parts as a whole. This course involves:

(a) the imagination reaching its maximal comprehension and striving to exceed it
(b) the failure of the imagination, so that it sinks back into itself
(c) its being transposed then into a certain emotional satisfaction.

(a) First moment: striving of the imagination.
On this course, it is a matter of "pushing . . . the comprehension of the many in an intuition to the limit of the power of imagination" (*CJ*, p. 110). Here "the striving toward comprehension surpasses the power of imagination" (*CJ*, p. 112). On this course, imagination thus "exhibits its own limits" (*CJ*, p. 114). In the striving toward the whole and in the failure to attain that whole comprehensively, there occurs what could be called an "experience of limitation."

It is not only a matter of the imagination reaching its limit. It is also, in the very way imagination reaches that limit, a matter of experiencing the *excess of nature*, its surpassing our imaginative capacity to grasp it. This excess of nature, disclosed only in the experience of limitation and irreducible to a determinate magnitude, is the unlimitedness, the infinity of nature: "Hence nature is sublime in those of its appearances whose intuition carries with it the idea of its infinity. But the only way for this to occur is through the inadequacy of even the greatest striving [straining] of our imagination to estimate the magnitude of the object" (*CJ*, p. 112).

Although Kant does not explain further, it is important to consider what the infinity of nature means here, that is, how nature appears here as infinite. It does not mean simply that the object goes on and on. However massive and hence sublime a mountain may be, it does not extend on and on forever. What is decisive is that this infinity of nature appears *in relation to* the striving of the imagination to apprehend it.

Specifically, it appears in relation to a situation in which imagination finds itself caught in a double bind: extending apprehension proper impairs comprehension, but extending comprehension (for example, by taking distance from the pyramids) impairs apprehension. So the infinity of nature means not that the object goes on and on but that the object withdraws from imaginative apprehension, holds itself in reserve, retreats.

(b) Second moment: failure of the imagination.

The experience within the apprehensive moment of the judgment of the mathematically sublime is both an experience of the limitation of the imagination and an experience of the excess of nature, of its unlimited surpassing of the imaginative capacity to grasp it. Hence this is an experience disclosing the *difference* between unlimitedly surpassing nature and the limited power of imaginative apprehension.

This disclosure is the site of the sublime, its site within experience or, rather, at that limit where sublime nature is engaged by our highest sensible power. What is disclosed at this site is precisely the difference between great and powerful nature and our highest sensible power, namely, imagination.

When this disclosure occurs in imaginative apprehension, the imagination is set into relation to reason. This relation, however, is not, as is the judgment of taste, an accord or harmony. Instead, it is a difference. In other words, what comes to be marked, disclosed, and ultimately felt is not accord but difference. Specifically, what is disclosed in/as this relation is the difference between the limited capacity of imagination and the unlimited demand of reason, between the limited grasp of the whole that imagination can achieve and the absolute totality demanded by reason.

In this connection, it is imperative to recognize the character of reason, its fundamental determination. The demand for totality is not just an act that reason performs. Rather, reason is precisely the demanding, the power of demanding, absolute totality. When reason comes on the scene, there is thereby a demand for totality; that is, reason occurs *as* the demand for totality. Yet no sensible object or group of such objects constitutes an absolute totality; rather, any absolute totality goes beyond the domain of the sensible, beyond to the supersensible. Thus, the demanding of absolute totality, that is, reason, is a supersensible power.

The determination of reason can also be described in another way, namely, by reference to the distinction between knowing and thinking. Although one can know only sensible objects, objects as they are given to and informed by the subject, thinking is not dependent on intuition: we can think anything as long as it is not contradictory. This power of thinking, if directed to absolute totality, is reason. Kant writes: "But—and this is most important—to be able even to think the infinite as a *whole* indicates a mental power that surpasses any standard of sense" (*CJ*, p. 111). Hence again, reason, the unlimited power to think the unlimited, is a supersensible power.

Thus it is a matter of the difference between our limited sensible powers (as limited by nature) and our unlimited rational, supersensible powers (which constitute our superiority over nature). Therefore, to put the first two moments together, the apprehension issues in the disclosure of the difference between limited imagination and unlimited nature, the natural difference. But, then, through this apprehension, imagination is set into relation to reason in such a way that another difference is disclosed, namely, the one between our limited sensible powers, especially imagination, and our unlimited supersensible powers, the rational difference.

The question is: how are these two differences and their respective disclosures related? How is it that the disclosure of the natural difference, through the experience of limitation in the face of the sublime, opens onto and leads to a disclosure of the rational difference?

This opening of the natural onto the rational, this movement by which the natural leads over to the rational, is precisely the transition by which the sublimity of the natural object passes over to a sublimity in the subject, so that the sublime in its true sense, in its proper determination, proves to lie in the subject rather than in the natural object.

Kant offers several important indications regarding this issue. He refers to the object of nature which is, strictly speaking, improperly called "sublime" and says that it "makes intuitable for us the superiority of the rational vocation of our cognitive powers over the greatest power of sensibility" (*CJ*, p. 114). He also refers to "ideas of reason, which, although they cannot be exhibited adequately, are aroused and called to mind by this very inadequacy, which can be exhibited in sensibility" (*CJ*, p. 99). And he says that "the subject's own inability discloses in him the consciousness of an unlimited ability which is also his, and the mind can judge this ability aesthetically only by that inability" (*CJ*, p. 116).

These passages say that what happens in the experience of sublime nature is that the difference between reason and our sensible powers—hence, the superiority of reason over sense—is rendered intuitive, sensibly presented, exhibited. In other words, in/through the natural difference, the rational difference is sensibly presented, intuitively exhibited.

Kant offers a still more decisive indication. Referring to ideas, he says: "The imagination strains to treat nature as a schema for them" (*CJ*, p. 124). So it is a matter of imagination using nature as a schema for the ideas. What occurs at the center of the judgment of the sublime, when imagination experiences its limitation over against infinite nature and is set into relation to reason, constitutes a schematizing in the strict Kantian sense. The difference between nature and the human sensible powers is taken as a schema for the difference between the sensible and the supersensible within the human being. That is, the excess of nature, its exceeding human sensible powers, is made to reflect and to exhibit intuitively the excess of reason, the superiority of the supersensible over the sensible.

As a sublime object such as a towering mountain rises beyond the limit of our imaginative comprehension, it draws us up to our higher vocation. More generally, as any sublime object—in its excess—withdraws into an incomprehensible distance, it draws us upward beyond sense to our higher supersensible vocation.

It is not unlike the function of the schema in the *Critique of Pure Reason*, which renders understanding intuitive by casting intuition in the shape of categorial determinations. The sublime object is a schema that, in its transition into the subject, connects our sensible power to reason, or rather, spans the distance between them. Through engagement with the sublime, there occurs a disclosure within the sensible of the very difference between the sensible and the supersensible.

Considered in much broader terms, this configuration and the disclosure that occurs within it indicate a profound affinity between Kant's analytic of the sublime and an analytic that runs throughout much of the history of metaphysics. Already in the Platonic dialogues there are outlined various sensible disclosures of the difference between sensible and supersensible—for example, the account of beauty as the shining forth of the supersensible in the sensible. Such an account reemerges in the thought of Kant's successors—for example, in Hegel's description of art as the sensible presentation of the idea. It is as if, behind the complex of analyses that Kant develops, the curtain opens upon the history of metaphysics so as to reveal in this respect the affinity of Kant's thought to the developments that constitute this history.

(c) Third moment: emotional satisfaction.

Let us begin with a passage contrasting the *movement* involved in the affective experience of the sublime with the *rest*, the restful contemplation, induced by the beautiful: "In representing the sublime in nature, the mind feels itself moved, whereas in an aesthetic judgment about the beautiful in nature it is in restful contemplation" (*CJ*, p. 115). The mind is moved not only in its recoil from excessive nature in an apprehending moment in which it runs up against its limit but also in the disclosure accomplished through the schematic use of nature, the disclosure of the rational difference. Indeed, it seems that this feeling comes into play preeminently in relation to such disclosure: "Hence nature is here called sublime merely because it elevates our imagination, making it exhibit those cases where the mind can come to feel its own sublimity, which lies in its vocation and elevates it even above nature" (*CJ*, p. 121). Thus Kant says explicitly: the disclosure accomplished by the schematic use of nature opens itself *to feeling*. In other words, the rational difference is revealed to feeling, is something felt.

Another passage formulates this even more succinctly and names the feeling that comes into play: "The feeling of the inadequacy of our power for attaining an idea that is a law for us is respect" (*CJ*, p. 114). This inadequacy or inadequation is precisely the difference that comes to be disclosed in the schematic use of nature, the difference between our limited sensible powers and our unlimited supersensible, rational powers. This difference is felt, disclosed to feeling, namely, to the feeling Kant calls "respect."

In the case of the sublime, the feeling is not—versus the judgment of taste—a simple feeling, not simply pleasurable. This results, in the first instance, from the fact that it is a feeling of difference rather than simply of accord, harmony, unity. But its complexity is seen especially in its division into two component feelings: the feeling of difference and a feeling of unity which comes to be conjoined, almost paradoxically, to the feeling of difference. The feeling of unity is expressed in the passage just cited in the phrase "law for us." The reference is to a law that would be purely rational and that would also be "for us," binding upon the human being, that is, a law to which we belong essentially, by which we are claimed, even though our sensible nature (especially our highest sensible power, imagination) remains always inadequate to this law, falls short of it.

Such a law can only be the moral law, and that is why the feeling is called "respect." It is the feeling in which both the separation of our sensible nature from that law and our essential belonging to it are felt.

In terms of Kant's practical philosophy, we cannot, as sensible beings, entirely free ourselves from the force of sense-inclinations such that our actions would be governed completely by the moral law; yet, as supersensible beings, we are bound by the law, subject to its demand.

The duality of the feeling of respect is a duality of pleasure and displeasure: "Hence the feeling of the sublime is a feeling of displeasure that arises from the inadequacy of the imagination, in an aesthetic estimation of magnitude, for an estimation by reason, but it is at same time also a pleasure, aroused by the fact that this very judgment, namely, that even the greatest power of sensibility is inadequate, is itself in harmony with rational ideas, insofar as striving toward them is still a law for us" (*CJ*, pp. 114–15).

Kant stresses that the feeling of difference and the feeling of unity are interrelated moments. The feeling of pleasure in unity is aroused, almost paradoxically, precisely by the feeling of displeasure in difference: "Hence our inner perception that every standard of sensibility is inadequate for an estimation of magnitude by reason is itself a harmony with laws of reason, as well as a displeasure that arouses in us the feeling of our supersensible vocation, according to which our finding that every standard of sensibility is inadequate to the ideas of reason is purposive and thus pleasurable" (*CJ*, p. 115).

It is a matter of a pleasure possible only through displeasure. And so Kant says: "And yet this same violence that is done to the subject through the imagination is still judged purposive for the whole vocation [*Bestimmung*: also, determination] of the mind" (*CJ*, p. 116).

* * *

Let me conclude our discussion of the judgment of the sublime by calling attention to two very significant passages that point still further into the nature of the sublime. The first passage marks the difference between the apprehension proper and the comprehension of a sublime object *as* corresponding to the opposition between progression and regression. The supervention of comprehension upon what has been successively apprehended produces a suspension of time:

> The comprehension of a multiplicity in a unity (of intuition rather than of thought), and hence the comprehension in one instant of what is apprehended successively, is a regression that in turn cancels the condition of time in the progression of the imagination and makes *simultaneity* intuitable. Hence (since temporal succession is a condition of the inner sense and of an intuition) it is a subjective movement of the imagination by which it does violence to inner sense, and this violence must be the more significant the larger the quantum that the imagination comprehends in one intuition. (*CJ*, p. 116)

In other words, when the sequence of moments of apprehension is comprehended as a whole, the sequential structure is cancelled, and within the comprehension all the moments are simultaneous. In suspending temporal progression, comprehension interrupts the form of inner sense and thus does violence to it. Whenever imagination comes on the scene, there will always be a threat of violence, which, however, is also purposive.

The second passage concerns the fact that in the judgment of the sublime we feel ourselves moved. This being-moved or emotion involves two opposed moments: repulsion from sublime nature and a certain attraction to it:

> This movement can (especially in its beginning) be compared to a shaking, that is, to a rapidly alternating repulsion from, and attraction to, one and the same object. That which is excessive for the imagination (up to which it is impelled in the apprehension of intuition) is, as it were, an abyss in which it fears to lose itself; yet, for the rational idea of the supersensible, it is not excessive but lawful to bring forth such a striving of imagination, and consequently here there is the same amount of attraction as there was of repulsion for mere sensibility. (*CJ*, p. 115)

VI. Interest in the Beautiful

Let us now talk about birds, about the beautifully colored feathers of birds, about birds themselves, real birds and fake birds, and, above all, about the songs of birds. In birdsongs, we find perhaps the most striking case of a mixing or crossing of nature and art: a purely natural creature, lacking reason and speech, nonetheless producing song. Indeed, they are songs we find beautiful—beautiful songs in which we may even take a considerable interest.

The beautifully colored bird feathers make their appearance in Kant's discussion of *interest* in the beautiful. Throughout the Analytic of the Beautiful, Kant stressed that a judgment of taste about the beautiful is always disinterested. That means we find no pleasure in the existence of the object but merely take its form up into freely playing imagination. We like it merely for its own sake, not because it satisfies some interest. Yet, in the course of the Analytic of the Beautiful, Kant refers to such interest-free beauty as pure beauty and distinguishes it from mixed beauty, in which a judgment of taste is connected with an interest in the beautiful object. From that point on, Kant is primarily concerned with mixed beauty. And once birds come onto the scene, he is concerned solely with mixed beauty, that is, a beautiful object to which is directed both a disinterested judgment of taste and an interest that takes pleasure in the existence of the object. In this analysis, Kant distinguishes between two kinds of interest: empirical interest, which pertains to our character as sensible beings together with other such beings (§41), and intellectual interest, which pertains to our character as intelligible or supersensible beings, as moral beings bound by the moral law. Both kinds of interest can be connected to a judgment of taste; that is, to the mere liking of the object for its own sake, for its beautiful form, there can be conjoined an interest, which is a taking of pleasure in the *existence* of the object. Such a conjoining requires that there be something else that links the judgment of taste to the interest in the object. The link may be something empirical, namely, an inclination inherent in human nature. This amounts to an empirical interest in the beautiful. Or the link may be something intellectual, namely, the will's being determinable apriori by reason, that is, by the moral law. This amounts to an intellectual interest in the beautiful.

With regard to empirical interest in the beautiful, Kant writes: "Only in *society* is the beautiful of empirical interest.... A person abandoned on some desolate island would not, just for himself, adorn either his hut or himself; nor would he look for flowers, let alone grow flowers, to adorn himself with them" (*CJ*, p. 163). Thus empirical interest in the beautiful is linked to sociability. Sociability is an inclination inherent in human nature that forms the link between the judgment of taste (mere liking) and a taking of interest in the existence of the object. How does this link function? The judgment of taste allows us to communicate our feelings. To say something is beautiful is to say that its mere apprehension evokes a pleasurable feeling of harmony. Thus, by allowing us to communicate our feelings, the judgment of taste serves to further our natural inclination to sociability, and so we take an interest in the beautiful.

Kant defines refinement as the skill to communicate one's feeling of pleasure in the beautiful to others, so as to feel in a certain community with them. Yet such refinement occurs only in an advanced stage of civilization. Prior to this, charm plays the same role, although less adequately, that will later be played by beauty. In other words, one takes interest in charms as furthering sociability—interest in such charming things as flowers, seashells, and beautifully colored bird feathers.

But, Kant says, this empirical interest is "of no importance for us here." Why? —Because it has no relation to reason, to the moral sphere, and hence does not provide any mediation between sense enjoyment and moral feeling and, ultimately, between nature and freedom. On the contrary, "in such an interest, taste caters to inclination" (*CJ*, p. 164). Kant's primary concern, then, is with *intellectual* interest in the beautiful, which he addresses in one of the most magnificent sections of the *Critique of Judgment*, §42: "On the intellectual interest in the beautiful."

Birds appear twice in this section. In the first scene, it is the beauty of the bird itself that is highlighted. In the final scene, it is the beauty of the bird's song. Both scenes, as we will learn, involve deception. Between these is another scene about the language of nature. So there are three scenes.

Before raising the curtain on the first scene, Kant addresses the question of whether taking an interest in the beautiful in general is a sign of good moral character. In this regard, he insists on the distinction between the beautiful in art and the beauty of nature. He maintains that in the case of art, there can be no assurance of any such connection. He refers to connoisseurs of art who "apparently as a rule are vain, obstinate, and given to ruinous passions" and who "can perhaps even less than other people claim the distinction of being attached to moral principles" (*CJ*, p. 165).

On the other hand, Kant insists that interest in the beauty of nature is indeed a sign of attachment to morality. "I do maintain that to take a direct interest in the beauty of nature (not merely to have the taste needed to judge it) is always a mark of a good soul and that, if this interest is habitual, if it readily associates itself with the contemplation of nature, then this indicates at least a mental attunement favorable to moral feeling" (*CJ*, pp. 165–66).

Kant specifies that the interest must concern the beautiful *forms* of nature and not the mere charms which nature tends to connect with these forms. So, as regards birds, the interest will need to be in the beautiful form of the bird, not just in the bird's beautifully colored feathers.

The first scene pictures a person who is alone and to that extent removed from all interests linked to society. He does not intend any communication with others concerning the things he is about to observe. One of these things is a bird. He contemplates certain natural things, the beautiful shape of a wildflower, of a bird, of an insect. His contemplation is one of admiration, of love, of wonder at these beautiful forms. Indeed, he would not want nature to be without them, even though they offer no prospect of benefit to him. Such comportment to nature is not merely a matter of a judgment of taste, although, as comportment toward beauty, it must include such a judgment as an independent component. But to the disinterested judgment of taste an interest is added, a direct interest that Kant calls, without further explanation, "intellectual": "Such a person is taking a direct interest in the beauty of nature, and this interest is intellectual. That is, not only does he like nature's product for its form, but he also likes its existence . . ." (*CJ*, p. 166).

Deception now makes its entrance. The scene is transformed into one in which the lover of the beautiful is tricked: artificial flowers are stuck in the ground, and artfully carved birds are set on the branches of trees. Yet the deception is only momentary. The lover of natural beauty quickly discovers the deceit. With this discovery, his direct interest in these things promptly vanishes, although it may be replaced by other types of interest, empirical interest. For example, if this Robinson Crusoe were to return to society, then his interest might be aroused in using such things as decorations.

Kant formulates as a conclusion what the events enacted in this scene have demonstrated, namely: "the thought that the beauty in question was produced by nature must accompany the intuition and the reflection" and, furthermore, "the direct interest we take in such beauty is based on that thought alone" (*CJ*, p. 166). Along with the intuition and the reflection, which constitute the judgment of taste, the love of beauty (intellectual interest in the beautiful) requires also the thought of the *natural* origin of the beauty.

Kant proceeds to raise the curtain on the second scene. The action with which the scene begins is meant to declare the superiority of natural beauty over that of art. The scene pictures a man leaving a museum in order to go forth into nature. He is a man of sufficiently refined taste as to be able to judge the beauty of the works of fine art that he observes in the museum. But he turns away from the beauties of art, turns instead to the beautiful in nature. He does so, as Kant—most remarkably—says, "in order to find there, as it were, a voluptuousness for his spirit in a train of thought that he can never fully unravel"

(*CJ*, pp. 166–67). One who makes such a turn, such a choice of nature over art, will be esteemed and considered to have a beautiful soul, surpassing anything that can be claimed by connoisseurs who remain indoors with their art. Kant then asks: what is the ground of this difference marked by the dramatic turn to nature?

Kant draws a distinction between the judgment of taste (aesthetic judgment, exercised without concepts) and intellectual judgment (moral judgment, proceeding from concepts and determining the will). Strictly speaking, neither type of judgment is based on an interest. But in the case of moral judgment, an interest *arises from* the judgment. This interest is an interest of reason: specifically, its interest that the ideas of practical reason such as freedom, God, and immortality have objective reality. Whatever attests to an objective reality of these ideas will be of direct interest to reason. That is to say, reason will take a direct interest in whatever trace or hint nature may show of its accord with the mind. Now, this interest, though arising in the sphere of moral judgment, undergoes a certain transference to the aesthetic sphere:

> Hence reason must take an interest in any manifestation in nature of a harmony that resembles the mentioned kind of harmony, and hence the mind cannot meditate about the beauty of nature without at the same time finding its interest aroused. But in terms of its kinship, this interest is moral, and whoever takes such an interest in the beautiful in nature can do so only to the extent that he has beforehand already solidly established an interest in the morally good. Hence if someone is directly interested in the beauty of nature, we have cause to suppose that he has at least a predisposition to a good moral attitude. (*CJ*, p. 167)

So the interest as transferred to the aesthetic sphere is in nature's visible and audible attestation of its harmony with our moral vocation, namely, that there is no conflict between, for instance, moral self-determination and the mechanism of nature. This supposes a predisposition to good moral character, and that is why intellectual interest in nature is indicative of a morally good character.

Artistic beauty, on the other hand, cannot function in such a way. For it is manifest that art is intentionally designed by the artist to produce aesthetic liking and hence does not attest to any harmony in nature. Thus judgment of artistic beauty is not connected with any direct interest such as that in natural beauty. Accordingly, everything hinges on the natural trace, the trace by which nature shows that it involves some sort of ground for assuming in its products a harmony with the requirements of practical reason, that is, the trace of spirit or reason in nature.

Yet nature does not *show* this ground as such. Nature does not make the harmony manifest from the ground up. It is precisely because of this not-showing of the ground that everything hinges on the natural trace, on a showing within nature of a trace of the ground. So here nothing is shown simply as such, but only by way of the trace inscribed in nature or, as Kant also says, by way of nature's writing, by way of the "cipher through which nature speaks to us figuratively in its beautiful forms" (*CJ*, p. 168).

Accordingly, in and through the beautiful forms of nature, something is said, something that could never be present or presented in nature as are those beautiful forms by which it is inscribed and thus meant. That is, the beautiful forms of nature constitute a language in which nature speaks to us. In contemplating the beautiful forms of nature, the lover of nature is reading, interpreting, the script of nature.

Can there be a *voicing* of what is thus written in nature? Does nature also give voice to what is written in its beautiful forms? Kant does not say. He does not identify a voice capable of translating nature's beautiful forms into speech—or into song. Instead, he introduces still another language of nature. This is a language accompanying the language of beautiful forms. It is distinct from this language while being nonetheless fused with it. It is a language that supplements the language of beautiful forms.

By introducing this second language of nature, Kant sets the stage for the final scene, the one in which the bird contemplated by the lover of nature finally breaks into song. Kant introduces the second language in relation to the charms of nature. Recall that these were previously distinguished rigorously from beautiful forms, as not pertaining to intellectual interest in the beautiful nor to purely aesthetic judgment. Such charms include the beautifully colored bird feathers. But now Kant observes that such charms are often found fused with beautiful forms.

He explains: such charms are matters either of color or of tone, since it is only in such sensations that a space opens for a reflection by which they are not merely felt but found charming, not merely present but significant: "For these are the only sensations that allow not merely for a feeling of sense but also for reflection on the form of these modifications of the senses, so that they contain, as it were, a language in which nature speaks to us and which seems to have a higher meaning" (*CJ*, p. 169).

Thus, in those sensations that constitute the charms of nature, there is an opening within sense. By virtue of this opening, enacted through reflection on the form of the modifications of the senses, the charming sensations *say something*, mean something. That is, they are not merely felt in their mute presence but are significant. And so, like the beautiful forms with which they are often found fused, they constitute a language to be read and interpreted in nature. Kant offers an interpretation of this sense-writing in nature: "Thus a lily's white color seems to attune the mind to ideas of innocence, and the seven colors of the spectrum, from red to violet, seem to attune it, respectively, to the ideas of sublimity, courage, candor, friendliness, modesty, constancy, and tenderness" (*CJ*, p. 169).

The curtain now rises on the final scene. It begins with a song. It is not one that would merely translate into the sound of a voice something already written in nature, but rather it is a song in which something would sound forth originally. It is a song in which something would sound forth vocally in the same way that, in the sense-writing of nature, something shines forth significantly in nature's charming script. We could say: it is nature's song that sounds, and, in sounding, it opens a space of signification and hence of interpretation. Thus: "A bird's song proclaims his joyfulness and contentment with his existence. At least that is how we interpret nature, whether or not it has such an intention" (*CJ*, p. 169).

Direct interest in nature's song, birdsong, requires—no less than is the case with nature's beautiful forms—the thought of a *natural* origin. As soon as deception is detected in this regard, as soon as art rather than nature proves to be the origin of a song that was mistakenly taken to be nature's own, interest vanishes completely, so completely that taste will no longer find anything beautiful nor sight anything charming:

> What do poets praise more highly than the nightingale's enchantingly beautiful song in a secluded thicket on a quiet summer evening by the soft light of the moon? And yet we have cases where some jovial innkeeper, unable to find such a songster, played a trick—received initially with the greatest satisfaction—on the guests staying at his inn to enjoy the country air, by hiding in a bush some roguish youngster who (with a reed or rush in this mouth) knew how to play that song in a way very similar to nature's. Yet as soon as one realizes that it was all deception, one will not long endure listening to this song that before he had considered so charming; and that is how it is with the song of any other bird. (*CJ*, p. 169)

VII. Art

Let us now move from birds to genius. This move spans the greatest of differences, even an abyssal difference: between nature and the supremely human, between the entirely natural and a creativity possible only through freedom. And yet, despite this difference, birds and the genius are in another respect alike, namely, in their expressive relation to nature.

When a bird sings or a genius composes music, what they put forth comes from nature. In the most elemental formulation, the difference between their productions is that between nature and art. It is with this difference that Kant begins the series of sections that concern art (§§43–54). Initially, he rigorously opposes nature and art. Then he proceeds to draw them together in certain distinctive ways, culminating in his development of the concept of genius. Here he renews—profoundly—the ancient question of φύσις and τέχνη.

§43. On art in general.

Kant begins with the general distinction between art and nature. Here art (*Kunst*) is taken in a very general sense, not specifically as fine art (*schöne Kunst*). Kant formulates the difference as follows: art is to nature as doing (*Tun*) is to acting (*Handeln*) or operating (or effecting—*Wirken*). The Latin formulation is clearer: art is to nature as *facere* (perform, execute, accomplish) is to *agere* (move, conduct). The respective products are work (*Werk, opus*) and effect (*Wirkung, effectus*).

So art *makes*, whereas nature merely drives or effects, as a cause bringing about an effect. But what is making? The word translates the Latin *facere*, which in turn translates ποιεῖν. Indeed, behind what Kant says, resides the classical determination of ποιεῖν: the maker has in advance a representation of what is to be made, a paradigm beheld by the "mind's eye," and then he makes the product in the image of the paradigm so that it comes to look like the paradigm. Here is how Kant expresses this determination: "we see art in everything that is of such a character that before it became actual its cause [maker] must have had a representation of it" (*CJ*, p. 170). On the other hand, Kant restricts or specifies this classical concept by insisting that, in the case of art, the production must occur through freedom and in relation to reason: "By right we should not call anything art except a production through freedom, that is, through a power of choice that bases its acts on reason" (*CJ*, p. 170). In this sense, art will always be the work of human beings, and, as linked to freedom, it is rigorously opposed to nature and to productions carried out by purely natural creatures such as bees.

Among human forms of production, Kant distinguishes art from science and craft. The crux of the distinction between art and science is that in the former, mere knowledge gained through science does not suffice, does not immediately give us the skill needed to make something. In other words, art indeed requires a prior representation, but the representation alone does not suffice for making the thing. As regards craft (*Handwerk*), Kant contrasts art to it as free versus mercenary, play versus labor. The making involved in art is agreeable on its own account. Crafting is disagreeable and is attractive only because of its effect, such as the pay received.

In relation to the second distinction, Kant brings out a very important point: even in free art, as opposed to craft, there is need for a certain constraint or mechanism. For example, poetry requires richness of expression, correctness of language, prosody, and meter. So even in free art, there is not sheer free creation but a making that is carried out within certain constraints.

Why are these constraints needed? Kant answers by introducing the concept of spirit: "Without this, the spirit, which in art must be free and which alone animates the work, would have no body at all and would evaporate completely" (*CJ*, p. 171). So constraint or mechanism provides the *body* of the artwork animated by *spirit*.

§44. On fine art.

In order to delimit fine art, Kant divides art in general into its species and subspecies: "If art merely performs the acts required to make a possible object actual, adequately to our cognition of that object, then it is mechanical art; but if what it intends directly is to arouse the feeling of pleasure, then it is called aesthetic art. The latter is either agreeable art or else fine art" (*CJ*, p. 172).

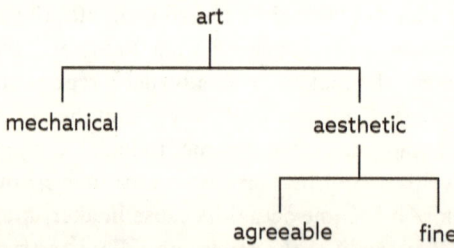

Here the classical concept of making—with the restriction Kant has placed on it—continues to operate: it is a matter of making an object actual in accord with a previous cognition of it. Everything depends on the intention that guides the making, whether it is simply to produce the object or to produce it in such a form that it arouses a feeling of pleasure. If that feeling is aroused simply by sensations, then it is agreeable art. Such is the case with Tafelmusik, namely: "a strange thing which is meant to be only an agreeable noise serving to keep minds in a cheerful mood and to foster the free flow of conversation between each person at the table and his neighbor, without anyone's paying the slightest attention to the music's composition" (*CJ*, p. 173). So this is a kind of music that is not fine art. Kant's remarks here foreshadow the precarious position of music in his system of the arts.

If the feeling of pleasure is aroused in and through reflective judgment, then we are in the presence of fine art.

§45. Fine art is an art insofar as it seems at the same time to be nature.

Up to this point, Kant has delimited fine art and has set art, including fine art, in opposition to nature. With fine art and nature posed in their difference and opposition, Kant now begins to draw them together, to introduce a certain crossing of art and nature, a crossing of each over to the other. More precisely, he shows how each must, in a certain respect, appear as, that is, look like, the other. Let us consider three passages in which Kant describes this crossing.

The first passage describes the crossing from the side of art: "In dealing with a product of fine art we must become conscious that it is art rather than nature; and yet the purposiveness of its form must seem as free from all constraint of chosen rules as if it were a product of mere nature" (*CJ*, p. 173). The second passage says: "Fine art must have the look of nature even though we are conscious of it as art" (*CJ*, p. 174). In the most celebrated formulation, Kant expresses this relation (of looking like) from both sides: "Nature, we say, is beautiful [*schön*] if it also looks like art; and art can be called fine [*schön*] art only if we are conscious that it is art while yet it looks to us like nature" (*CJ*, p. 174).

So the crossing of fine art and nature is such that each, while remaining itself and while we are aware of it as itself, must take on the look of the other.

Beautiful nature must look like art. The point is that in order to be judged beautiful, nature must appear as purposive with respect to our cognitive powers. But that means nature must appear as if it had been made in just such a way as to conform to and evoke the play of our cognitive powers, that is, look as if an artist—though perhaps a divine one—had made it in this way.

Art—though we know it to be art—must look like nature. The point is that art must appear as *freely* purposive (purposive without a purpose) with respect to our cognitive powers. Even though we know that, as art, it is not freely purposive but has been intentionally made by the artist, it does accord with our cognitive powers and so looks like nature. Kant says: "Even though the purposiveness in a product of fine art is intentional, it must still not seem intentional" (*CJ*, p. 174). In other words, it must look like nature.

§46. Fine art is the art of genius.

Kant now takes the relatedness, crossing, intertwining of art and nature even further by introducing the concept of genius. Kant begins with a very precise statement concerning what genius is and how it is related to nature and to art: "Genius is the talent (natural endowment) [*Naturgabe*: natural gift] that gives the rule to art. Since talent is an innate productive ability of the artist and as such belongs itself to nature, we could also put it this way: genius is the innate mental disposition (*ingenium*) through which *nature* gives the rule to art" (*CJ*, p. 174).

Thus the relatedness amounts to this: it is from nature, by way of genius, that art receives the rule that determines it.

Kant immediately develops several points. He begins by insisting that all art requires rules. These serve as the foundation through which a product, if it is to be called "artistic," is "first of all represented as possible" (*CJ*, p. 175). This follows from the classical concept of making: if something is to be produced (for example, an artwork), it must be represented in advance (beheld by the mind's eye) as merely possible. The rules constitute, in effect, this prior representation.

This representation, however, these rules, cannot be based on and expressed in a concept, for the beauty of a product cannot be derived from any concept. Here again it can be said: there is no concept of beauty. So this prior representation is not a conceptual representation. It is not as if the artist first looks to a concept of the object and then produces an actual exemplification of it. Thus Kant says that art (the artist) cannot devise, think out, the rules by which the product is to be brought forth.

Yet there must still be a rule, a rule must be given, according to which the product, the artwork, is brought forth. Genius is the talent that gives the rule. That is—in terms of the classical notion of making—genius gives in advance the rule from/through which the artwork is brought forth.

But genius is *itself given*. It is a natural endowment, a *Naturgabe*, a gift of nature. It is a productive power that is inborn in the artist, bestowed on him by nature. It is "nature in the subject" (*CJ*, p. 175). Thus nature gives the gift of genius, and genius gives the rule to art. In other words, genius is the inborn disposition, "nature in the subject," through which *nature* gives the rule to art.

Kant notes three immediate consequences. First, genius is not a predisposition or talent for learning a skill by which, through the application of rules, something would be produced. Instead, genius is a talent for producing something without any determinate, conceptualizable rules being given. According to Kant, the foremost property of genius is originality.

Second, originality alone does not suffice, since there can also be original nonsense. For this reason, certain works of genius must serve as models, must be exemplary.

Third, to say that genius is a gift of nature does not simply mean it derives from nature. In addition, operating within the artist, it operates in the *mode of nature*, as nature in the subject, not in the mode of cognition or freedom. We could also say: genius is in excess of the subject, adherent to the subject yet not appropriable. Accordingly, a genius does not know and cannot describe how he brings about his products, nor can he bring them forth at will. So Kant says: "it is rather as *nature* that genius gives the rule. That is why, if an author [*Urheber*: originator, creator] owes a product to his genius, he himself does not know how he came by the ideas for it" (*CJ*, p. 175).

§47. Elucidation and confirmation of the foregoing explication of genius.
Kant marks certain limits of art, specifically as art of genius. First, he refers to the peculiar historicity of art. Science continues without limit to perfect our knowledge. (This is a very classical conception of science as it progressed from Descartes to Galileo and Newton. Today, granted certain ideas of the metaphysical foundations of science and of scientific revolutions, this view of science could not simply be assumed.) In contrast, art has a boundary beyond which it cannot go, a boundary that it has probably long since reached.
Though Kant does not elaborate, he is suggesting that art progresses only up to a certain point and that, beyond this limit, it could achieve no greater perfection. Artworks could only, in a sense, repeat what art had already achieved. Here Kant anticipates Hegel's thesis of the pastness of art.
Second, the artist's skill, insofar as it is derived from genius, cannot be communicated, taught, handed on, the way scientific knowledge and methods can be passed down, each great scientist, as Newton said, standing on the shoulders of his predecessors. Nature confers its gift of genius directly on each individual artist, and this gift dies with him. On the other hand, there is a certain indirect communication possible, a certain way of handing something down in art. Although the rule cannot be put in a formula and conceptualized as a precept, it can in a sense be abstracted from the work. That is, one can obtain a certain sense of it by considering the work. Thus the products of genius can become exemplary, can serve as models against which other persons can test and measure their talent, although Kant admits: "How that is possible is difficult to explain" (*CJ*, p. 177).
Kant's formulation regarding such exemplary works, regarding how they are to be used, is significant. He says that others are to let the exemplary work "serve them as their model, not to be copied [*Nachmachung*] but to be imitated [*Nachahmung*]" (*CJ*, p. 177). With this formulation, Kant introduces a new orientation to *mimesis*. An inferior form of *mimesis* (mere copying) is rejected—but then precisely in order to affirm a superior form (imitation). One finds this notion expressed in almost exactly the same way by Coleridge and throughout much of Romanticism. It is also found, if more elaborated, in German Idealism.

Third, finally Kant returns to mark again a limit he touched on earlier, namely, that genius alone does not suffice to produce beautiful art: "Genius can only provide rich material for products of fine art; processing this material and giving it form require a talent that is academically trained" (*CJ*, p. 178). What is preeminently developed by this academic training is taste and the ability to conjoin taste with genial production: "The artist, having practiced and corrected his taste by a variety of examples from art or nature, holds his work up to it [his taste] and, after many and often laborious attempts to satisfy his taste, finds the form which is adequate to it" (*CJ*, p. 180).

In summary of this §, let us note how Kant has subtly altered and displaced the classical conception of making, at least as pertaining to fine art. According to that conception, the artist must have a prior representation of what is to be made. But it transpires that this is precisely what he does *not* have. Although the work is brought forth according to rules and is not sheer accident, the genius does not have these rules in view. Instead, they merely "pass" through him from nature.

Here let me refer to the example of Paul Klee. In "On Modern Art," a lecture Klee delivered in 1924 in Jena in conjunction with an exhibition of his works, he offers the simile of a tree to illustrate the artist's engagement in nature:

> He has such good orientation [in nature] that he is able to bring order to the flux of appearances and experiences. This orientation in the things of nature . . . , this order with all its limbs and branches, I would like to compare to the root structure of the tree.
>
> From that structure juices flow upward to the artist, passing through him, through his eye.
>
> He is therefore standing in the place of the trunk.
>
> Moved and compelled by the power of those streaming juices, he conducts what he is looking at into the work.
>
> Like the crown of the tree, unfolding into visibility in every direction through time and space, that is how it also goes with the work.
>
> *Über die moderne Kunst* (Bern: Benteli, 1945), p. 13

Thus, like the relation of roots to trunk to crown of a tree, so is the relation of nature to the artist to the work of art. The trunk, the artist, is the conduit allowing the passing through of streaming juices.

Yet, on the side of nature, if nature is capable of giving the rule to art and giving genius such that genius equals nature in the subject, then nature can hardly still be conceived as a merely mechanical complex. The conception of nature has begun to shift in the direction of purposiveness. Indeed, this shift is already initiated when Kant refers to the fact that beautiful nature looks like art while still remaining nature.

§49. On the powers of the mind which constitute genius.

Kant says there are works that can to some extent be considered fine art, since they measure up to the judgment of taste and so are beautiful but of which we say: they have no spirit. This suggests that fine art in the full sense must not only be beautiful but must have spirit.

We can suppose that spirit is given as/through genius. But what is spirit? Kant says it is "the animating principle in the mind" (*CJ*, pp. 181–82). So spirit is what animates, enlivens, gives vitality to, quickens, the mind. It sets the mind in motion in such a way that thought is stimulated and is expanded, extended, beyond its usual compass.

Nevertheless, granted its animating effect, what specifically is spirit? Kant identifies it as "the power of presenting aesthetic ideas" (*CJ*, p. 182). So in order to determine what spirit is, we need to consider what an aesthetic idea is and what its presentation involves. Kant provides an explicit definition: "By an aesthetic idea I mean a representation of the imagination which prompts much thought but to which no determinate thought whatever, no concept, can be adequate, so that no language can fully express it and allow us to grasp it" (*CJ*, p. 182).

So an aesthetic idea is a representation of imagination in the subjective sense of the genitive, a presentation *by* the imagination. But Kant has already said that spirit is the power of presenting aesthetic ideas. Thus we see immediately: spirit is—or is very closely linked to—imagination. Furthermore, an aesthetic idea is a representation that prompts (*veranlassen*: occasions, motivates, brings about, calls forth, evokes) much thought. Yet such an idea is a representation to which no determinate thought, no concept, can be adequate, can match up to. It is a representation that cannot be comprehended in a concept. It is a representation that *exceeds* every determinate thought. Thus language cannot fully express it, or, to translate more literally: "No language can fully reach it and render it understandable." Why? —Because what can be expressed in language, what is meant by words, is precisely a concept or combination of concepts. An aesthetic idea, on the other hand, is a representation that escapes language, that exceeds the expressive possibilities of language.

Kant contrasts aesthetic ideas with rational ideas. Whereas an aesthetic idea is a representation of imagination to which no concept is adequate, a rational idea is a concept to which no intuition, that is, representation of imagination, can be adequate. So an aesthetic idea is the counterpart or inverse of a rational idea.

Kant describes the way imagination presents aesthetic ideas: imagination produces, creates, such ideas. It creates "another nature out of the material that actual nature gives it" (*CJ*, p. 182). Here again we see a connection between fine art and nature: creative imagination takes up the material that nature offers through experience and from this material creates a second nature. In doing so, imagination proceeds in part analogically, so that the second nature is, to a degree, like the first. And yet the imagination also follows higher principles, ones of reason rather than of nature, and then it recasts the material of the first nature "into something quite different, namely, into something that exceeds nature" (*CJ*, p. 182). Thus these representations venture beyond the limits of experience, and that is one of the reasons Kant calls them "ideas." The other reason is that no concept is adequate to them.

Now we come to a crucial point: although an aesthetic idea exceeds every concept, it is always set forth in conjunction with a concept. That is, an aesthetic idea is not set forth in some remote and independent sphere apart from concepts and from the experience of first nature. Instead, an aesthetic idea is always paired with a concept, and so it is always an idea "about" something. Kant uses here the term *unterlegen*: the aesthetic idea is "set under" the concept. Yet this does not mean that idea and concept are simply matched, for it is characteristic of an idea to exceed every concept.

It is precisely this movement of exceeding that is decisive. Set under the concept and exceeding it, the aesthetic idea "aesthetically expands the concept itself in an unlimited way" (*CJ*, p. 183). Accordingly, it is as if, set under the concept, the excessive idea stretches the concept beyond what it can comprehend, expands the concept beyond itself. When this happens, the imagination is creative, and reason is made to think more than can be comprehended in the mere concept.

This process, by which the mind is animated to think in excess of the concept, might also occur in another, slightly different way. Instead of setting under the concept an aesthetic idea paired with the concept in the sense of representing it, being "about" it as such, the imagination may set certain partial representations alongside the concept, namely, representations that express the implications of the concept and its kinship with other concepts.

These representations are called "aesthetic attributes" (*CJ*, p. 183)—as when, to the concept of Jupiter, there is added the god's eagle with the lightning bolts in its talons. Yet the effect is the same: these attributes present "something that prompts the imagination to spread itself over a multitude of kindred representations which arouse more thought than can be expressed in a concept determined by words" (*CJ*, p. 183).

Therefore, "in brief, an aesthetic idea is a representation of the imagination which is conjoined with a given concept" (*CJ*, p. 185). Kant continues: "Hence it is a representation that makes us add to a concept the thoughts of much that is unnameable [unspecifiable—*Unnennbares*] but the feeling of which quickens [enlivens—*belebt*] our cognitive powers and connects language, which otherwise would be mere letters, with spirit" (*CJ*, p. 185).

Thus Kant comes back to the question of language. On the one hand, the aesthetic idea exceeds the grasp of language. It cannot be reached, encompassed, rendered understandable, by language in its normal logical, denotational function. And yet, on the other hand, it is as though the aesthetic idea has the effect of stretching language beyond these limits, such that it would be a matter not of the letter, of what is merely said, but of the spirit.

Finally, Kant returns to the question of genius and says that the mental powers which, in a certain relation, constitute genius are imagination and understanding. Yet everything depends on this relation, which is a double exceeding: on the one hand, imagination, freed of the cognitive bond to the understanding, goes beyond the concept and supplies, "in an unstudied way, a wealth of undeveloped material for the understanding, which the latter disregarded in its concept" (*CJ*, p. 185). But then, in turn, the understanding takes up this material so as to enliven its own power and be drawn beyond itself.

So we could say that genius is excess in the play of imagination and understanding. It is the gift of nature operating in the subject in such a way that imagination exceeds the sphere of understanding and thereby draws the understanding itself beyond that sphere. As such, genius makes it possible for us to discover ideas for a given concept and to find a way of expressing these ideas along with the concept so as to communicate the mental attunement that these ideas produce.

* * *

The final sections (§§51–53) of the Analytic of Aesthetic Judgment are devoted to the division, combination, and comparison of the arts. Kant begins—quite remarkably—with a definition of beauty that replaces, displaces, and exceeds the concept of beauty as mere correlate of the judgment of taste. He says that beauty is the expression of aesthetic ideas. So beauty in the full sense, whether in art or in nature, embodies spirit.

This definition is the key to Kant's division of the arts. He mentions in two footnotes (*CJ*, pp. 190, 192) that his classification is not intended to be definitive. He writes: "It is only one of a variety of attempts." Or, again, "the reader should judge this classification only as an attempt to combine the fine arts under one principle—in this case the principle of the expression of aesthetic ideas (by analogy with a language)—rather than regard it as a decisive derivation."

Because artistic beauty is expression, Kant draws on the analogy between art and expression. That is, he carries out a division of expression as speech and then divides the arts along the lines of that division.

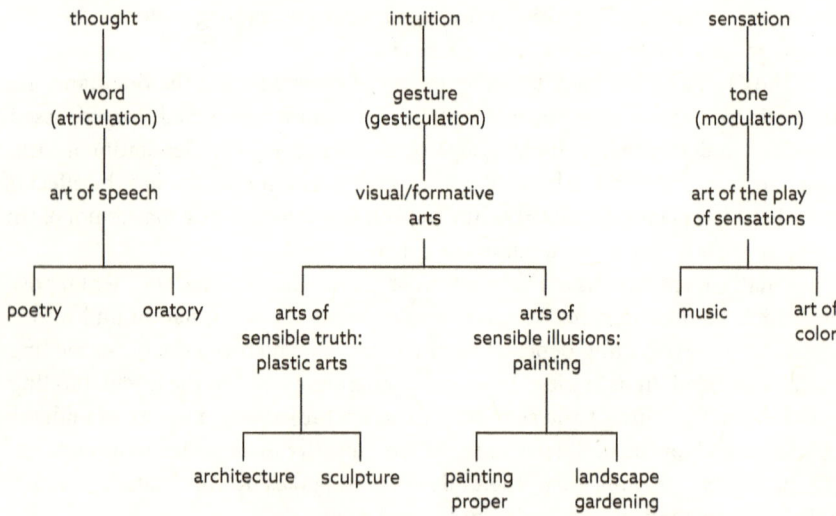

I will highlight only a few issues. First, Kant declares (in §53) that among all the arts, poetry holds the highest rank. Poetry is distinctive in its capacity to expand the mind and set the imagination free. Kant says: "Poetry lets the mind feel its ability to use nature on behalf of and, as it were, as a schema of the supersensible. Poetry plays with *Schein* [letting appear, shining, deception], which it produces at will, and yet without using it to deceive us, for poetry tells us itself that its pursuit is mere play."

It should be noted that by his reference to "a schema of the supersensible," he hints at a connection between poetry and the sublime (*CJ*, p. 197).

Second, to our current sensitivities it seems rather odd that Kant includes, alongside painting proper, landscape gardening, to say nothing of the decoration of rooms with tapestries, with bric-a-brac, and with all beautiful furnishings whose sole function is to be looked at, as well as the art of dressing tastefully with rings, snuff-boxes, etc. But what is most curious is that painting proper proves not to be contained entirely within the boundary meant to delimit it. For in fact—even if design and hence form are essential to painting—it involves also the art of color. Thus, painting is separated from itself, dissevered, so that it falls partly among the visual arts and partly among the arts of the play of sensations. This separation points to the question of whether form or color is primary in painting, a question that Hegel will take up and will resolve in favor of color.

Third, the case of music is also curious. Here everything depends on whether it is just a play of sensations or a formal (beautiful) play of sensations. Only in the latter case can music be considered a fine art. That is, in the play of sensations produced by music, there must be a formal element as a result of which the work could be judged beautiful. The question is whether one merely hears, or also reflectively judges, music.

Fourth, Kant refers to a special affinity between poetry and music or, more specifically, between linguistic expression and tone. He writes: "Every linguistic expression has in its context a tone appropriate to its meaning. . . . The art of music [tone] employs this language all by itself in its full force, namely, as a language of affects" (*CJ*, pp. 198–99.). This says that for every linguistic expression, there is a tone belonging to it. This, in turn, implies that when the linguistic expression is spoken, this tone is also sounded in unison with it. Music separates the tone from the linguistic expression and sounds it all by itself—as music. In this way, music—at least some kinds of music—has its origin in language.

VIII. Conclusion to the Course

At the outset of the *Critique of Judgment*, Kant announced that the goal was to complete the critical enterprise by bringing together the theoretical and the practical, understanding and reason, nature and freedom. We have observed in various contexts how, in subtly different ways, such connections have been established. They occur above all in relation to the purposiveness of beauty, most purely in the beauty of nature. But connections occur also with the sublime, with the way in which sublime nature can serve as a schema of reason itself. They occur also in relation to genius and spirit, in which nature proves to be operative in the subject creatively rather than mechanically.

Yet, perhaps—granted all this—the *Critique of Judgment* is even more significant for what it opens up than for the closure it brings to the critical system. It opens philosophical thought to the beauty of nature and art, so that nature and art are no longer simply regions of objects to be grasped conceptually in philosophical theories. Instead, they prove such that they can draw thought out, extend it beyond its conceptual limits, let it exceed itself.

The *Critique of Judgment* also opens thought to the imagination. Imagination is no longer relegated to being an inferior power, even a distorting and misleading influence to be kept at a distance from rigorous philosophical thought. Instead, imagination can convey thought further, can render it ecstatic. In thus showing how imagination expands thought, Kant has also expanded the very sense of imagination in ways that we have, it seems, only now begun to recognize and take up.

Let me return, then, to a figure I mentioned at the outset. It is the figure Heidegger provides to illustrate the situation with respect to Kant's thought. Even the greatest of those who followed Kant merely leaped over him. Far from overcoming Kant, they simply abandoned the essential foundation of his thought. Indeed, they could hardly be said to have abandoned this foundation, because they never really took it up but merely skirted it. Can we say, then, that for us too, as for the German Idealists, "Kant's work remains like an unconquered fortress behind a new front"?

In any case, I hope we have succeeded in taking a few steps back—or perhaps ahead—toward the site of that fortress.

Part Four.
The Truth of Beauty

Lectures presented at the Collegium Phaenomenologicum
Città di Castello, Italy
July 2011

I. Introduction

Within the general framework of this year's Collegium, expressed in the title "Philosophy, Truth, and the Claims of Art," I propose to take up the specific theme of "the truth of beauty." I will do so in connection with Kant's *Critique of Judgment*.

The *Critique of Judgment* is a strange book; one can say with only the slightest hyperbole: it is uncanny. To those who know something of the first two *Critiques*, much of its language and conceptuality is familiar. It appears merely to extend the critiques of understanding and of reason to the third, intermediate cognitive power, namely, judgment, and thereby "conclude the entire critical enterprise" (*CJ*, p. 7). On the other hand, even from a preliminary, extrinsic perspective, there are some very strange features, giving the book an aura of uncanniness, of disjointedness in a systematic context where it would least be expected.

It is as if the book sometimes falls back beneath levels it has already attained and sometimes races on ahead of itself—also as if it often diverges from what would seem to be its prescribed course. I will mention three (fairly extrinsic) points:

(1) At the end of the Introduction, Kant provides a table listing all the mental powers: powers of knowledge (cognitive powers), the feelings of pleasure and displeasure, and the power of desire. The cognitive powers include understanding, judgment, and reason. What is strange is that imagination is not to be found in this table, despite the fact that in the *Critique of Judgment*, at least in its major part, the Critique of Aesthetic Judgment, the power that figures most prominently is the imagination. It is, then, as if what comes to light in the analysis with regard to the imagination warps or disjoints the framework from which these analyses begin, as if imagination, which hardly figures at all in the beginning, comes to commandeer the analysis.

(2) At the end of the Introduction, there is a table showing the "Division of the Entire Work." In it there is a curious omission. The table shows the Analytic of the Sublime being immediately followed by the Dialectic of Aesthetic Judgment. But in fact, between these, there is a section of more than 50 pages entitled Deduction of Pure Aesthetic Judgments. It is in this section that the entire discussion of art occurs, and indeed it is in many respects the heart of the *Critique of Judgment* as a whole. Strange! The very heart of the work is omitted from the table of contents, as if it did not fit within the framework from which the work begins.

(3) Again something quite strange—and of enormous significance—is indicated in a statement in the first Introduction, the one Kant originally composed and then eventually rewrote. This statement needs to be seen against the background of Kant's basic, most general conception of philosophy. This is the statement: "Philosophy is the *system* of rational cognition [*Vernunft-Erkenntnis*: rational knowledge] through concepts" (*CJ*, p. 385). In distinction from the system (philosophy proper), critique merely investigates the idea of such a system by establishing the possibility and limits of rational knowledge through concepts.

Since there are two kinds of concepts, those of understanding and those of reason, such critique is carried out by the *Critique of Pure Reason* and the *Critique of Practical Reason*. These constitute the propaedeutic to the two parts of the system: metaphysics of nature and metaphysics of morals. So there is a certain asymmetry involved in the project of a *third* critique, although Kant justifies it by reference to the fact that there are three cognitive powers. But what is strange and brings out the asymmetry is what Kant says about the primary theme of a third critique, namely, aesthetic judgment: "Aesthetic judgment, on the other hand, contributes nothing to the cognition of its objects; hence it belongs only to the critique that is the propaedeutic to all philosophy" (*CJ*, p. 35).

So the entire investigation in the *Critique of Judgment* belongs only to the propaedeutic, is not yet philosophy proper, and, as preparatory, does not even correspond to a part of philosophy. Why? It is because aesthetic judgment yields no knowledge, no rational knowledge through concepts. In other words, in carrying out an aesthetic judgment with regard to an object, one gains no knowledge at all about the object. (This is a central issue to which we will return.) So it is as if the *Critique of Judgment*, since it deals with a kind of relation to objects that is totally different from rational knowledge of objects through concepts, falls completely outside philosophy.

* * *

These features indicate that the course of the third *Critique* is not simply a linear development and that its topography is of such complexity as not to be easily charted. The work seems to have a kind of *inner dynamism*; as it engages its basic issues, its *Sachen*, it is driven on in ways not readily foreseeable and sometimes at variance with its systematic constraints. Our concern will be to measure the extent to which and the ways in which this inner dynamism drives the *Critique of Judgment* beyond the standpoint from which it is launched, that is, to see how this text exceeds itself and opens onto something beyond or outside the completion of the critical enterprise.

II. Truth

It may also seem strange that we will focus of the specific theme of "the truth of beauty." For this is not properly a theme of the *Critique of Judgment*. Nowhere in the text does Kant address this theme as such. Indeed, he does not ever address the theme of truth; that is, he does not take up the question of truth, the question, "What is truth?" In the *Critique of Pure Reason*, Kant does *touch* on this theme, and yet, rather than taking up the question of truth, he simply cites a traditional conception, which he says he is assuming, presupposing without further discussion: "The nominal definition of truth, that it is the agreement of knowledge with its object, is granted and presupposed" (A58/B82). We could then justifiably say that Kant evades the question of truth. But why this evasion?

In the *Critique of Pure Reason*, Kant defends this evasion by referring to the sagacity displayed by knowing which questions can reasonably be asked. And yet, we might wonder: at the outset of a critique of *reason*, can it be known which questions are or are not reasonable? Or could this be determined only *on the basis of* a critique of reason? Nevertheless, Kant is quite sure that pursuing the question "What is truth?" is not the right course, which is to pass over this question and turn immediately to the issue, not of truth itself, but of its criterion. In a rare moment of humor, Kant says that entanglement in the question of truth could even have the effect of "presenting... the ludicrous spectacle of one person milking a he-goat and another holding a sieve underneath" (A58/B82–83).

In Kant's *Logic*, the precariousness of engaging in the question of truth becomes even clearer. Here, too, Kant cites the definition of truth as the agreement of knowledge with the object. He continues: "My knowledge, then, in order to pass as true, shall agree with the object. I can, however, compare the object with my knowledge only by knowing it. My knowledge thus shall confirm itself, which is yet far from sufficient for truth. For since the object is outside me and the knowledge in me, I can judge only whether my knowledge of the object agrees with my knowledge of the object" (*Logic*, tr. R. S. Hartman and W. Schwarz, Indianapolis: Bobbs-Merrill, 1974, p. 55).

So here, according to Kant, there is a circle, one impossible of solution. The taking up of the question of truth, even to the extent of thinking through what the definition really means, leads into an impossible circle. Hence Kant moves on immediately in the *Logic* (p. 55) to the issue of a *criterion* of truth: "For that is the meaning of the question: what is truth?" Here the evasion is clearly marked.

What I want to ask is this: granted Kant's evasion, does the very force of his analyses in the *Critique of Judgment* have the effect of reopening the question of truth and of setting in motion advances that exceed the perspective of the *Critique of Pure Reason*? According to that first *Critique*, truth is a character of knowledge, namely, its agreement with the object, and so Kant uses the expression "the truth of knowledge." Now, can one justifiably speak of the truth of something other than knowledge? For example, of things, of art, of beauty?

Instead of simply following Kant in his evasion of the question of truth, let us for a moment dwell with the question and consider some implications of the conception Kant presupposes. That will help us understand both the initial standpoint from which the third *Critique* proceeds and how in general an exceeding of this standpoint is achievable.

Truth is the agreement of knowledge with its object. But what is the object of knowledge? What can be an object of knowledge? For Kant, the objects of knowledge are appearances, objects as they appear to us through the mediation of the categories and the forms of intuition. The totality of these objects equals nature. Nature is "the sum total of all objects of sense" (*CJ*, p. 13). According to the *Critique of Pure Reason*, "By nature . . . is meant the sum of appearances insofar as they stand, in virtue of an inner principle of causality, in thoroughgoing interconnection" (B446). This is the conception of nature as pure mechanism, even though conceived as mechanism of appearances rather than of things in themselves. Nature is devoid of all features other than the causally determined properties treated by physical science.

What happens in the *Critique of Judgment* is that Kant discovers a way to take seriously certain other features we experience in nature, such as beauty and sublimity. Kant discovers that these are not merely subjective and empirical but that they have a transcendental ground, are governed by an apriori principle. Thus there is some basis for our judging certain things to be beautiful or sublime, even if there is no cognition. To this extent, nature proves to exceed its purely objective, mechanical, causally determined character. This is, then, one kind of advance the *Critique of Judgment* will carry out. It will do so through an analysis of aesthetic judgment, since it is in such judgment that these features are disclosed.

Truth is the agreement of knowledge with its object. In other words, truth consists in a certain relatedness of knowledge to its object. This relatedness is not simply an external connection between two distinct things, for knowing is *not* a thing. Instead, knowledge agrees with its object and so is true precisely when, in and through the knowing, the object is revealed. True knowing is an intending of, an opening upon, the object, which means the object is thereby revealed.

Now, once knowledge is understood in this way as a disclosive comportment, the question can be posed: are there other forms of relatedness or comportment that also—if in a different respect—disclose the object? Aesthetic judgment is precisely such a form of comportment in which the object can be disclosed—as beautiful. So this judgment is a form of relatedness that is like knowledge in that it reveals the object, yet it is also other than knowledge.

If we extend the traditional, presupposed conception of truth to include other ways of revealing things, that is, other ways of relating disclosively to things, ways other than knowledge, then we can give a sense to the phrase "the truth of beauty." The truth of beauty is the agreement or accord that must be displayed between a certain comportment and a beautiful thing, the comportment in and through which the thing reveals itself as beautiful. This accord is analogous to the one between knowledge and its object, thus analogous to the truth of knowledge. Such comportment to beauty occurs in what Kant calls "aesthetic judgment" or, more precisely, the "judgment of taste."

III. Aesthetic Judgment

LET US CONSIDER what Kant means by aesthetic judgment and specifically by aesthetic judgment with regard to beauty, that is, the judgment of taste. I will mention four points.

(1) Aesthetic judgment is a form of reflective judgment. The latter is defined by Kant as follows: "Judgment in general is the ability [power, capacity] to think the particular as contained under the universal. If the universal (the rule, principle, law) is given, then judgment, which subsumes the particular under it, is determinative.... But if only the particular is given and judgment has to find the universal for it, then this power is merely reflective" (*CJ*, p. 18).

In reflective judgment, only the particular (either the specific or the singular) is given and judgment must find the universal under which to subsume it. Note that Kant extends the sense of universal beyond that of mere concepts. He mentions rule, principle, law. For example, the subsumption would be as follows: from some phenomenon to a specific law to a more universal law. This implies that aesthetic judgment proceeds from the particular, and in fact, as we will see, it proceeds from the singular.

(2) Aesthetic judgment involves purposiveness. More precisely, in aesthetic judgment, the object judged, the singular, proves to be purposive. In section IV of the Introduction to the *Critique of Judgment*, Kant provides a precise yet very abstract definition of purpose and purposiveness. To put it as simply as possible, a purpose is that for the sake of which something is made. Whatever is of such a character that it serves a purpose is purposive. More precisely, whatever by virtue of its character *could* serve a purpose, whether it does or not, is purposive. Still more precisely, whatever appears as *suited* to serve a purpose (as if it were made for that purpose) can be called purposive, even if in fact no conception of purpose was involved in its fabrication. Hence, it is possible to have "purposiveness without a purpose" (*CJ*, p. 65).

In aesthetic judgment, the object proves to be purposive without a purpose. This means that it appears so suited to our mental powers that it is as if it had been made in accord with—made to accord with—those powers. An object that appears as having such purposiveness, such accord, such *truth*, reveals itself thereby as beautiful.

(3) Aesthetic judgment is distinct and different from cognition (knowledge) and yet has a decisive connection to it. We saw already how this difference is marked in the Introduction. Let us now look at the formulation in the Preface. There Kant says about aesthetic judgments: "For although they do not by themselves contribute anything whatever to our cognition of things, they still belong to the cognitive power alone . . ." (*CJ*, p. 6). This says that aesthetic judgment is distinct from knowing and yet is effected precisely through the power of knowing. In other words, aesthetic judgment is an exercise of a power of knowing which produces not knowledge, but something else distinct from knowledge. We could say that aesthetic judgment, although different from knowing, is bound to it, has a certain affinity or proximity to knowing. It is within the space of this affinity or proximity that many of the most important moves—indeed, the most excessive moves—of the *Critique of Judgment* take place.

We will want to watch very closely what happens in the space of this proximity, this space that both disjoins and conjoins knowing and aesthetic judgment. In anticipation, let me discuss one indication. As a subsuming of the particular under a universal, judgment is intrinsically an operation of thought, a conceptual operation belonging to cognition. So, even the phrase "aesthetic judgment" already poses a tension, since "aesthetic" refers to sense in opposition to thought, concept. It is remarkable, then, that Kant characterizes our comportment to beauty, which is sensuous comportment, as judgment. The appropriateness lies solely in the affinity between this comportment and cognition. But, insofar as there remains an irreducible difference, comportment to the beautiful cannot remain simply a kind of judgment. Instead, as the analysis is carried through, the character of this comportment as judgment will be displaced. That is to say, there will occur a kind of erasure of the judgment in aesthetic judgment—even as still, in a certain way, the structure of judgment or a trace of it will remain.

(4) If we put the first three points together and extend them slightly, we gain an outline of the structure of aesthetic judgment with regard to beauty. There is the singular object, which is given and which we apprehend. The object proves to be purposive, that is, in accord with certain of our cognitive powers. Through the display of this accord (truth), the object reveals itself as beautiful. This accord, like all such accord, is accompanied by a positive affectivity, that is, by a feeling of pleasure. So the structure of aesthetic judgment involves three moments:

(a) the object is apprehended
(b) an accord with our cognitive powers is displayed
(c) a feeling of pleasure is produced.

Let us consider this structure more closely. Aesthetic judgment has to do with the object only as intuitively apprehended. Specifically, it has to do only with the *intuitive form* of the object. It does not have anything at all to do with the sensory or material content, with what in the object, as given, is merely a matter of sensation. In aesthetic judgment, the sensory content is completely disregarded for the sake of the pure intuitive form.

Kant contrasts this formal intuitive apprehension with the case in which, rather than being merely apprehended, the object is known, cognized. Cognition involves both intuition and concept: intuition through which objects are given and concepts through which they are thought. For example, I see an object, have an intuition of it, and then, in an act of recognition, I refer that seen object to the concept "tree." Then I know, as I say: This thing is a tree. So, in general, cognition involves both intuition and concept and occurs through the referral of the intuition to a concept.

On the other hand, in aesthetic judgment, there is no cognition of the object, not even of its form. That means the apprehended form of the object is *not* referred to a concept. So, the way the form is taken up in aesthetic judgment will be different from a referral to and subsumption under a concept.

Note an apparent aporia here. As a type of reflective judgment, aesthetic judgment must involve thinking the particular as contained (subsumed) under the universal. And yet, since it is not cognition, aesthetic judgment does not involve the subsumption of a particular under a universal concept. So how is its character as reflective retained? What is the relevant universal, and how is the particular related to it? We will come back to these questions.

* * *

Let us turn now to the key paragraph (*CJ*, pp. 29–30, section VII of the Introduction), which begins: "When pleasure is connected with the mere apprehension (*apprehensio*) of the form of an object of intuition and we do not refer the apprehension to a concept so as to give rise to determinate cognition. . . ." Here Kant is laying out the structure of the apprehension occurring in aesthetic judgment:

(1) apprehension of the form of an object
(2) pleasure connected with this apprehension
(3) but without any cognition; the apprehension is not referred to a concept.

The passage continues: "then we refer the representation not to the object but solely to the subject. . . ." That means the representation, the apprehended form, is not used for cognition of the object. Instead, the representation is referred "solely to the subject." In other words, it is taken solely in its relation to the subject, as purposive with respect to the subject, as displaying a certain accord with the subject's cognitive power.

Kant continues: "and the pleasure cannot express anything other than the object's being commensurate with the cognitive powers that are, and insofar as they are, brought into play when we judge subjectively, and hence the pleasure expresses merely a subjective formal purposiveness of the object." This says that the pleasure expresses—is produced as a result of—the accord of the object (its pure form) with the cognitive powers, that is, its subjective purposiveness. Note that in reflective judgment, the cognitive powers are not simply, inactively, dormantly there but rather are *in play*.

Let us consider more precisely the apprehension of the form of the object. What is the character of this apprehension? Up to now, it has seemed to be merely a matter of intuition. Certainly, it is an act taking place at the level of intuition and, in particular, prior to any thought, any concept, indeed without even being oriented toward a concept to which it might subsequently be referred. Yet this apprehension, unlike sheer sense intuition, is not merely receptive, for rather than intuiting the object, it apprehends only the form. That is, in and through this apprehension, the form is detached from the object itself, separated from the sensory content.

Such apprehension requires imagination. Thus the passage continues by alluding to the "apprehension of forms by the imagination" or, to translate more literally and precisely, the apprehension takes the forms up *into* the imagination (*in die Einbildungskraft*).

What then happens once the forms are taken up in this way? The passage continues: "For this apprehension of forms into the imagination can never occur without reflective judgment comparing them, even if unintentionally, at least with its power to refer intuitions to concepts." So once the forms are apprehended, they are compared to the power by which intuitions are referred to concepts. But that power, the power of concepts, is primarily the understanding. Thus once the forms are taken up into imagination, these forms (held in imagination) are compared to the understanding. In other words, imagination (as holding these forms) is referred to the understanding.

Accordingly, the passage continues: "If in this comparison the imagination (as the power of apriori intuitions) [Here Kant expresses the mixed, receptive-active character of the imagination.] is, through a given representation, unintentionally set into accord [*Einstimmung*: harmony] with the understanding (as the power of concepts), and thereby a feeling of pleasure is aroused, then the object must be regarded as purposive for the reflective judgment." This shows more clearly the character of the accord at the center of aesthetic judgment. In this judgment, the form taken up into imagination proves such that imagination is thereby (by holding this form) set in accord with the understanding. And when there is such accord between imagination and understanding, a feeling of pleasure is aroused.

Then the object—by virtue of having such form—will have proved to conform to our cognitive powers.

* * *

Having outlined the basic structure, Kant, in section VII of the Introduction and in the Analytic, proceeds to introduce several further developments. I will discuss only four of them.

(1) Aesthetic judgment is not based on any concept and does not produce a concept. In different terms, an aesthetic judgment is always singular. The singular form of this singular object proves to set imagination in accord with the understanding. But there is no cognition, no concept under which the singular is subsumed.

(2) When the form of the object sets the imagination in accord with the understanding and so arouses a feeling of pleasure, the object is said to be beautiful. We would then assert that the truth of beauty lies in the accord between the object's form as taken up into imagination and the understanding. So the truth of beauty, like the truth of knowledge, consists in a certain *Einstimmung* or *Übereinstimmung* between the cognitive powers and the object. What distinguishes these two truths is the specific structure of the *Übereinstimmung* and especially that the truth of beauty involves no concept and remains at the level of singularity.

(3) Even though an aesthetic judgment is singular, it has a certain universality, a "subjective universality," in the sense that it can lay claim to everyone's assent. This universality constitutes still another affinity between aesthetic judgment and cognition.

Kant approaches the issue of universality from several different perspectives. In one of these approaches in section VII of the Introduction, he clarifies not only this issue but another one equally important for us:

> In the same way, someone who feels pleasure in the mere reflection on the form of an object, without any concern about a concept, rightly lays claim to everyone's assent, even though this judgment is empirical and singular. For the basis of this pleasure is found in the universal, although subjective, condition of reflective judgments, namely, the purposive accord [*zweckmässige Übereinstimmung*] of an object (whether a product of nature or of art) with the mutual relation of the cognitive powers (imagination and understanding) that are required for every empirical cognition. (*CJ*, p. 31)

Kant is saying here that the purposive accord of the object is its accord with the mutual relation between imagination and understanding, *as* they are related in all empirical cognition. More specifically, what happens in the aesthetic judgment is this: imagination takes up the form of the object into itself, and thereby that form is set in accordant relation to the understanding. Imagination takes the form up into the very same relation imagination and understanding must have in cognition in order for cognition to occur, although in aesthetic judgment there is no cognition. In other words, imagination and understanding are set in this relation in such a way that what occurs is not cognition but merely *play* between them, free play.

We could say, then, that apprehended form proves accordant with what is universal in the subject; indeed, not just *is* universal and hence shared by all and possessing the universality of aesthetic judgment but is the very *source* of universality, the origin from which all universality arises.

This result can be extended in two ways. First, in this very significant move, Kant shows that in aesthetic judgment, the accord between imagination and understanding is the same as the accord in knowledge, except that no concept is involved and so there is no referral to a concept. Thus here the affinity is enhanced between aesthetic judgment and cognition. That is, there proves to be still closer proximity between these two kinds of comportment to objects. Second, once the relation between the mental powers, as evoked through the apprehension of the form, is recognized as the origin of universality, then it is clear how aesthetic judgment is a kind of reflective judgment. In aesthetic judgment, a particular (the singular form of a singular object) is referred to (taken up in relation to) not just a universal but to the very origin of universality, that is, referred to universality itself.

(4) The fourth development concerns feeling. Kant reiterates that in aesthetic judgment, the apprehended form, that is, the representation, sets the cognitive powers in free play, since there is no concept involved and hence no determinate cognition. Then Kant observes: "Hence the mental state in this representation must be a *feeling* of the free play of the representational powers in connection with the given representation and directed to cognition in general" (*CJ*, p. 62, emphasis added). So whereas in cognition, there is a knowing directed to the objective thing, in aesthetic judgment, there is a feeling directed to the beautiful thing, but directed to it *through* the feeling of free play, accord, that it evokes. Kant calls it even the feeling "of the accord in the play of the mental powers" (*CJ*, p. 75). Or again: "Here the subject feels itself, namely, how it is affected by the representation" (*CJ*, p. 44). Kant is referring to the "feeling of life," which is a "feeling of pleasure" (*CJ*, p. 44).

Here we begin to see that the feeling of the accord and the feeling of pleasure are not two separate feelings. There is not first a feeling of the accord and then consequently, as produced, a feeling of pleasure. Rather, when the accord is felt, it is felt *with pleasure*. That is, pleasure refers not to the object of the feeling but to its "quality." The object of the feeling is the accordant free play of imagination and understanding. Kant says that we come "to feel the representational state with pleasure" (*CJ*, p. 159).

We can summarize Kant's development of the structure of aesthetic judgment as follows. At first, this structure appeared to involve three distinct moments: apprehension, reflection, and feeling of pleasure. But it eventually proved to be a highly *unified* structure. When the form of the object is taken up into imagination, that power is thereby set into accordant free play with the understanding. In its very initiation, this accordant free play is felt with pleasure, in a feeling that is also reflexive, namely as a feeling of oneself, a life-feeling. What forms the center of this unified structure is the double accord, and this accord constitutes the truth of beauty.

Furthermore, recalling that the truth of beauty lies in the accord and is realized in the free play of imagination and understanding, we can say: the truth of beauty is felt with pleasure. It is a truth that, despite its proximity to knowing, is felt rather than known. In the feeling of this truth, the thing reveals itself as beautiful, and at the same time, in this very feeling, one feels oneself, one's life. In other words, there occurs an enlivening, a quickening of life.

Here, then, there is an erasure of the judgment in aesthetic judgment, inasmuch as judgment (conceptual act) is displaced by feeling. Yet there remains a trace of the structure of reflective judgment inasmuch as a particular (singular form) is referred to universality itself, the origin of universality.

IV. The Turn in the Analysis of Aesthetic Judgment

Most of the Analytic of the Beautiful is concerned with amplifying the general structure of aesthetic judgment and drawing out consequences. Kant rigorously distinguishes this mode of comportment, the pure judgment of taste, from cognition of an object and also from other kinds of affective comportment to things, namely, from a liking for things that are agreeable or pleasant, things that please the senses or things we like because of their charm (which also has to do with sense), and from a liking for things that are good. Kant observes that an orientation to the good always involves concepts: to consider something good, I must know what it is supposed to be, its purpose; that is, I must have a concept of it.

Kant contrasts such things with those that can be called beautiful: "Flowers, free designs, lines aimlessly intertwined and called foliage, signify nothing, depend on no determinate concept, and yet they please us" (*CJ*, p. 49).

Throughout this discussion, Kant stresses that form alone entitles something to be called beautiful. Only the form can evoke the felt accordant free play through which the object is revealed as beautiful. Neither the sense-content nor the concept has the slightest bearing on beauty.

Let us now focus on a strange turn the *Critique of Judgment* takes, in a direction that seems counter to its previous course. Throughout almost the entire Analytic of the Beautiful, Kant insists on the purity of the judgment of taste—that it not be contaminated by an admixture of concepts or of sensory content. And yet, before the analysis is even quite finished, indeed long before Kant finally stops circling back to it, he begins to refer to cases in which there is in fact an admixture of a conceptual aspect. This turn is clearly marked at the beginning of §16: "There are two kinds of beauty: free beauty (*pulchritudo vaga*) [*vagus*: vague, unfixed] and merely dependent beauty (*pulchritudo adhaerens*). Free beauty does not presuppose a concept of what the object is meant to be. Dependent beauty does presuppose such a concept as well as the perfection of the object in terms of that concept" (*CJ*, p. 76).

Kant adds: "When we judge free beauty (according to mere form), then our judgment of taste is pure" (*CJ*, p. 77). This is to be contrasted with judgments in which we judge the object both with respect to form and also with respect to its perfection, its matching up to its concept.

This terminology and all that preceded would seem to posit a priority of free beauty over dependent beauty. Yet Kant's examples might make us wonder, for free beauties include things like flowers and foliage on wallpaper, whereas the beauty of a building or of a human being is a dependent beauty, involving both form and perfection. In fact, by the end of §16, Kant grants the superiority of dependent beauty: "It is true that taste gains by such a connection of aesthetic with intellectual liking, for it becomes fixed . . ." (*CJ*, p. 78). There is a gain "when the two states of mind harmonize" (*CJ*, p. 78).

So, contrary to what the previous analysis suggests, virtually everything from this point on involves *not* maintaining the purity of aesthetic judgment but rather mixing or conjoining such judgment with other kinds of comportment. This becomes eminently clear in Kant's discussion (§17) of the ideal of beauty (highest example, exemplary beauty). It transpires that the ideal is not a free beauty (there is no ideal of beautiful flowers) but a dependent beauty (that of a human being). The ideal thus corresponds to a double (coupled, mixed) comportment: pure aesthetic judgment (feeling of accord evoked by form) and determinate conceptual judgment with regard to the perfection of the object.

V. Couplings

Let us look at several couplings and identify the modes of comportment involved and the manner in which the moments are conjoined. We want to see what comes to be revealed—or in some other way brought forth—through these compound modes of comportment and to observe especially how this exceeds mere formal beauty. We will consider:

(1) Intellectual interest in the beautiful
(2) Artistic production
(3) The artwork.

(1) Intellectual interest in the beautiful.

There is a coupling of aesthetic judgment (judgment of taste) with intellectual interest in the beautiful. Recall a feature of the judgment of taste as developed in §§2–4. This judgment is a *disinterested* liking of the object. That means the judgment of taste is engaged merely with the detached form and has no interest in the existence of the object. So in this coupling, there is conjoined to the judgment of taste—although as a distinct moment—a taking of interest in the beautiful object.

Kant describes this interest as intellectual. Here "intellectual" refers to reason and to our moral vocation as free, supersensible subjects. Kant's point is that as rational, we take an interest in whatever trace or hint nature may show—through its beautiful forms—of its accord with the domain of freedom. More precisely, anyone of good moral character, that is, anyone in whom rational, free self-determination is operative, will take such an interest and so will couple this taking of interest with his disinterested comportment to the beautiful.

Yet if it should turn out that this trace is not natural but contrived, then the intellectual interest will immediately cease. This demonstrates that such interest requires the thought of the *natural* origin of the beauty. That is, along with the judgment of taste and the taking of interest, there must also be a thought of the natural origin. That is the point of the famous story Kant tells at the end of §42: if the song of a nightingale proves to have been produced by a boy playing a prank, these sounds that a moment ago were so charming will immediately become unendurable.

If we now ask what is revealed, brought forth, through this complex comportment, then we are merely asking what guise the natural trace assumes. Most remarkably, Kant says it assumes the guise of "a cipher-writing through which nature speaks to us in its beautiful forms" (*CJ*, p. 168). So in and through the beautiful forms of nature, something is said, something that could not simply be presented. That is, the beautiful forms of nature constitute a language in which nature speaks to us. In contemplating the beautiful forms of nature, the lover of nature is reading, interpreting, the script of nature.

Furthermore, and just as remarkably, Kant introduces still another language of nature, one that accompanies and supplements the language of beautiful forms. It is a language distinct from the language of beautiful forms yet nonetheless is fused with it. This second language is that of the charms often connected with beautiful forms. Indeed, charms are a matter of sense-content, so here we see how, in this complex comportment, the merely formal is exceeded. For here occurs a sense-content that is not merely sensed but is significant, thus constituting "a language in which nature speaks to us" (*CJ*, p. 169). Kant offers some examples: the lily's white color attunes the mind to ideas of innocence, etc. But, above all, there is the bird's song (*CJ*, pp. 94, 169).

So in cases of these couplings, the beauty of nature is no longer simply its beautiful form; instead, in the more complex comportment involved in this beauty, it is form and its accompanying charms that are beautiful and also assume the guise of these languages in which nature speaks to us. Natural beauty thus exceeds mere form by assuming the guise of a λόγος of nature.

(2) Artistic production.

When Kant finally turns to art and artistic beauty, he focuses not on our receptive-imaginative comportment to art but especially on the productive comportment, the creative activity, by which artworks are brought forth.

Kant's entire analysis here is set against the background of the classical conception of ποίησις: the maker has, in advance, a representation of what is to be made, a paradigm in the mind's eye, and then he makes the product in the image of the paradigm. Kant himself expresses it this way: "we see art in everything that is of such a character that before it became actual its cause [maker] must have had a representation of it" (*CJ*, p. 170). The first question is then: in the case of the production of a work of fine art (*schöne Kunst*), what are the modes of comportment and/or activity that must be involved? One required mode is aesthetic judgment, the judgment of taste. Kant stresses that the artist must develop taste to the highest degree, which requires academic training carried out by study of exemplary works. Only in this way is the artist capable of giving form to the artistic material he would bring forth in the artwork. Kant describes how this occurs: "The artist, having practiced and corrected his taste by a variety of examples from art or nature, holds his work up to it [his taste] and, after many and often laborious attempts to satisfy his taste, finds the form which is adequate to it" (*CJ*, p. 180).

Yet artistic production requires that another moment be conjoined with the highly developed judgment of taste. Kant does not describe how this other, productive moment operates and provides no analysis comparable to that of the judgment of taste, for its operation is essentially concealed. Not even the artist in whom it is instantiated has any insight into how it operates. This other moment, the moment of originality, Kant calls "genius": "Genius is the talent (natural endowment) [*Naturgabe*: natural gift] that gives the rule to art. Since talent is an innate productive power of the artist and as such belongs itself to nature, we could also put it this way: genius is the innate mental disposition (*ingenium*) through which *nature* gives the rule to art" (*CJ*, p. 174).

So this moment is constituted by a double giving: nature gives genius, and genius gives the rule to art. In other words, it is from *nature*, by way of genius, that art receives the rule determining it.

Kant immediately develops several points. He begins by insisting that all art requires rules. These serve as the foundation through which a product, if it is to be called "artistic," is "first of all represented as possible" (*CJ*, p. 175). This follows from the classical concept of making: if something is to be produced (for example, an artwork), it must be represented in advance to the mind's eye as merely possible. The rules constitute, in effect, this prior representation.

This representation, however, these rules, cannot be based on, that is, expressed in, a concept, for the beauty of a product cannot be derived from any concept. So this prior representation is not a conceptual one. It is not as if the artist first looks to a concept of the object and then produces an actual exemplification of it. Thus Kant says that art (the artist) cannot devise, think out, the rules by which the product is to be brought forth.

Yet there must still be a rule, a rule must be given, according to which the artwork is brought forth. *Genius* is the talent that gives the rule. That is to say, in terms of the classical concept of making, genius gives in advance the rule from/through which the artwork is brought forth.

But genius is *itself given*. It is a natural endowment, a *Naturgabe*, a gift of nature. It is a productive power inborn in the artist, bestowed on him by nature. Let me highlight three consequences:

First, to say that genius is a gift of nature does not simply mean that it derives from nature but also means that, operating within the artist, it operates *in the mode of* nature, not in the mode of cognition or freedom. In this regard, Kant uses the phrase "nature in the subject" (*CJ*, p. 175). It is not as though the subject receives the gift and then, having appropriated it, goes about producing his work through a cognitive or at least self-transparent activity. The one with genius does not *know* how he brings about his product: "Genius itself cannot describe or indicate scientifically how it brings about its products, and it is rather as *nature* that genius gives the rule. That is why, if an author [*Urheber*: originator, creator] owes a product to his genius, he himself does not know how he came by the ideas for it; nor is it in his power to devise such products at will" (*CJ*, p. 175). So we could say that genius is in excess of the subject. It is adherent to the subject, operative as nature within the subject, but not appropriable by the subject.

Second, in this analysis, the classical conception of production—as it pertains to fine art—has undergone a decisive mutation. According to that conception, the artist must have a prior representation of what is to be made. It now transpires that this is precisely what he does *not* have. Although the work is brought forth according to rules and not just arbitrarily, not by sheer accident, the genius does not have these rules in view. Instead, they are "in him" only as nature. We could say that they merely "pass through him" from nature.

Last, if nature is capable of giving the rule by which beautiful art is brought forth, then nature can no longer by conceived as the mere causal nexus it was taken to be in the *Critique of Pure Reason*. That is, if nature can operate within the subject so as to give rules the subject himself cannot give and to which he is blind, then nature must have a capacity that exceeds mere mechanism.

(3) The artwork.

In and through an artwork, thus brought forth tastefully by genius, what is revealed, disclosed, expressed?

The work appears of course as beautiful, since its production will have been governed by a judgment of taste. Kant observes, however, that there are works that measure up to the judgment of taste but of which we say that they have no spirit. This suggests that fine art in the full sense must not only be beautiful but must also have spirit.

What is spirit? According to Kant, it is the power of presenting aesthetic ideas (*CJ*, p. 182). Thus for an artwork to have spirit means it presents aesthetic ideas. In fact, it turns out that the beauty of an artwork is intimately bound up with its presentation or expression of aesthetic ideas. And it is this bond that leads Kant finally (§51) to redefine beauty in a way that exceeds the formal determination in the Analytic of the Beautiful: beauty is the expression of aesthetic ideas. What, then, is an aesthetic idea? Kant provides an explicit definition: "By an aesthetic idea I mean a representation of the imagination which prompts much thought but to which no determinate thought whatever, that is, no concept, can be adequate, so that no language can fully express it and allow us to grasp it" (*CJ*, p. 182). So an aesthetic idea is a representation of (subjective genitive) imagination, a representation *by* the imagination. This indicates that in genial production, the mental power that is operative is imagination. Although nature gives the rule, it is imagination that effects the production.

Furthermore, an aesthetic idea is a representation that prompts (*veranlassen*: occasions, motivates, brings about, calls forth, evokes) much thought. Yet such an idea is a representation to which no determinate thought, no concept, can be adequate, can match up to. It is a representation that cannot be grasped, comprehended, encompassed in a concept. It is a representation that *exceeds* every determinate thought. Thus language cannot fully express it, or, to translate Kant's phrase more literally: "No language can fully reach it and render it understandable." Why? —Because what can be expressed in language, what is meant by words, is precisely a concept or combination of concepts. An aesthetic idea, on the other hand, is a representation that escapes language, that exceeds the expressive possibilities of language.

Now we come to a crucial point: although an aesthetic idea exceeds every concept, it is always set forth in conjunction with a concept. That is, an aesthetic idea is not set forth in some remote and independent sphere apart from concepts and the experience of nature. Instead, an aesthetic idea is always paired with a concept and so is always an idea "about" something. Kant uses here the term *unterlegen*: the aesthetic idea is "set under" the concept. Yet this does not mean that idea and concept are simply matched, for it is precisely the character of an idea that it exceeds every concept.

It is just this movement of exceeding that is decisive. Set under the concept and exceeding it, the aesthetic idea "aesthetically expands the concept itself in an unlimited way" (*CJ*, p. 183). Accordingly, it is as if, set under the concept, the excessive idea stretches the concept beyond what it can comprehend, expands the concept beyond itself. When this happens, the imagination is creative and reason is made to think more than can be apprehended in the mere concept.

VI. Conclusion to the Course

So finally, what about the truth of beauty? Or, more precisely, what about the truth that determines our comportment to the beautiful, that determines it as comportment to the beautiful? Now, it seems, we can say: this truth consists not only in the accord of the free yet measured play of imagination with understanding but also in the excess of the imagination, that is, in the movement by which imagination, through aesthetic ideas, so exceeds the concept that it draws knowing beyond itself.

In the end, the truth of beauty is such that we, rational and cognitive subjects, yet also sensuous ones, are drawn beyond what we are, drawn to exceed ourselves.

Editor's Afterword

This volume of John Sallis' Collected Writings presents his lecture courses on Kant. The first three main Parts of the volume correspond respectively to courses on the *Critique of Pure Reason*, on Kant's practical philosophy (*Foundations of the Metaphysics of Morals* and *Critique of Practical Reason*), and on the *Critique of Judgment*. Part Four again takes up the *Critique of Judgment* but this time with a focus on a particular theme, namely, the connection between truth and beauty.

The discussion herein of the *Critique of Pure Reason* deals only with the Aesthetic and Analytic. The entire second semester of the course on this *Critique* was devoted to the Dialectic, and those lectures form the basis of Sallis' already published *The Gathering of Reason* (see above, footnote 1, p. 99).

Only minor editorial intervention was required in preparing the courses for publication. The notes Sallis lectured from are written in a clear longhand and are almost always formulated in full sentences. I was privileged to attend Sallis' courses on Kant at Duquesne University, and my transcription of the lectures as delivered enabled me now to supplement Sallis' notes when he departed from them in oral presentation. Sallis himself has approved the final text. I articulated the courses into outline form, provided a key to the citations of Kant's works, and verified all the references to Kant. Finally, although Sallis' notes display few colloquialisms, I needed to make some changes in phraseology and diction, as might be expected in the transition from oral delivery to printed page.

I thank John Sallis for entrusting this volume of his Collected Writings to me, and for very helpful comments on the penultimate version of the entire text, I am indebted to one of his current graduate assistants, now writing her dissertation under his direction at Boston College, my daughter Christine Rojcewicz.

Richard Rojcewicz

Index

Page numbers in italics refer to diagrams.

absolute totality, as demand of reason, 162, 228
academic training of talent, 244, 268
aesthetic, as investigation of sensibility, 20–40; as judgment of taste, 153, 191–225, *201, 240, 257*; aesthetic ideas, 183, 245–47, 270
agreeableness, as a liking based on sensation, 214, 217–18, *240*, 241, 265
analogies of experience, 79, 86–87
analytic, versus synthetic, 12–13
anticipations of perception, 79, 82–87
antinomies, as disrupting the unity of reason, 10–11, 106; first antinomy, 10; as cradle of the critical philosophy, 23; third antinomy, 110–13, 142, 151; antinomy of practical reason, 163–65
apodicticity, 32
appearances, versus things in themselves, 15–16, 24, 97, 188; as matter and form, 25, 31; outer versus inner, 35–37; primary qualities as, 38; self-intuition as, 39, 66–67, 141, 160; as of some thing appearing, 58–61, 91, 189; and the transcendental object, 62, 95; affinity of, 72; subsumption of under categories, 74, 83; time as universal form of, 75, 85; versus noumena, 151, 191; nature as sum of, 181, 256
apriori, versus aposteriori, 12–13, 33, 45
Aquinas, 52
architectonic, 4, 15, 21
architecture, *217, 248*; architectural metaphor, 15–16
Aristotle, 18, 51–52, 192
arts, classification of, 217, 241, 247, *248*
association of representations, 71
astronomy, 13, 187
autonomy, versus heteronomy, 122, 136, 150; formula of, 132–33; as foundation of morality, 137; as supreme principle of morality, 138; as the causality of freedom, 138–40
axioms, of time in general, 36; of intuition, 79–82

Baumgarten, 15, 84, 215
beauty, analytic of, 205–20; as symbol of morality, 181; free versus dependent, 218, *219*, 265–66; interest in, 233–38; truth of, 253–72
birds, birdsongs, 218, 233–38
British Empiricists, 71
Brouwer, 34
Burke, 182, 215

categories, as pure concepts, 44; table of, 49–51; deduction of (*see* transcendental deduction); determination of, 73–93; practical, 154–55, 166
causality, as problem of connection between object and representation, 9; Humean attack on the concept of, 89–90; and third antinomy, 111–12; that of freedom versus that of nature, 138–41; as noumenal, 151–54; as free, 155; and antinomy of practical reason, 167; of God, 171
charm, 216–18, 222, 224, 234–35, 237, 265, 268
Christ, 123
cipher-writing, 237, 268
Clarke, 27–28
cognitive powers in aesthetic judgment, 189, 197, 200–10, 241, 253–63
Coleridge, 183, 243
color, as sensation, 35, 38; mere charm of, 217; of bird feathers, 233–37; art of, 238; color (Hegel) versus form (Kant) as primary in painting, 248; as a language of nature, 268

communicability of mental state, 216
constraint, in morality, 126, 136, 160; in artistic production, 211, 240
contemplation, as disinterested liking, 213
Copernicus, Copernican revolution, 13–16, 45, 77, 100, 187
crafts, 240
critique, as self-critique of reason, 7, 11, 39, 254; of dialectical illusion, 42; as topology of pure understanding, 93; sense of with respect to practical reason, 107–10; of teleological judgment, 119; sense of with respect to taste, 179–180, 186, 222

dance, 217
deduction, juridical sense of, 56; of the categories (*see* transcendental deduction); of the principles of pure practical reason, 150; of pure aesthetic concepts, 253
Derrida, 3
Descartes, 26, 243
desire, versus action from duty, 119–22; as determining only hypothetical imperatives, 147; higher faculty of as pure reason, 148, 192; the good as necessary object of, 153; for happiness, 162–63; as basic power of the soul, 193; reason as legislative of, 197; as absent in the judgment of taste, 215; and the dynamically sublime, 223
detachment, in theoretical knowledge, 106; in praxis, 107–08, 118, 138
Dewey, 105
dialectic, transcendental, as negative part of the Doctrine of Elements, 20–21, 43, 98–99, 101, 106, 190; of pure practical reason, 161–73; of aesthetic judgment, 253
dignity, versus price, 134, 137, 160
divine sensorium, 27
domain, its specific sense, 186
duty, 119–20, 123–24, 130–31, 158

Eberhard, 10
empirical reality, 35. *See also* transcendental ideality
Enlightenment, 181
epoché, 214

examples, role of in morality, 123–24, 131, 135, 138; for aesthetic clarity, 208
experimentation, 13; thought experiment, 29, 156

fact of reason, as consciousness of moral law, 149–52, 161, 173
faith, 11
Feder, 113–14
feeling, as practical sensibility, 157–61; for the beautiful and sublime, 180; of pleasure, 192–203; of the free play of the representational powers, 206–14, 259–66; of the sublime, 223–27, 230–31
Fichte, 67, 179, 184, 189
Flatt, 114, 150
freedom, transcendental concept of, 112–14; as lawful, 138–40; and moral law, 149–54; postulate of, 167–69; as influencing nature, 190–93; art as production through freedom, 223–40
free play among the cognitive powers, 183, 205–16, 263–65
function, as act of reflection, 45–46

Gadamer, 3
Galileo, 38, 181, 195, 243
Garve, 4, 113
gathering (λέγειν), of theoretical reason as a gathering of appearances, 17–18, 86, 101; of practical reason as a self-gathering, 165–66
genius, 239–47, 269–70
geometry, 21, 32–36, 81
German Idealism, 39, 67, 179–84, 191, 243
God, 6, 15, 22–27, 56, 92, 98, 113, 236; does not think, 22; death of, 24; existence not part of the concept of, 92; practical postulate of, 170–73. *See also* divine sensorium; original intuition
the good, as based on the moral law rather than vice versa, 153–54; liking for, 214–19, 265. *See also* good will; highest good; supreme good
good will, 117–21, 135, 147, 154; absolutely good will as holy will, 136–39
Greeks, 13, 18–19, 23, 101, 105, 165, 185, 296

happiness, 118, 127, 147; as forming together with virtue the highest good, 162–67, 171
Hegel, 183–84, 214, 248
Heidegger, 3, 18–19, 184–85, 189, 191, 250
hermeneutics, 3–4, 101, 184
Herz, 8
heteronomy, 122, 136, 150; as the lawfulness of natural causality, 138
Heyting, 34
highest good, 162–72
Hobbes, 182
holy will, 126, 136, 150
Horace, 113
Hume, 89
Husserl, 41
Hutcheson, 137

illusion, dialectical, 11, 42, 93, 99, 106, 145, 162
image, sensible manifold as, 59–60, 71; versus schema, 74–75; time as pure image, 74, 82; result of productive imagination, 183; in classical paradigm of making, 239, 268
imagination, as power of spontaneous receptivity, 40, 155; as power of synthesis, 48–60; as power of projecting moral maxims, 155–56; as central to the experience of the beautiful and the sublime, 182–83, 202–16, 221–33, 245–53, 261–64, 270–72
imitation, in morality, 123; of exemplary works of art, 243
immortality of the soul, 6, 112–13; practical postulate of, 169–70
imperatives, 124–43
Inaugural Dissertation, 7–9, 21–28, 94–95
incentive, 157–59
inclination, 120–22, 158–59, 189, 215, 231–34
incongruent counterparts, 30
Instrumentalism, 105
intellectual intuition, 22, 95–96, 142–43. *See also* real use of the intellect
interest, defined, 168; as a liking for the existence of the object, 213–15; intellectual interest in the beautiful, 233–38, 267
intuition, as immediate relation to objects, 22–23; space and time as pure intuitions, 25–40; as connected to thought through the imagination, 55–72
Intuitionism (mathematics), 34

Jacobi, 189
judgment, as mediate knowing of an object, 45–49, 194; table of, *47*; Doctrine of, 73–92; practical, 121, 156, 236; reflective versus determinative, 180, 195–99; aesthetic, 191–225, 236–50, 258–64
justice, 107

Klee, 244

landscape gardening, 248, *248*
language, and nature, 234, 237, 268; in poetry, 240; and aesthetic ideas, 245, 247, 270–71; and music, 249
Leibniz, 10, 21, 27–28, 53
Levinas, 105, 174
life, 211–12; feeling of, 263–64
liking, for the beautiful, 212–13; for the agreeable or the good, 214–15; universal, 215–16
Locke, 26, 38
λόγος, -οι, 18, 54–55, 101, 106–07, 165

magnitude, as representation of space, 31–32; as *quantitas* versus *quantum*, 80–81; intensive versus extensive, 83–85; of sublime nature, 222–27
Marx, 105, 174
mathematics, 6, 13, 33–34, 81, 100. *See also* geometry
maxim, 119–23; as subjective principle versus command, 129–30, 146; as universalizable, 133–35, 139, 148–49, 156, 189; of a holy will, 136
mechanism, nature as, 181, 210, 236, 256; as the constraint required by art, 240; nature as exceeding mechanism, 270
metaphysics, as general problem of the *Critique of Pure Reason*, 6–18, 187; metaphysical expositions, 26–32; general versus special, 15, 21, 98; of nature, 15, 79, 254; of morals, 15, 107, *116*, 129, 138, 254; no possible metaphysics of the beautiful, 215

method, 4, 11–14, 71, 109, 114–15; transcendental doctrine of, 16, 33, 145; artist's skill versus, 243
Middle Ages, 116
mimesis, 243
monads, monadology, 7, 10, 53
Monet, 209
moral law, as requiring affirmation of freedom, 112–15; formulas of, 128–36; as fact of reason, 149–52; as objective determining ground of the will, 158–61
motion, 36–37, 181
music, 217, 239, 241, 248, 249

nature, and modern science, 13–14, 38; the understanding as lawgiver of, 78–79; as causal mechanism, 181, 210, 236, 256; moral formula of the law of, 130–31, 156; in German Idealism, 181–82; the beauty and sublimity of, 181–92
need, 113, 118, 124
Newton, 27, 79, 181, 195, 243
Nietzsche, 24, 105, 174–75, 189
noumenon, 8; positive versus negative sense of, 96–98; and phenomenon, 110–11; free agent as belonging to a noumenal order, 151–52; in resolution of antinomies, 110–13, 163–65; as substratum of natural things, 191

objectivity, the critical problem as a problem of, 16–17, 91, 100; of objects of experience, 57; practical, 153
obligation, 116, 136
Ockham, 53
ontology (general metaphysics), 15, 98
original intuition, 22–26. *See also* intellectual intuition
originality, as foremost property of genius, 242, 269

painting, 209, 217, 248, *248*
pantheism controversy, 180
personality, 160
phenomenon, as object of sensibility, versus noumenon, 8, 94–97, 110–11, 166–67
physics, 6, 83, 116, 125, 181, 195

Pistoris, 114, 151, 154
planets, 14, 187–88. *See also* astronomy
Plato, 4, 7, 18, 54–55, 106, 116, 142, 165, 230
play. *See* free play
pleasure, feeling for as one of three powers of the soul, 193; negative pleasure, 224
poetry, 217, 240, 248–49, *248*
Pollock, 209
postulates, of empirical thought in general, 79, 91–92; of practical reason: freedom, 167–69; immortality of the soul, 169–70; existence of God, 170–72
powers of the soul, 197. *See also* cognitive powers
pragmatism, 105, 174
presence, to self, 1, 18, 29, 39, 71; and λόγος, 18, 101; space as a condition of, 29; and absolute knowledge, 68
proof, meaning of, 83
purposiveness, of reason, 119; versus moral goodness, 120; nature as purposive, 190, 196, 225; as suitability to a purpose, 198, 258; as without purpose, 198–200; subjective versus objective, 201, 220; of the subject with respect to the object, 203; of the object with respect to the subject, 204–13, 259–60; and the good, 214, 265; of form alone, 216, 241; the sublime as contrapurposive, 224; art as freely purposive, 241; of beauty, 250; and aesthetic judgment, 258
psychologism, 41
pyramids, 226–28

qualities, primary versus secondary, 38
quality, category of, 47, 53, 75, 79; as including reality, 84–85

rational cosmology, 15, 111
reality, versus actuality, 84; existence not a real predicate, 92
realm of ends, 128, 133–35, *134*
real use of the intellect, 8–9, 23, 95
reason, self-critique of, 7–18; as power of gathering into unity, 165–66, 223; as pure thought versus schematized thought, 106; as legislative for the power of desire,

197–99; the unlimited demand of and the sublime, 228–30
receptivity and spontaneity, 21, 40. *See also* sensibility
refinement, 234–35
reflection, 44–48, 71–73, 197–99, 235–37; reflective judgment, 195–97, 200–04, 241, 258–64
Reinhold, 179, 189, 197
respect, as moral feeling, 157–85, *161*; for the law, 120, 157; for persons, 132; as rational sensibility, 145; as intellectual contentment, 165
Robinson Crusoe, 235
Romanticism, 181–84, 243
rules of the pure thought of an object, categories as, 44, 75, 81–94. *See also* schematism

Schelling, 67, 179, 182–84, 191
schema, versus image, 74; as apriori determination of time, 75; as the ruling of the ruled (appearances) by the rule (category), 81–94; schematized thought, 98, 106, 152; as "type" of the natural law, 156; nature as schema of ideas, 229–30; poetry as schema of the supersensible, 248; sublime nature as schema of reason, 250
schematism, 73–75
Schiller, 182
scholasticism, 51–54
science (natural, physical, mathematical), 13, 38, 78–79, 181, 256
Scotus, 52–53
sculpture, *248*
self-love, 120–21, 147, 159
sensation, as result of affection, 24–26; as not yielding apriori knowledge, 35; as the matter of appearances, 37; as atomistic, disordered array, 58, 71; intensive magnitude of, 82–83; as lacking extensive magnitude, 83; as corresponding to the real, 84; as irrelevant to aesthetic judgment, 201, 237; formal play of, 248
sensibility, as receptivity, 7, 38; not simply confused understanding, 20; pure forms of, 25; as limited by the positing of the noumenon, 97–98; practical sensibility, 157–66; and the sublime, 229
seriousness, 223–24
Sextus Empiricus, 116
Silber, 156
skepticism, 112; moral skepticism, 123–24; skeptical Platonism, 142
sociability, 234
Socrates, 54, 106–07, 165
space and time, metaphysical and transcendental expositions of, 26–37
Speusippos, 116
Spinoza, 180
spirit, as animating, as power of presenting aesthetic ideas, 240, 245–47, 270
Stoics, 116
St. Peter's, 227
the sublime, versus the beautiful, 180; three moments in the judgment of, 221–22; mathematical versus dynamical, 222–26; as contrapurposive and producing negative pleasure, 224, 231; not in the object itself but in the mind, 224, 229; as subordinate to the beautiful, 225; as repelling and attracting, 232; and poetry, 248; as schema of reason itself, 250
supersensible, 15, 24, 114, 142, 151; versus the sensible, 191, 228; reason as a supersensible power, 228–30; humans as supersensible beings, 233, 267; poetry as schema of, 248
supreme good, 162
synthesis, defined, 48; as threefold connection between pure concepts and objects, carried out by imagination, 58–67; productive versus reproductive, 70; transcendental versus empirical, 85–86
synthetic apriori, *12*; as formula of the critical problem, 13, 100; geometry as, 32–33; axioms of time in general as, 36; the system of principles as, 75–78; categorical imperative as, 141
system, 15–16, 43, 78–79, 112, 115, 133, 254

Tafelmusik, 241
talent, as innate productive ability of the artist, 242–42, 269; academic training of, 244, 268; talents of the mind, 118; duty to develop one's, 131
taste, as discrimination with regard to beauty, 179, 205–20, 244, 258; apriori principles operative in, 186; versus judgments about the sublime, 203, 221–28, 231; and intellectual interest, 267–69
teleology, teleological judgment, 119, 189, 200, *201*, 222
thing in itself, 8, 15–16, 30–38, 61, 95–97, 110, 188–91, 256
time, as universal form of intuition, 37, 70, 75; as pure image of all objects of the senses in general, 74; transcendental determinations of as the schemata, 75, 82–94; the totality of and holiness, 170–71. *See also* space and time
Tittel, 114
transcendental, defined, 24
transcendental aesthetic, 20–40, 48, 59, 70, 80, 157
transcendental analytic, 41–93; division of, 48, 81; as critical general metaphysics, 98
transcendental apperception, 62–72, 86–89, 141, 155, 165–66, 174
transcendental deduction, 55–72; difficulty of, 55; task of, 56–57; from above, 69–70; from below, 70–72
transcendental dialectic, 18, 23; preview of, 98–99
transcendental exposition, of space, 32–34; of time 36–37
transcendental freedom, 110–11
transcendental ideality, 35, 38. *See also* empirical reality
transcendental ideas, 143
transcendental imagination, 58, 66, 70, 75, 156
transcendental intuition, 69
transcendental logic, 20, 42–44, 47, 49, 56
transcendental metaphysics of nature, 79
transcendental object, 60–63, 95–101
transcendental philosophy, history of, 51–54
transcendental praxis, 142, 151, 161, 174–75
transcendental schema, 70–75, 156
transcendental synthesis, 59–60, 67, 70, 85–86
transcendentals, 51–54
tribunal, 7, 56
truth, and principle of contradiction, 76; domain of understanding as land of, 93, 99, 145; and Socrates' second sailing, 106; and presumed identity with knowledge, 191; Kant's evasion of the question of, 255–56; of beauty, 257–59, 262–64, 272
typic, 156

understanding, versus sensibility, 20–21; as subordinate to intuition, 23–25; as birthplace of pure concepts, 42–55; as thought of the transcendental object, 60–63; as faculty of rules, 73–97; nature as its domain, 187–91, *190*, 195–97; as legislative of the cognitive powers, 197–99; as in accord with the imagination in judgments of taste, 203–16, 261–72
universality, as criterion of apriori knowledge, 12; of concepts, 33, 106, 165; of law, 130–35, 156; of reflective judgment, 180, 195–97, 208; of aesthetic judgment, 200, 203–04, 215–16, 218, 262–64
unthinkability, 29

virtue, 107; and moral feeling, 137; as continuous progress toward the moral ideal, 150, 164; as supreme good, 162; forming together with happiness the highest good, 162–67, 171

whole and part, 4, 184. *See also* hermeneutics
the will, reason as ruler of, 118–26; autonomy of, 135–38; as determined by law rather than by desire, 147–74
Wolff, 21, 76, 84

Xenocrates, 116

JOHN SALLIS is Frederick J. Adelmann Professor of Philosophy at Boston College. He is author of more than twenty books, including *Light Traces*, *The Return of Nature*, and *The Figure of Nature*.

RICHARD ROJCEWICZ edited the previously published volume III/10 of John Sallis' Collected Writings, *The Logos of the Sensible World: Merleau-Ponty's Phenomenological Philosophy*. Rojcewicz is the translator of numerous works by Martin Heidegger and Edmund Husserl and author of *The Gods and Technology: A Reading of Heidegger*.

www.ingramcontent.com/pod-product-compliance
Lightning Source LLC
Chambersburg PA
CBHW030611230426

43661CB00053B/1937